The Left in the Shaping of Japanese Democracy

Arthur Stockwin, as much as any Westerner living, made the Japanese Left a compelling concern for the political scientist and historian alike. This Oxford *Festschrift* seeks to honour him with a set of essays that reach beyond all previous studies of this great movement.

Part I focuses on left-wing thought. Christopher Goto-Jones probes the texts and reputations of two-left wing 'martyrs' of Imperial Japan: Jun Tosaka and Kiyoshi Miki; Rikki Kersten retraces the career of Hitoshi Asō, the leftist leader who controversially embraced the Army as an agency of anti-capitalist revolution; and David Williams mobilises Hobbes, Carl Schmitt and Foucault to dissect the Left's understanding of constitutional sovereignty.

Part II addresses the post-war scene. Robert Aspinall examines the rise and fall of Nikkyō-sō, the militant teachers' union; Koichi Nakano reveals the Left's impact on conservative efforts to privatize the state sector; and Sarah Hyde recounts the strange but sudden death of parliamentary socialism.

In Part III, 'Settling Accounts', Leonard J. Schoppa highlights the embrace of the free market by former leftist politicians; Williams returns the study of the Japanese Left to its critical roots via a post 9/11 critique of American Empire; and Junji Banno offers a passionate 'last judgment' on the fate of the Left in Japanese politics.

Rikki Kersten is Professor of Modern Japan Studies at Leiden University, the Netherlands. She is the editor of our Routledge/Leiden Series in Modern East Asian History and Politics.

David Williams, one of Europe's leading thinkers on modern Japan, is the author of *Japan: Beyond the End of History*, *Japan and the Enemies of Open Political Science* and *Defending Japan's Pacific War*, all published by Routledge.

Routledge/Leiden Series in Modern East Asian History and Politics
Series editor: Rikki Kersten

Through addressing ideas about history and politics in the modern period, and by encouraging comparative and inter-disciplinary work amongst East Asian specialists, the Routledge/Leiden Series in Modern East Asian History and Politics seeks to combine Area Studies' focus on primary sources in the vernacular, with a distinct disciplinary edge.

The Leiden Series focuses on philosophy, politics, political thought, history, the history of ideas, and foreign policy as they relate to modern East Asia, and will emphasise theoretical approaches in all of these fields. As well as single-authored volumes, edited or multi-authored submissions that bring together a range of country specialisations and disciplines are welcome.

Political Philosophy in Japan
Nishida, the Kyoto school and co-prosperity
Christopher S. Goto-Jones

The Left in the Shaping of Japanese Democracy
Essays in honour of J. A. A. Stockwin
Edited by Rikki Kersten and David Williams

The Left in the Shaping of Japanese Democracy

Essays in honour of J. A. A. Stockwin

Edited by Rikki Kersten and David Williams

Routledge
Taylor & Francis Group

LONDON AND NEW YORK

Universiteit Leiden

First published 2006
by Routledge
2 Park Square, Milton Park, Abingdon, Oxon, OX14 4RN

Simultaneously published in the USA and Canada
by Routledge
270 Madison Ave, New York NY 10016

Routledge is an imprint of the Taylor & Francis Group

Transferred to Digital Printing 2009

Typeset in Times by
RefineCatch Ltd, Bungay, Suffolk

British Library Cataloguing in Publication Data
A catalogue record for this book is available from the British Library

Library of Congress Cataloging in Publication Data
The left in the shaping of Japanese democracy : essays in honour of
  J.A.A. Stockwin / edited by Rikki Kersten and David Williams.
      p. cm. – (The Leiden series in modern East Asian politics and history; 2)
      Includes bibliographical references and index.
      1. Political culture–Japan.   2. Socialism–Japan.   3. Japan–Politics
      and government – 1945– 4. Japan – Foreign relations. I. Stockwin,
      J. A. A. (James Arthur Ainscow) II. Kersten, Rikki, 1960- III.
      Williams, David. IV. Title. V. Series.
  JQ1681.L44 2005
  320.51'3'095209045–dc22   2005009856

ISBN10: 0–415–33434–9 (hbk)
ISBN10: 0–415–33435–7 (pbk)

ISBN13: 9–78–0–415–33434–1 (hbk)
ISBN13: 9–78–0–415–33435–8 (pbk)

Publisher's Note
The publisher has gone to great lengths to ensure the quality of this reprint
but points out that some imperfections in the original may be apparent.

Contents

Contributors

Christopher Goto-Jones is Associate Professor of the History of Ideas in Modern Japan at Leiden University.

Rikki Kersten is Professor of Modern Japan Studies at Leiden University.

David Williams is Senior Lecturer in Japanese Studies at Cardiff University.

Robert W. Aspinall is Professor in the Department of Social Systems, Shiga University.

Koichi Nakano is Associate Professor of Political Science at Sophia University.

Sarah Hyde is Lecturer in the Politics and International Relations of Japan at the University of Kent.

Leonard J. Schoppa is Associate Professor in the Department of Politics at the University of Virginia.

Junji Banno is Emeritus Professor at Tokyo University.

A tribute to Arthur Stockwin

Rikki Kersten

Summing up the achievements of one's professor, mentor and friend seems an incredibly cheeky thing for a student to do. And yet, as most people in Japanese Studies will agree, Arthur Stockwin has made it rather easy. In terms of tangible achievements, publications, the numbers of DPhil and PhD graduates who now work both within and outside academe, teaching and professional administrative roles, even the brute compilation of lists of each of these activities, will testify to his professional contribution to Japanese Studies. The hard thing is to try to convey, to those who have not worked with Arthur during his career, how the breadth of his humanity has made these other achievements resonate in our own professional lives. This is not about being a 'nice guy'; rather, what Arthur has represented for many of us is a profound intertwining of value integrity with impeccable scholarship. Arthur Stockwin is a scholar who knows where he stands as a human being, and he has built his scholarship and teaching around this, while retaining his empirical, scholarly quality. This is something to which most of us aspire, especially once we have met him and worked with him. To pre-empt the thrust of this assessment of his professional career, this is his lasting contribution to the field.

The tangible contributions almost speak for themselves, though they are worth examining, to show what is possible in one professional life. This book began with a different intention, namely to assess the field of Japanese political science, and approaches to the subject, during the course of Arthur's career. Ultimately, this found expression in one of Arthur's most recent publications, the *Dictionary of the Modern Politics of Japan*.[1] In the end, persuaded by convincing arguments on the part of my co-editor, I agreed that the thread that really binds Arthur's academic work is his analysis of and the attention given to the Left in Japanese politics, ideas and foreign policy. A quick glance at the disciplines covered by his graduates underscored the kind of structure that a book in his honour should take. Namely, one of disciplinary breadth, incorporating the history of ideas on the Left, political science and foreign policy. In his scholarly publications and public lectures, Arthur has given depth to each of these areas. Without him, the profile of Japanese politics would be monochromatic indeed, with the spotlight focused on the winners, and our understanding of the full picture considerably impoverished as a result. Power is not contained and constrained by those who formally hold the reins. Understanding politics and political culture demands that we look at the negotiation, compromises and fuzzy edges that accompany power and its exercise, and in Japan this means we must look at the Left as a central player in the power game of Japanese politics. Through his life-long dedication to this subject, Arthur has helped us understand Japanese politics as a whole, not just one heroic corner of it.

Arthur's journey to Japanese Studies partly explains his breadth in terms of disciplines and interests. It was a rather long and winding road, which took him from Oxford, through Bodmin Moor, Russian language training, to Australia, and back to Oxford again (with side-trips to France).[2] We are struck when reading about Arthur's journey that he was one of the pioneers of modern Japan Studies, in that he realized that fluency in Japanese language and actual experience in-country over regular, sustained periods, were essential to academic integrity. He was one of the first post-Occupation generation of Japan scholars to do this, and it has since become unthinkable for us to do anything else. And he did it by ship! This first foray helped produce both a thesis, and a pioneering work on the Japan Socialist Party's foreign policy.[3]

On a deeper level, Arthur has shown through his personal example that it is possible to have genuine dialogue with Japanese experts on Japan, moving analysis beyond the clinical subject–object plane, and onto the human one of communication, discourse, and disagreement when required. All too often, we find ourselves theorising and debating only amongst ourselves, the outsiders, about Japan. Performing in Japanese academic settings can be daunting, and the experience dispiriting, as on top of the politesse of Japanese academic exchange, we find ourselves swimming through a fog of discourse that is not like ours at all. Some Western scholars conclude that it is easier to stay away, in familiar academic environments, speaking our own language. But Arthur has shown through his incredible network of friends and colleagues in Japan, his active academic engagement with them, and his participation over the years in the Japan Political Science Association, that it is possible to theorise eyeball to eyeball, to argue and tease, with results that enrich and inspire. Because Arthur has done it, I for one am going to keep trying.

Through his geographical reach, as well as through his scholarship, Arthur has also achieved something tangible for the field in another way. He has opened up what David Williams has called 'the Australia-Europe axis' in Japanese Studies. While North American Japanese studies dominates the field, there is now, thanks to Arthur's personal example and through his nurturing of a significant number of scholars (some of whom are US nationals), an alternative presence that does not speak to quite the same refrain, within the same parameters, or amongst the same institutional cultures. Whether it be through the history of ideas, a serious treatment of the Left as a political and foreign policy force, or in addressing shared concerns (such as

One Party Dominance, or 'Immobilism'), Arthur has helped establish a broader spectrum of opinion and analysis.[4] The field can only be richer because of it.

Not many of us can boast of a bricks and mortar legacy for our labours. Building on the foundations provided by the late Dick Storry, Arthur Stockwin consolidated the original Nissan Institute of Japanese Studies at Oxford, located at Church Walk, when appointed as Director (and Professor of Japanese Politics). Then, defying the odds, Arthur successfully negotiated with the Nissan Corporation for another donation, this time to build from the ground up, a purpose-built new Nissan Institute (at Winchester Road). Incorporating the Japanese collection of the Bodleian Library, this new Institute breathed new life into Japanese Studies, providing light and airy spaces in which to gather, think and debate. The Nissan Lecture Theatre (still known in some circles as 'The New Lecture Theatre') contributes to the life of St Antony's College, on whose land it stands, and widens the welcome to the community beyond the college gates. Unbeknownst to many, this move from Church Walk to Winchester Road also inspired Arthur to new heights in his epic poetry, with odes written to 'the Nissan Ghost' who had to follow his 'family' around the corner, and deal with a different reality. The Ghost went back to the bosom of the Latin American scholars who became the new inhabitants of Church Walk, but I am ever hopeful that he will make a friendly return to Winchester Road one day. There is no doubt that the many visiting Japanese Fellows welcomed being removed from the notorious church bell that marked the hours at Church Walk, and ensconced in their new apartment at Winchester Road, were able to be identified by their sunny demeanours rather than their sleep-deprived faces.

Academic achievement can be assessed in terms of sheer weight – how many books, articles, and so on. Arthur can hold his own here, as his sole-authored and collaborative book projects attest. One of these, *Governing Japan: Divided Politics in a Major Economy*, in its various editions has become a standard textbook in the teaching of Japanese politics around the world.[5] Moreover, comparing these editions offers us insight not only into Arthur's thinking on Japan over two decades, and on the shifting concerns of Japanese politics, but also on the state of the field over that period. As the titles of these texts indicate, Arthur was intent in the first and second editions on transcending the 'harmony' stereotype that stuck to Japan, linking the fundamental divisions that made Japanese politics tick to the phenomenal growth in Japan's economy up to the late 1980s. In 1975, the relevance of Japan to us all was assumed, and Arthur felt no need to justify why Japan was worthy of serious academic attention. His periodization took in history up to the end of the Second World War, then the Occupation, bringing us up to the oil shocks of 1973. After elucidating the structures and institutions of Japanese politics (notably the constitution and Article 9), Arthur devoted the last three sections to domestic and foreign policy issues, and future 'dilemmas'. Here he identified 'the central paradox of Japanese politics' as a division between those who see 'the cohesive nature of "consensus politics" and explain Japan's "economic miracle" . . . in terms of a national capacity for subordinating individual gratification to the common good', and those who 'are more impressed by the constant faction fighting, the apparent lack of agreement between Left and Right on the basic rules of politics competition'.[6]

In 1999, with a title adjusted to suit the circumstances of a decade of economic stagnation, the textbook begins with a reminder of why Japan and the study of its politics still matters, and should continue to matter. The structure of this book assumes much greater sophistication in its audience, and more attention is paid to Japan's parliament and bureaucracy in the institutional section. The periodization is adjusted also, this time into 1945–1960, 1960–1989, and the 1990s. In this text, the key concern is the nature and substance of Japan's democracy in the eyes of academic analysts, as it travels through a succession of imposed paradigms (democracy, modernization, New Left, Number 1, revisionism, and its clash with 'rational choice'). Arthur plumps for 'patterned pluralism', the term coined by Krauss and Muramatsu, so that we can 'step back from established theories of politics and adopt an approach which is sensitive both to the formal and informal rules of the system and also to the cultural nuances of political behaviour'.[7] Japan has in this book become an analytical challenge, just as it is in danger of being perceived in the wider world as a has-been nation, with the field condemned to the periphery – in the minds of some – through its association with a 'declining' economy. Arthur's judgement that Japan may be an 'imperfect democracy', but a substantial democracy nonetheless, has been a major inspiration for this volume.

Just as the study of the Left and its foreign policy was given impetus by Arthur Stockwin's work, other areas have also become established through his contributions. Australia–Japan relations, Japan–Soviet relations (particularly the Northern Territories issue), reform in Japanese politics, and democracy in Asia have been integrated into his opus. The study of factionalism and factions, and the phenomenon of opposition in Japan, stand as the most formative scholarly legacies of his work, alongside his core concern of the politics of the Left. In all of these fields, Arthur has led large numbers of DPhils to successful completion. His many students will chuckle at his recollection of his own experience of being supervised at the Australian National University by the meticulous David Sissons, and at his own recognition that 'my own graduate students may feel that I absorbed his precise concern with language, punctuation and footnoting, and came to apply it pedantically to them'.[8] Perhaps in retirement, though this will be occupied with completing several DPhil supervisions for the medium term, Arthur will return to his theoretical work on the nature of opposition in Japan, while he surveys the mountain-scape of the French countryside. Then again, he has certainly earned the right to enjoy joining his wife Audrey at potters' markets, haggling in French with the locals (and getting on top of French politics while he is at it).

The wheels of academe remain greased through the often thankless, but nonetheless necessary, burden of administration. Arthur has starred in several countries in this realm: in the Japanese Studies Association of Australia, as President of the British Association of Japanese Studies, the Management Advisory Council of Tokyo University, the Japan Foundation Endowment Committee in Britain, as a key figure in the selection of Swire Fellows, and through years of commitment to the running of St Antony's College, Oxford. Above all, his general editorship of the Nissan Institute Routledge Japanese Studies Series, with 60 books published to date, will stand as a most imposing and impressive contribution to the field of Japanese Studies. Indeed, he has been so successful in inspiring publications, and so meticulous in his collection of clippings from the *Asahi* for the entire length of his career, that special care had to be taken when, to the disbelief of all who are familiar with his library and files, builders designed a library in his home that could hold his entire collection.

Those of us who teach will sport several Arthur Stockwin publications in our own collections, too. Beside the three editions of his Japan politics textbook, Arthur has also performed the great service of producing the kind of resources that make life easier for teacher and student alike. *The Dictionary of the Modern Politics of Japan* is the latest and most comprehensive of these, though his substantial contributions to *Political Parties of Asia and the Pacific*,[9] *The Kodansha Encyclopedia of Japan*[10] and *The Cambridge Encyclopedia of Japan*[11] remain standard entries on any course outline on Japanese politics and history.

In his valedictory lecture at the Nissan Institute on 30 May 2003, Arthur traversed the ground that has been covered by scholars of Japan over the past decades, and offered one of his clearest statements yet about the state of reform, and of the field, in Japanese politics.[12] Having observed Japan move from the status of miracle nation, through Japan bashing, and on to 'Japan passing', there was no question that political scientists and historians of Japan now need to fight their corner, and assert the ongoing importance of understanding Japan in the post-Cold War, unipolar world. The facile dismissal of Japan as a nation of 'relevance' on the basis of economic performance alone is not merely wrong, but as Arthur tells us, it would make us miss one the most exciting periods in the history of political reform in modern Japan. There is no mistaking the tone of foreboding in Arthur's closing lines: 'There is danger in the near-collapse of the political Left and the consequent upsetting of a political balance that, however inefficient it was in certain ways, at least provided a check against the ambitions of the Far Right.'[13] Reform could go in any direction, and much could be done in the name of reform that more accurately reflects a crisis mentality and extremist solutions to perceived crisis, than it might a genuine, systemic and attitudinal shift. Lurking at the crux of real reform though is the very existence of the Liberal Democratic Party (LDP), with it's 'spider's web of vested interest linkages and "iron triangles" ',[14] and the concurrent weakness of the opposition.

Despite the fascinating dynamics of the LDP operating in coalition, these are mutually reinforcing structural problems that point to one conclusion: while the LDP exists in its current form, albeit in coalition, real reform will not happen. Add to this the upheavals and instability underscoring North East Asian security, the rise of China and the policy challenges in managing deflation that confront the economies that are enmeshed with Japan's, and Arthur believes nothing less than radical reform will secure Japan's democracy in this context.

This is the baton that Arthur Stockwin has handed over to us, to his students and colleagues. He has given us a professional foundation, analytical tools, and a love of the perplexing entity that is Japan. Following and elucidating the progress and pitfalls of Japanese politics, particularly as it flirts with fundamental reinvention, is not a bad way for us to continue the Arthur Stockwin School.

Notes

1 London, Routledge, 2003.
2 For his own account of his encounter with Japanese Studies, see J. A. A. Stockwin, *Collected Writings of J.A.A. Stockwin, Part I, The Politics and Political Environment of Japan*, in *The Collected Writings of Modern Western Scholars on Japan*, Volume 10, London, Japan Library, 2004, pp. 1–16.
3 J. A. A. Stockwin, *The Japanese Socialist Party and Neutralism: A Study of a Political Party and its Foreign Policy*, Melbourne, Melbourne University Press, and London and New York: Cambridge University Press, 1968.
4 J. A. A. Stockwin, A. Rix, A. George, J. Horne, D. Ito and M. Collick, *Dynamic and Immobilist Politics in Japan*, Oxford, Macmillan, 1988.
5 Published in Oxford by Blackwell, 1999. This was the third edition of a textbook first published under the title of *Japan: Divided Politics in a Growth Economy*, published in New York by Norton and Norton in 1975 (and by Weidenfeld and Nicolson outside of the US), and thereafter in a revised version under the same title in 1982.
6 Stockwin, *Japan: Divided Politics in a Growth Economy*, New York, Norton and Norton, 1975, p. 243.
7 Stockwin, *Governing Japan: Divided Politics in a Major Economy*, Oxford, Blackwell, 1999, p. 221.
8 See Stockwin, *Collected Writings*, Volume 1, p. 3.
9 Haruhiko Fukui (ed.) *Political Parties of Asia and the Pacific*, 2 vols. Westport and London, Greenwood Press, 1985.
10 *The Kodansha Encyclopedia of Japan*, Tokyo and New York, Kodansha, 1983.
11 Richard Bowring and Peter Kornicki (eds) *The Cambridge Encyclopedia of Japan*, Cambridge, Cambridge University Press, 1993.
12 'Why Japan Still Matters', subsequently published in *Japan Forum*, Vol. 15 No. 3 2003, pp. 345–360.
13 Ibid., p. 357.
14 Ibid., p. 354.

An Oxford *Festschrift*

The book in brief

David Williams

Festschrift – A volume of writings collected in honour of a scholar. *OED*

The *Festschrift* has no natural place in the complex psychology of the relationship between teacher and student. The urge to instruct, to lead intellectually, to assert one's authority, to leave one's stamp and to defend the orthodox thrust of one's original insight clashes inevitably with the student's need to question, to rebel, to subvert authority, to resist being stamped and to challenge orthodoxy and the originality of others. Given these conflicting pressures, what hope is there for unity of community, of shared celebration, of honour dutifully offered and generously received: all the impulses that define the successful *Festschrift*?

The answer lies, and this *Festschrift* illustrates the necessary dynamic, in the system of instruction: the scope of the area of special interest, the discipline of a shared ideological outlook and the flexibility of approach that alone can withstand the struggle that each generation wages to makes its voice heard. Every chapter of this *Festschrift* reveals different versions of the original problem and its solution. Indeed, the first three contributions on left-wing political thought offer an effective demonstration, precisely because so unexpected, of just how much flexibility the teacher–student relationship must display if the long, and often contentious, march towards a successful *Festschrift* is to be achieved.

Thus, the three essays that form Part I of this *Festschrift* – 'Left-wing thought from the Russian Revolution to the war on terrorism' – represent a radical departure from the main concerns and ambitions of the Arthur Stockwin School of Japan Studies, but Oxford itself prepared the ground for this innovation. There, the study of history and politics has, during the past century, developed a natural partnership. Indeed, the brick wall that distinguishes the labours of the historian and the political scientist at Oxford has been kept porous, thus encouraging the specialist in one field to make himself at home in the other.

Such porosity is at work in Christopher Goto-Jones's doctoral research on Kitarō Nishida and the wartime Kyoto School, and Rikki Kersten's on one of postwar Japan's most influential political thinkers: Masao Maruyama. The result is that the history of political ideas has become a fruitful wing of the Stockwin School. The magical influence on the Oxford scene of such magisterial figures as Sir Isaiah Berlin and Leszek Kolakowski has offered a classic precedent and stimulus for such fruitfulness; but Stockwin's decision to supervise these projects was crucial.

In his article 'The Left hand of darkness', Goto-Jones navigates the troubled and treacherous waters of Pacific War revisionism by gently probing the texts and reputations of two of interwar Japan's most famous left-wing 'martyrs': Jun Tosaka and Kiyoshi Miki. Both thinkers have been more frequently discussed and idealised than read carefully. Goto-Jones has helped to loosen the vice of Pacific War orthodoxy in ways that may encourage others to commit their scholarly energies to the mammoth undertaking of rethinking the entire Western understanding of what kind of society wartime Japan was and what role that country's thinkers really played in the crucial years between 1931 and 1945.

Closer to Arthur Stockwin's own rather more orthodox view of the Pacific War, Kersten, in her essay 'Painting the Emperor red', shows the kind of restlessness in the face of established opinion that all historians display when the revisionist urge begins to be felt. In her research on Hisashi Asō, perhaps the most unsettling example of political apostasy (*tenkō*) in prewar Japan, she insists that we take a harder look at the reasoning and motivations behind the dramatic decision of this great leader of the Japanese Left to lend his support to the army as an agency of anti-capitalist revolution. The harsh assessment of Asō by left-wing intellectuals after 1945 reflects, in Kersten's view, all the comfortable securities and perfect hindsight of the postwar condition, thus obscuring the realities with which Asō and his fellow leftists had to grapple.

If Goto-Jones and Kersten remind us of the impact of the Russian Revolution on the progressive Japanese intellectual during the Taishō (1912–1926) and early Shōwa (1926–1941) eras, I have sought, in my chapter, 'The Japanese evasion of sovereignty', to link the explosive power of Weimar German thought to the Japanese Left's fitful struggle with constitutional sovereignty after the Second World War. As the most enthusiastic of believers, among all the contributors, in the substance of Japanese thought, I seek to test the quality of Japanese ideas against the powers of three of Europe's most influential theorists of political realism: Thomas Hobbes, Carl Schmitt and Michel Foucault. Again, the terrain, the subject matter and the conclusions depart radically from Stockwin's own, but the insistence that the Japanese left-wing intellectual merits the closest analysis reflects his lifelong regard and concern for the fate of Japan's progressive-minded democrats.

The three articles that form the second part of this *Festschrift* – 'The metamorphosis of the Left in postwar Japan' – plunge the reader deep into the field of special interest that has dominated Stockwin's own writing about Japan: party politics and the politician as policymaker. In his chapter 'The rise and fall of Nikkyōso', Robert Aspinall, whose uncompromising left-wing stance most closely approaches that of Stockwin himself, traces the trajectory of one of the most important mainstays of the democratic Left among all Japan's militant unions: Nikkyōso, Japan's once powerful education union.

In his overview of the '1955 system', from its inception to its 1993 demise, Aspinall links developments in the Japanese educational scene with the fate of the Japan Socialist Party and the labour movement as a whole. The result is a dynamic portrait of four decades of Japanese politics grounded in the facts of a single educational movement.

In '"Democratic government" and the Left', Koichi Nakano offers a subtle analysis of the delayed but impressive impact of left-wing politicians on the restructuring of Japanese political institutions and policy philosophies that began to take shape under conservative hands from the 1980s. In contrast with the mantra of efficient bureaucracy that has so coloured the Japanese approach to policy in the past, Nakano seizes on the idea of 'democratic government' as one of the great gifts that the Left has bequeathed to future evolution of public policy in a post-socialist Japan. In ways entirely unanticipated by the political conservatives who have made the administrative agenda their own, Nakano's meticulous research reveals that the Left has quietly shaped, at some points decisively, the trajectory of this national effort by a troubled political establishment caught in troubled times to reform itself.

The strange but sudden death of parliamentary socialism is treated in Sarah Hyde's chapter, 'The end-game of socialism'. Like Stockwin, she is a committed bean counter, quite rightly insisting that democracy is indeed about numbers. Reviewing the often bewildering series of Diet alignments and realignments that accompanied the eclipse of the Japan Socialist Party, she traces the rise of the Democratic Party of Japan to its new position as the nation's chief opposition force. One of the rare non-partisan political scientists among Stockwin's students, she affirms her membership of his tribe by her energetic attention to the facts, thus allying empiricism with progressivism, in the Stockwin mode.

Having focused on the detail of politics and policy change in Part II, the assessment of the role of the Left in the consolidation of Japanese democracy is broadened in Part III, 'Settling accounts: globalization, American empire and history's judgement'. In 'Neoliberal economic policy preferences of the "New Left"', Schoppa expands the scope of the range of approaches and subject matter most obviously associated with Arthur and his students to include 'political economy' by linking economic policymaking with the attitudes and ideologies of individual Diet members and the parliamentary groupings to which they belong. In the process, the traditional Oxford commitment to comparative politics is affirmed and the ghetto outlook that so often defines the Japanese Studies approach is effectively breached by putting the economic orientation of members of the DPJ, for example, in an international context.

In 'After Abu Ghraib', I seek to return the study of the Japanese Left to its roots in the Cold-War era critique of American imperialism by focusing on the realities of the American 'hyper power' (Hubert Védrine) so boldly revealed in the wake of the 9/11 attacks on Manhattan and Washington DC. A rarity among scholars associated with the Stockwin School, I have long stressed the importance of right-of-centre perspectives and interpretations of Japanese political reality. But here I announce my own *tenkō* from Right to Left. My insistence on seeing the issue of the 'Left and Japanese democracy' as an aspect of area studies proper, highlights one of the sometimes neglected dimensions of Stockwin's approach to the study of Japanese politics. Furthermore, as we live in what has been called 'the age of Edward Said', I believe that it is necessary to focus attention not only on the object of our study – that is Japan – but also on the observer, the Westerner identifying the facts, making the analysis and drawing the conclusions about an Asian society. Hence my insistence that Western as well as Japanese intellectuals are involved in this enterprise.

Finally, in 'The Left in the Shaping of Japanese Democracy', Professor Junji Banno has contributed a 'last judgement' on the fate of the Left in Japanese politics. His analysis is, as always, pointed and unsparing. As a political historian, he settles scores, personal and historical, as he traces the arc of the Japanese parliamentary Left from the unlikely electoral surge of 1937 to the ballot box debacles of the 1990s. This comrade-in-arms of Stockwin offers us an unflinching but never despairing assessment of the great movement in Japanese political life that Arthur Stockwin, as much as any Westerner living, has made a vital and stimulating concern of the political scientist of Japan.

Acknowledgements

The editors extend their sincere appreciation to the Great Britain Sasakawa Foundation and to the Isaac Alfred Ailion Foundation for their generous support for the workshop on 'The Left in the Shaping of Japanese Democracy', held at Leiden University between 6 and 8 June 2003. Professor Glenn Hook helped give shape and ballast to the discussions which led to this *Festschrift*, an idea originally proposed by David Williams when he worked with Glenn at Sheffield University. The Leiden workshop also benefitted enormously from the labours, often behind the scenes, of Iben Molenkamp and Karin Aalderink.

Turning to the production of this book, the editors express their gratitude to Peter Sowden at RoutledgeCurzon, who first encouraged the project, and to Stephanie Rogers of Routledge, who has seen the project through to final fruition. Robin Reilly also provided useful editorial advice on the finer arts of editing, by respecting, the labours of the professional scholar.

At Oxford, a special word of thanks is owed to Dorothy Storry and Roger Goodman, who not only warned us about the perils of producing a *Festschrift* but also provided sound advice on how to succeed in this often delicate task. Jane Baker of the Nissan Institute rendered, as always, sterling secretarial assistance. Finally, we wish to thank Professor Stockwin who let us get on with the task while aiding our efforts at every turn.

The content of each chapter is the sole responsibility of the author.

Japanese usage and style

Throughout this book, we have followed the style employed at *The Japan Times*, in which Western and Japanese names are given in English order, that is personal name followed by family name. This departs from the conventions of Japan Studies, and our reasons for doing so are as follows. First, attempting to reproduce the Japanese convention of family name first, personal second, works against the natural order of English, thus producing horrors such as 'Mishima Yukio's novels', where Yukio is the Japanese novelist's personal name. Second, confronted with 'Maruyama Masao', Western readers without Japanese often conclude, quite understandably, that this influential political thinker's family name is Masao. Third, and even more disconcerting, one discovers that undergraduate students of the Japanese language often make the same mistake well into their courses. Finally, the attempt to reproduce Japanese usage in English is largely to blame for the typographical nightmare that is the English side of the Japanese business card, where one confronts a chaos of font sizes and faces. All this trouble could be eliminated if we would follow the style of *The Japan Times*. We propose that we return to it.

Macrons have been employed reluctantly for all Japanese words except for 'Tokyo' and 'Kyoto'.

Part I

Left-wing thought from the Russian Revolution to the war on terrorism

1 The Left hand of darkness

Forging a political Left in interwar Japan

Christopher Goto-Jones

The translation of a physical direction into a political stance was one of the great terminological victories of the French Revolution.[1] However, searching for the 'political Left' in a non-European context is complicated by the profusion of other directions that are granted political significance. In the case of interwar Japan, intellectuals and political leaders were striving to make sense of a new universe of political ideas and organizational models, largely imported from Europe at the turn of the twentieth century. For many such thinkers, the most salient and useful directions in political thought were 'East' and 'West,' no matter how vulgar these terms might have been. 'Left and Right' appeared to be internal concerns or subdivisions of the 'West,' and it took a number of years for the Japanese academe to really appreciate the substantive ideological and philosophical distinctions between these two stances. Even then, there remained little consensus about how the Right–Left spectrum might be mapped onto the political formations of the 'East.' In particular, looking back through the rich philosophical traditions of Japan, it was not immediately obvious where to locate the various schools of Buddhist, Confucian, or Shintō-derived political ideas. Were these on the 'Left' or the 'Right,' or did they somehow transcend this schema altogether?[2]

Political directions were not limited to the physical. An overriding concern in the late 1930s was the political and cultural significance of temporal direction: 'modernity' and 'tradition' became the catch-words of political affiliation. History and historiography became pivotal political tools. Japan's rapidly expanding empire was categorised popularly as 'anti-Western' or as an attempt to 'overcome modernity,' rather than necessarily as a Rightist or imperialist adventure.

It is within this multi-directional context that we must locate the early years of the 'Left' in Japanese politics. Such a context not only provides a wealthy tapestry of political ideas, but it also creates a knot of methodological problems for the contemporary historian to unravel. A central dilemma is flagged by the treatment of this period in the postwar literature: until quite recently, the interwar and wartime period has been seen as a 'dark valley' (*kurai tanima*), haunted by the spectres of apostates (*tenkōsha*) who betrayed their 'Leftist' credentials to accommodate the imperial state.[3] The darkness of this valley has been considered almost absolute, with few or no lights of Leftist resistance burning in the shadows.

There are a number of possible reasons for this presentation of the interwar period. The first is simple: it is possible (albeit unlikely) that there really was no significant Leftist movement or discourse in the 1920s to 1930s. The second reason is concerned with the state of the Left in the early postwar: compounded by an acute sense of embarrassment about their failures during the war period, postwar Marxists such as Kazuto Matsumura (1905–77) have sought to represent postwar Japan as a radical new stage in the development of the Left in Japanese history, pushing the interwar under the carpet of history. Gayle refers to a 'general mood of amnesia' settling over the Marxist Left with the termination of the war.[4]

On a more general level, a third possible reason concerns the controversial question of war guilt. Here the influence of the transwar, 'Leftist' political thinker Masao Maruyama is critical. In his celebrated analysis of Japanese ultranationalism and fascism, Maruyama suggests that it is impossible to pin responsibility for Japanese aggression on any single individual or group.[5] Instead, Maruyama implicates the Japanese spirit itself – the people of interwar Japan simply were not spiritually or intellectually equipped to prevent the slide into the abyss. The political Left failed to propagate the necessary sense of autonomous subjectivity (*shutaisei*) in Japanese society. Buried beneath a system of irresponsibilities, nobody in interwar or wartime Japan could dissent – it was unthinkable.[6] For Maruyama, as for postwar Marxists like Katsumi Umemoto (1912–74), a vital first task for the progressive Left after August 1945 was to transform the 'common sense' (*jōshiki*) of the Japanese people; if progressive intellectuals could not succeed in disseminating *shutaisei* into the psyche of the Japanese, then Japan would never really escape from the dark valley.[7] Interestingly, as we will see, many of Maruyama's and Umemoto's concerns about the subjectivity of the Japanese people (*taishū*) had already been expressed by Kiyoshi Miki and Jun Tosaka, from the forgotten depths of the dark valley.

A final possible reason for the presentation of the interwar period as relatively barren of Leftist political ideas is because contemporary historians have been mistaken about the appropriate focus of their excavations. From the comfort of a postwar liberal hegemony, commentators have mined the 1920s and 1930s for signs of a familiar, fully formed, ready-made political 'Left.' However, given the tremendous intellectual and political complexity of the period in question – a veritable barrage of Left, Right, East, West, modern and traditional – this hardly seems like a reasonable (or historiographically consistent) expectation. Why, for example, should we assume that the political Left of 1920s Japan would embrace both liberalism and Marxism together? How sophisticated might be a Marxist, anti-liberal and anti-Western position? Is it really necessary (or appropriate) to assume that Leftist political thought could not have been nationalist or even imperialist simultaneously?

This chapter will explore the work of two leading 'Leftist' intellectuals from the interwar period, Kiyoshi Miki (1897–1945) and Jun Tosaka (1900–45). Both identified themselves as Marxists for varying periods during their careers, and both would be imprisoned because of this identification – indeed, both would die as political prisoners in the final months of the war in 1945. The twin stories of Miki and Tosaka reveal a great deal about the Left in interwar Japan, both in terms of its intellectual integrity and its political fate. In particular, whilst Miki and Tosaka would share a common identification in terms of the Left–Right political spectrum, their ideas would develop in different directions along the East–West and modernity–tradition axes. Whilst Tosaka would remain a thorough-going materialist until his death in the summer of 1945, providing a rare and brilliant light of dissent during the dark oppression of the war years, Miki would allow his communist ideas to evolve to participate in the cooperativist ideology of the pseudo-fascist *Shōwa kenkyūkai*. Nonetheless, Miki's apparent *tenkō* would not prevent him from continuing to identify himself with the 'Left' and neither would it prevent the authorities from arresting him on charges of violating the anti-Communist Peace Preservation Law (*Chian ijihō*) on 25 March 1945.[8]

Rather than writing Miki off as a *tenkōsha*, I suggest that a great deal can be learned about the composition of the interwar Left by considering the continuities in his thought across the alleged apostasy. Indeed, it should be one of the monuments of the political Left in 1920s and 1930s Japan that it was broad and sophisticated enough to encompass both Miki and Tosaka. Hence, rather than dismissing this period as a dark valley for the Left, I suggest that it provides a number of important insights into the particular intellectual form taken by the Left in Japanese history – a broad and slightly unconventional Left that might usefully be seen as the predecessor of original postwar movements, such as Kōjin Karatani's New Associationist Movement. That said, I certainly do not contend that the interwar Left should be excused its often complicit position in the imperial regime. I merely observe that being complicit and being Leftist need not necessary be considered mutually exclusive in the intricate context of interwar Japan.

Locating Miki and Tosaka in the activist Left

Masao Maruyama has noted that the 1920s saw Marxism sweep 'through the Japanese intelligentsia like a whirlwind,'[9] stoking the fires of Leftist activism but also generating a variety of ostensibly 'Marxist' positions. Indeed, across the political spectrum in the 1920s and also in the 1930s, it would have been hard to find an intellectual who did not broadly agree with Marx's basic diagnosis of the problems of capitalist society – the atomization and alienation of the individual due to his/her commodification. However, only some intellectuals would subsequently identify themselves as Marxists, others would be content simply to call themselves 'Japanese' and to define their opposition to capitalism in terms of Japan's increasing opposition to the culture and power of the West, emblemised by capitalism.

Even those thinkers who did choose to identify themselves as Marxists or Communists did not always expound ideological positions that we would immediately recognise as Marxist. Certainly Marx, famous for not being a Marxist himself, would have been rather surprised to see some of the ideas whirling around in his name. Perhaps the archetypal 'Marxist' from just before this period might be Hajime Kawakami (1879–1946), who managed to be a self-proclaimed Marxist for nearly a decade before he mentioned class conflict or historical materialism.[10] In the classic work of his early period, *Bimbō monogatari* (A Story of Poverty, 1917),[11] Kawakami established his influential vision of Marxism as a moral philosophy – the problems of the unequal distribution of wealth should be solved through the exercise of moral will on the part of the affluent. In many ways, Kawakami's 'idealist' Marxism set the tone for a generation of young Japanese Marxists, for whom the political Left became tantamount to expounding ethical politics. For Kawakami and many others (including Miki) it was the humanist side of Marx that was most appealing[12] – in his later work Kawakami would concern himself with demonstrating that Marx's principal concern had not been with material things but rather with human relationships. This concern for the 'lacuna' in Marxism would also be characteristic of the early postwar Marxists in Japan, some of whom (such as Katsumi Umemoto) would seek to fill the humanist void with idealist devices that would have been readily familiar to Miki and the interwar Kyoto School of Kitarō Nishida.[13]

The intellectual make-up of the political Left in Japan underwent a gradual process of transition, as leading figures such as Kawakami began to shift their positions in response to the criticisms of a younger generation of Marxist scholars such as Miki, Tosaka and Kazuo Fukumoto (1894–1983), many of whom had made the pilgrimage to Germany, where they had studied at the cutting edge of modern philosophy.[14] The Communist movement in Japan was also given new energy by developments in the international arena. Future leaders of the Japan Communist Party (established July 1922) such as Hitoshi Yamakawa (1880–1958), would be inspired by the Bolsheviks' seizure of power in the Russian Revolution of October 1917. For Yamakawa, the Bolshevik Revolution demonstrated the power and efficacy of direct action to produce political change, and he argued that it should provide a model for the action of the Japanese proletariat. Implicit in Yamakawa's view was the idea that the Meiji Restoration had been truly revolutionary and that it had established Japan as a modern, bourgeois capitalist state – hence, Japan was ready for the final revolution. This view would become central to the identity of the *Rōnō* (Labour-Farmer) faction of the JCP, although it would never dominate the party line. Indeed, by about 1926 Yamakawa's position had been effectively refuted by Kazuo Fukumoto and his *Kōza* (Lecture School) faction, which maintained that the Meiji Restoration had been incomplete, and that any socialist revolution in Japan would have to be preceded by a proper modern, democratic revolution to remove the last vestiges of feudal organization from Japanese society.[15]

The Yamakawa-Fukumoto debates were indicative of some of the key theoretical concerns of the Japanese Left in the 1920s. However, the concern for ideological purity appears to have been translated into a preference for intellectual struggle over political praxis. For some postwar commentators, this intellectualization of the Japanese Left was a key factor in its impotence: 'it turned the JCP into a confederation of mandarins and quite possibly made the Marxist movement of Japan the most theoretically sophisticated in the world.'[16] In the Thesis of 1927, the Comintern criticised the JCP (and Fukumoto himself) for its over-preoccupation with dogma, theory, and abstraction – although it did tacitly confirm the *Kōza* position that Japan retained too many elements of feudalism for an immediate socialist revolution.[17]

The 1927 Thesis did not act to reduce the theoretical sophistication of the Japanese Left. Instead, intellectuals such as Miki and Goro Hani, previously associated with Fukumoto, began to question the hegemony of Moscow and its ability to dispense wisdom to non-European nations with their own particular contexts and particularities. If anything, this nudge from the international Communist movement actually made the Japanese Left strive for even greater levels of theoretical sophistication, and it certainly prompted intellectuals like Miki and Hani to broaden their understanding of the parameters of the political Left. In particular, the question of the need for national unity began to compete with issues of class conflict for priority in the discourse.[18]

In October 1928, Miki and Hani founded a new journal with the idea of providing a public forum for the theoretical Left. The title, *Shinkō kagaku no hata no moto ni* (Under the Banner of the New Science), was self-consciously drawn from Fukumoto's earlier journal, *Marukusushizumu no hata no moto ni* (Under the Banner of Marxism), and the shift from 'Marxism' to 'New Science' was deliberate. Whilst it is possible that the new title was simply necessitated by the increasingly strict application of the anti-Communist Peace Preservation Law of 1925, which saw the mass arrest of Leftist leaders in 1928 (the so-called '15 March Incident' in which 500 people were arrested as Communists), Miki and Hani appear to have designed the title to encourage participation from a wide range of the intelligentsia – not just JCP members.[19] Indeed, in the editorial postscript to the second issue of the journal the publisher Isamu Kobayashi acknowledged that: 'we do not adhere to a single perspective even on Marxism, which is of most importance within the framework of the New Science . . . Rather, we seek not to introduce in these pages a primer, an outline, or a commentary on Marxism, but instead to construct a point of view with Marxism as the backdrop.'[20]

The quest to 'construct a point of view with Marxism as the backdrop' was shared with Miki's long-time friend and colleague, Jun Tosaka, who also wrote for the New Science journal. The two men had met in their student days in Kyoto Imperial University, where both were drawn by the lure of the biggest names in philosophy (Kitarō Nishida and Hajime Tanabe – the latter joining the philosophy department just after Miki became a student there in 1917) and in Marxism (Hajime Kawakami was Professor of Economics). Miki was a few years Tosaka's senior, indeed he was already in the graduate school at Kyōdai when Tosaka first enrolled as a young student in 1921. After graduation, both men would find themselves in Tokyo – in fact, Miki would be replaced by Tosaka as professor of philosophy at Hōsei University, when the former was forced to resign his post after having been arrested in May 1930 under suspicion of donating money to the JCP. Ironically, Tosaka himself had been arrested only two months earlier, having given shelter to an active member of the JCP. In any case, Tosaka was also dismissed from his position at Hōsei at the start of 1934 – the university cited his political views as the reason. Miki and Tosaka would continue to move in the same social circles and even to collaborate on roundtable discussions (*zadankai*) at least until the end of the 1930s, by which time Tosaka was constantly in and out of jail and Miki was beginning his flirtation with the state in Prince Fumimaro Konoe's *Shōwa kenkyūkai*.

Partly due to pressure from the Higher Thought Police, but mostly thanks to internal fragmentation and disunity, the *Shinkō kagaku sha* did not last very long. In fact, the last issue of the journal was published in December 1929; Miki and Hani merged their Society into the new Proletarian Science Research Institute (*Puroretaria kagaku kenkyūjo*). However, this turned out to be a disastrous move for Miki. Just as the broad theoretical sweep of the JCP and even the *Shinkō kagaku sha* had produced tensions and personal rivalries, so it was with the new Institute. Within only a year of its foundation, the influential Marxist intellectual Shiso Hattori (1901–56) attacked Miki's ideas for being bourgeois and even democratic – Miki was forced out of the Proletarian Science Research Institute. At about this time, Miki held a series of high profile roundtable discussions with Kitarō Nishida, perhaps the most famous philosopher in Japanese history but a central target of attacks from the Marxist Left.[21]

After Miki Left the Proletarian Science Research Institute, it reformed into the *Yuibutsuron kenkyūkai* or *Yuiken* (Research Group on Materialism) in 1932 – again dedicated to the construction of a 'point of view with Marxism as the backdrop.' The *Yuiken* not only included Hattori but also two of Miki's oldest friends, Goro Hani and Jun Tosaka. Indeed, Tosaka would remain one of the key driving forces behind the *Yuiken* and its journal (which changed its name from *Yuibutsuron kenkyū* to *Gakugei* (Science and Art) in 1938), until it was forcibly disbanded by the police in the so-called *Yuiken* Incident of November 1938, two months after Miki had joined the *Shōwa kenkyūkai*.

Between communism and cooperativism: Miki, Tosaka and the elasticity of the theoretic Left

During his time at Kyoto Imperial University, Miki told his friend Jun Tosaka that he intended to become a 'better Fukumoto.'[22] At this time, Miki was becoming increasingly involved with Hajime Kawakami – indeed, his mentor Kitarō Nishida had recommended him to direct Kawakami's new research group on Hegel's dialectics – and his ambition appears to have been to become the leading left-wing intellectual of his day. In many ways, Miki would succeed in this ambition: whilst Miki never had the charisma of the activist and party leader, his work brought the philosophy of Marx to the attention of a much wider audience than Fukumoto ever could.[23]

Miki established his theoretical position in an influential series of four essays, *Yuibutsushikan to gendai no ishiki* (Historical Materialism and Contemporary Consciousness) published between 1927 and 1928.[24] The contrast between Miki's concern for materialism in these essays and his dismissive attitude towards materialism in his masterpiece of 1932, *Rekishi tetsugaku* (Philosophy of History), is often cited as indicative of his alleged *tenkō* whilst imprisoned for Communist sympathising in May 1930. It is interesting to reflect, however, that the trajectory of Miki's Marxism was anti-materialistic from the start, at least to some extent.[25] One of Miki's principal concerns in the essays of 1927/8 was to free Marxism from what he called the metaphysical (*keijijōgakuteki*) aspects of materialism. In this way he hoped to shift intellectual inquiry away from questions of matter and substance, and towards social concerns and (in particular) social consciousness.

Ironically, it was the publication of these important and influential texts that began the marginalization of Miki from the mainstream of the JCP and the Communist Left – although there is little evidence to suggest that Miki himself was concerned by the question of his 'orthodoxy.' Whilst Miki may have found support for his position in the texts of Marx himself (some of which he translated into Japanese for the first time – for example, *Die Deutsche Ideologie*[26]), he was implicitly rebuked by Moscow and thus criticised by the more orthodox members of the Japan Communist Party.

Jun Tosaka, who penned the closest thing to a Japanese 'German Ideology' in 1935 (*Nihon ideorogii-ron*),[27] would become increasingly critical of Miki's slide away from materialism and into what he termed liberal-humanism (which he identified as a methodology opposed to materialism). For Tosaka, there was nothing to stop a liberal philosopher slipping into Japanism (fascism) entirely on the basis of feeling or a character flaw, whereas the embrace of materialism required a commitment of reason and logic.[28] In fact, as we will see, Miki's character would become central to the political impact of his thought, as his personal ambition drew him into the service of the state.

The central problems for Miki *qua* Marxist were his conceptions of man and of history. Echoing his one-time teacher in Kyoto, Hajime Kawakami, Miki was most interested in the humanistic side of Marx's writing and hence appeared to reject the essential significance of historical materialism. Even worse (from the perspective of the more 'orthodox' Marxists), Miki's conception of man appeared to borrow quite heavily from the Kyoto School idealism of his mentor, Kitarō Nishida.

The question of the place of 'man' in Marxist theory is by no means simple, and the kind of opposition that we see between Miki and the more mainstream Marxists of the late 1920s (including Jun Tosaka) can be seen rehearsed throughout the postwar period in Europe as well as Japan. In many ways, Miki's unconventional Marxist humanism highlights one of the great theoretical disputes in Marxist discourse, and might be seen as greatly enriching the Left in interwar Japan (although this was certainly not appreciated at the time). Perhaps the clearest exposition of this debate would not appear until the mid-1970s, when Lucien Sève published his landmark text, *Marxisme et théorie de la personnalité*.[29]

Sève highlights two traditions in the interpretation of man in Marxist theory. For the first, which we might simplistically associate with Miki himself, 'Marxism is essentially defined as a *humanism*, i.e. as a philosophy of the progressive realization of the "whole man" throughout history . . . [Man] is not reducible to the relations of production but is always defined by free-choice and the creative project . . . [To] proceed in this direction it would be necessary to develop a whole Marxist theory of *subjectivity* and . . . in failing to do so Marxism is mutilated.'[30] Interestingly, as we have already suggested, this quest to fill a perceived humanist-subjectivist lacuna in Marxism, might be seen as a central characteristic of Japanese Marxism, both pre- and postwar.[31]

The second view of man in Marxism, which we might simplistically attribute to Miki's critics, including Jun Tosaka, refutes the first, arguing that Marx changed his position fundamentally in his mature works, abandoning the psychologism of the *1844 Manuscripts* on which the humanists draw so heavily. 'It is said that Marx entirely displaced the terrain of his analysis from the human essence to social relations . . . More fundamentally still, according to this interpretation, *it is the very concept of man which no longer finds a place in mature Marxism* . . . Individuals can only intervene in Marxist theory *in so far as they personify social relations*, hence, in so far as they *are not* psychological subjects.'[32] Any and every theory of subjectivity is outside of Marxism – it is abstract humanism or *ideology*.

It is not the case, however, that Miki's reading of Marx was restricted to the latter's youthful (pre-Marxist?) works – indeed he translated into Japanese the pivotal texts that Engels himself famously claimed 'deposited the brilliant germ of the new world outlook,' that is the mature historical materialism of Marx.[33] Like Sève over forty years later, Miki would be dissatisfied with the unsynthetic opposition between these two 'Marxist' positions, and he would construct a sophisticated theory of man that sits somewhere in between these two extremes.[34]

Hence, Miki's 'anthropological Marxism' was not a simple attempt to construct a psychological explanation of the predicament of modern man;

neither did it seek to marginalise the importance of social relations and historical process. Indeed, in many ways, Miki's Marxism was at the cutting edge of interwar political philosophy – drawing inspiration from eminent contemporaries like Nishida, Tetsurō Watsuji (1889–1960) and Martin Heidegger as well as from Marx himself.

The philosophical debt owed to Kitarō Nishida is immediately apparent at the foundations of Miki's *ningengaku no marukusushugi*, where he rests his entire system upon the concept of *kiso keiken* (or *kisoteki keiken*) – basic experience. There is a clear terminological and conceptual affiliation between *kiso keiken* and Nishida's revolutionary concept of *junsui keiken* (pure experience).[35] Nishida's term referred to the undifferentiated moment of experience prior to conscious deliberation (and, for Nishida, prior to the self), and Miki's fledgling Marxist concept, *kiso keiken*, resonated closely with this, despite the pristine (even essentialist) idealism implied by Nishida *tetsugaku*. For Miki, however, the substance of this basic experience was historical rather than essential – it changed according to developments in the *actual* world (*genjitsu*) – and it was the experience of the proletariat that was basic to the modern period.

Miki's emphasis on historical construction clearly represents a Marxist-influenced reinterpretation of Nishida's 1920s idealism, detaching foundational reality from the quasi-mystical 'place of nothingness' (*mu no basho*) and pinning it quite firmly to the pragmatic demands of the present.[36] In making this move, Miki appears dubious about the possibility of universal principles – suggesting that 'all thought systems were ideologies that could vary with the different demands of each era' and 'that the individual by himself embodied no ultimate values outside of his social and historical context.'[37]

It is in this way that Miki claims to have established a Marxist anthropology, since he is centrally concerned with the historical and social evolution of *ways of being* (*sonzai no shikata*, or sometimes *sonzai no moderu*). In language reminiscent of Heidegger, Miki expresses the nature of the individual as: 'I exist; I exist with others and amongst other things . . . existence becomes realised in our negotiations.'[38] Hence, Miki effectively conflates a humanist reading of Marx (emphasising his ideas about individual identity grounded in his/her material, socio-economic relationships) with a cultural-constitutionalist (*kyōyōshugi*) position (emphasising the location of an individual within the socio-cultural matrix of the period).[39]

For Tosaka, however, such a conflation of contexts would be a mistake. In an effort to clarify the terminology of the Left, Tosaka argues that there are two realities: *genjitsu* (reality) and *jissaisei* (actuality). The former refers to the socio-cultural context of the individual (represented by the institutional state, *kokumin*), and it was thus characterised by an 'unbelievably distorted liberalism' that has become characteristic of the commonsense of our society (*shakai no jōshiki*).[40] *Jissaisei*, on the other hand, was the contextual product of historical materialism – unpolluted by the ideological taint of *genjitsu* (represented by the historical or ethnic state, *minzoku*).[41] By conflating the two,

Miki stretched the elasticity of the theoretic Left further than Tosaka would have liked.

For Fletcher, Miki's efforts to contextualise the individual effectively 'stressed the allegiance of the individual to a larger group . . . the needs of the nation over those of the individual.'[42] However, Fletcher is wrong to suggest that the slippage between Miki's anthropological Marxism and totalitarianism is simple: Miki is explicit about the dialectical processes involved in the continuous, mutual invention (*hatsumei*) of the nation and the individual. Unlike the anthropology of Watsuji, for example, which emphasised the essential, timeless connections between climate, culture and character, Miki is clear that individuals are not determined by their environment, but that they negotiate (*kōshō*) with it in different ways at different times.[43] Like Marx and Hegel (to whom he refers constantly), Miki's logic is dialectical.

Unsuprisingly, Tosaka is also critical of romantics like Watsuji for failing to understand the relationship between the individual and their environment. For Tosaka, however, the problem is not so much the lack of dialectical method (which is really a Hegelian critique), but rather the methodology of philology. Tosaka argued that liberalism (and therefore Japanism, since the two are variations on a theme for Tosaka) is characterised by its philological and hermeneutic method,[44] which allows historians to substitute material reality for 'literary representations and images,' thus constructing a 'false' or 'ideological' history as a tool of bourgeois interests in the present. Actual (*jissaisei*) history *produces* the present and is not a product of it.[45] Hence, to the extent that Tosaka defines liberalism methodologically, he places Miki on the cusp of theoretic liberalism – perilously close to the slide into the abyss of Japanism.

Fortunately, Miki's anthropological Marxism does not end with his conception of *kiso keiken*, but rather this is merely its beginning. He builds on it in two additional stages – a primary logic (*dai ichiji rogosu*) and a secondary logic (*dai niji rogosu*) – both of which move beyond the fundamentals of man's *actuality* (*genjitsu* – already tainted by the everyday for Tosaka) and into the arena of his everyday existence.

The first stage is identical with anthropology itself – 'the primary logos is born directly from raw, foundational negotiations.'[46] In other words, it is the individual's initial 'self-interpretation' (*jiko kaishaku*) when confronted with basic experience.[47] Nonetheless, because of its conscious nature, this primary logos is still distanced from basic experience itself – it represents the individual's first attempt to make sense of his/her interactions with a basic reality that is beyond (or prior to) his/her language and comprehension. Primary logos is the Left hand of a foundational darkness.

The second stage is the sociological consequence of the first. Miki characterised the secondary logos in terms of ideology, which he differentiated from anthropology by its diminishing proximity to basic experience: ideology transmuted or mediated (*baikai*) the direct expression of the primary logos through the vocabulary and categories of the social sciences and philosophy.

For Miki, there was a correct relationship between basic experience, anthropology and ideology. The basic experience of 1920s Japan was identified with that of the proletariat, and Miki believed that this should act on the world through the self-interpretation of clear-minded individuals. Subsequently, 'the structure of anthropology acts to regulate the structure of ideology,'[48] and thus social discourse and social movements should reflect shifts in the basic experience of the people. However, this 'correct relationship' between experience and action (i.e. the correct form of the genealogy of theory – *riron no keifugaku*) was an ideal, and Miki was well aware that it might break down in practice.

Miki noted that 'Marx criticised Feuerbach's anthropology for being abstract (*chūshōteki*), just as the latter considered Hegel's idealist philosophy to be abstract,'[49] and so Miki was concerned that a barrier might develop between the basic experience of the proletariat and the invention of an ideological form suited to its needs. This barrier could be constructed through the ossification of the secondary logos into an abstract and non-negotiative ideology. The result, of course, would be a non-responsive, ahistorical ideology or modern consciousness (*gendai no ishiki*) that acted to suppress and dominate exactly those people who should be creating it. Any system of thought that did not negotiate directly with the basic experience of the proletariat constituted a dangerous abstraction – Jun Tosaka would call it 'bourgeois philosophy,' and would suggest a link between this, liberalism and the 'many types of fascist ideology that saunter about [Japan] in the middle of the day.'[50]

Even more profound than the problem of the ossification of ideology was the 'despotic position'[51] of logos and language itself, since ideology rested and relied on logos for its existence: just as ideology could become an abstract barrier between man's understanding of the world and his actual experience of it, so too could language fulfil this function. Hence Miki would call on intellectuals to search for a new logos – a fresh language that the people of Japan could use to break down the barriers between themselves and reality, barriers erected and defended by modern society itself.[52]

Not many of Miki's Leftist contemporaries interpreted his agenda as a call for the development of a revolutionary vanguard movement. Indeed, as we have seen, his approach was generally denounced by fellow Marxists who did not appreciate his focus on consciousness and ideology. Miki's position appears to have been somewhat contradictory: whilst it is clear that he viewed Marxism as an analytical tool rather than a manifesto for action (*à la* Georg Lukács), suggesting that the material dialectic itself would resolve any contradictions between basic experience and social existence, he also suggests that historical materialism was the *ideal* form of the present – i.e. the basic experience of the proletariat *should* be directly translated into ideology via logos – but that the present failed to live up to this ideal, hence necessitating willed change. This second position completely undermines the significance of materialism since it implies that materialism has little (or no) determining influence on the social world. Hence, Miki managed to alienate both the left-wing radicals (and Yamakawa's *Rōnō-ha*), who called for revolutionary action *and* theoretical Marxists (such as Jun Tosaka and some members of the *Kōza-ha*) who fully embraced the significance of materialism. In a manner not unfamiliar to Hajime Kawakami, Miki occupies an ambiguous space in Marxism, filling a perceived lacuna with human agency inspired by moral ideals. In Tosaka's terms, Miki stretched the left into Liberalism – and that was a dangerous thing to do.

Between or beyond Left and Right?

It may be the case that Miki's leftist contemporaries did not appreciate his anthropological Marxism, but activists and thinkers towards the Right of the political spectrum were keen to develop the trajectories of his ideas. Certainly his philosophy was more promising in this regard than that of Tosaka. For many observers in the 1930s, it seemed that Miki was partaking in the quasi-nihilistic discourse of the Kyoto School – the terminological affinity between *kiso keiken* and *junsui keiken* was clear and the substantive differences between these concepts were rather more inaccessible.[53] Even conceptually, however, Miki leaves some room for uncertainty about the actual nature of *kiso keiken* – it appears dark, hidden and ineffable in most of his texts, leaving the door open for romanticism. In addition, Miki's close personal relationship with Kitarō Nishida seemed to associate him with other students of his mentor, such as Keiji Nishitani, Masa'aki Kosaka and Kōyama Iwao, who were unself-conscious about the nationalistic implications of Nishida *tetsugaku*.

Miki himself helped the political Right to develop another of the trajectories from his Marxist thought. In his seminal essay from 1932, *Fuan no shisō to sono chōkoku*, written two years after his imprisonment for contributing funds to the JCP, Miki develops his critique of logos as a source of oppression and despotism in modern Japanese society. Whilst he warned against the development of a philosophy of anguish (*fuan no tetsugaku*), as witnessed in Germany, which was characterised by a loss of faith in reason, he was also quite clear that logos was not sufficient to the needs of Japanese society at that time. Miki called on intellectuals to produce a 'new thinking' that would unite logos and pathos – overcoming the philosophy of angst dialectically.[54] Later in the 1930s, following in the direction feared by Tosaka's methodological critique, Miki would phrase his overcoming in terms of the need to transcend Marxism and Liberalism – his communism was gradually transmuted into cooperativism (*kyōdōshugi*).[55] In the social discourse of the early 1940s, this overcoming would become conflated with the drive to 'overcome modernity.'[56]

Clearly, Miki's critique of the place and value of logos played directly into the hands of the ultra-nationalists, who were constructing vulgar oppositions between the 'rational West' and the 'spiritual East.' However, it also had an important theoretical consequence that pulled Miki's thought dangerously into the direction of fascism. It would certainly be wrong to argue that Miki's work in the early 1930s was fascist, but it is true that it contained trajectories that would lead in this direction. In Tosaka's terms, Miki had stretched the political Left in the wrong direction, opening the door to liberalism, which he saw as leading the way to Japanism.[57] He asserts that the step from one to the other is more a matter of taste than logic – hence, Miki's liberal thought could not defend itself against the manipulations of the Japanists.

In a controversial thesis in the mid-1990s, Zeev Sternhell argued that fascism was actually a revision of Marxism, enacted under specific socio-historic and intellectual conditions. 'Fascist ideology cannot be described as a simple response to Marxism, its origins . . . were the direct result of a very specific revision of Marxism. It was a *revision* of Marxism and not a *variety* of Marxism or a *consequence* of Marxism.'[58] Whilst Sternhell was explicit that he was referring exclusively to European fascism (and his goal was to distinguish it from Nazism, which, he suggested, had nothing to do with Marxism at all), his argument sheds some light on interwar Japanese history.

For Sternhell, fascism was an 'antimaterialist and antirationalist' revision of Marxism, combined with an organic sense of nationalism. Sternhell suggests that such a form 'involved both the non-conformist extreme Left and the nationalist Right' and 'allowed the association of a new kind of socialism with radical nationalism.'[59]

Unlike Tosaka, Miki might be well categorised as part of the 'non-conformist' Left in interwar Japan. His thought moved in anti-materialist directions from the start, and anti-rationalism was certainly a conclusion drawn from his work by others (even if it was not his intention). Furthermore, both Miki and Tosaka might be considered representative of the political Left in interwar Japan in terms of their nationalism.

Miki's 'leftist' nationalism was rather more unconventional than that of Tosaka, although, following Lenin, they would both insist on the importance of a properly historicised nation. For Miki, however, the nation should be considered as an undivided whole. In particular, Miki would argue that Marx himself had been trapped by the logos of the eighteenth century, and that the concept of class (and class conflict) was not applicable to twentieth-century Japan. Indeed, Miki's later cooperativism was explicitly formulated as the resolution of two bourgeois evils: capitalism and class conflict. Factionalism and partisan politics were part of the ossified secondary logos; they had to be overcome. It was the duty of intellectuals to reconceptualise man in accordance with the basic experience of the present, not to reiterate conceptions from the past.[60]

One of the consequences of this conception of the nation, embraced by the *Shōwa kenkyūkai*, was the apparent vulgarization of the previously sophisticated, dialectical conception of the relationship between man and society. The elevation of the needs of the nation over those of the individual in this leftist discourse could have found its genesis in Miki's anthropological Marxism, wherein the individual was a negotiated entity, owing its existence and nature to its relational position.[61] By the time he wrote *Shinnihon* in 1938, however, this process of negotiation had become a unilateral process of determination – the ossified state defined the individual in accordance with its own (abstract) needs.

It is interesting to reflect that this intellectual shift was as much a product of socio-historic forces as internal logic – it is really a question of intellectual history. As Fletcher notes, participation in the *Shōwa kenkyūkai* 'guaranteed protection from censorship and distribution of their proposals to the highest levels of government,'[62] but it also carried with it the obligation to vulgarise sophisticated theoretical positions into terms acceptable (and comprehensible) to the authorities. Fletcher notes that the closer the *Shōwa kenkyūkai* 'thought they were getting to political power, the more they phrased their proposals towards achieving these goals.'[63] In other words, Miki's faith in the ability of intellectuals to change the political system in the direction of his anthropological Marxism was confronted by the power of the state.

Meanwhile, Jun Tosaka, who refused to participate in governmental or pseudo-governmental bodies such as the *Shōwa kenkyūkai*, evidently suspicious of the ability of (even well-meaning) intellectuals to reform the state from within, was dying in prison. Like Miki's, although in a very different way, his ideas were trumped by the material power of the state.

Conclusion – the Left hand of darkness

It is certainly not the case that the dark valley of the interwar period was bereft of a political Left. Indeed, the Left was an expansive and sophisticated arena, defined to some extent by Miki at one side and Tosaka at the other. That said, it is also not the case that these leftist intellectuals necessarily provided bright lights of reason or dissent in the darkness. Indeed, in many ways Miki represented the Left hand of darkness, building a theoretic road between the Marxist Left and the nationalist Right, via an emphasis on the humanist and anthropological aspects of Marx. Interestingly, he could shift his position without a significant intellectual reversal or *tenkō*. Tosaka was a rare individual, both as a courageous man in the face of oppression and as a dignified intellectual who remained true to his materialist convictions.

For Miki, as for many Japanese Marxists before and since, the Left encompassed Marxism and liberalism, unified by a concern for humanism, unity and social harmony, and stretched to include Japanism at the extremes. For Tosaka, on the other hand, the Left was anti-liberal, anti-idealist and anti-imperialist. Both thinkers combined a concern for nationalism with a disdain for capitalism and 'modernity,' and both believed that a vanguard of intellectuals would be needed to salvage Japanese society – resulting in an over-intellectualised Left separated by a great abyss from the people it was trying to represent. Tosaka once lamented that the liberals found 'the masses to be worth less than a cup of black tea.'[64]

Despite their different theoretical positions and political actions, both would end their lives as political prisoners in a Japanese prison. The imperialist state found the whole theoretical space between the two thinkers *too leftist*, while commentators today struggle to locate an interwar Left at all.

Notes

Much of this chapter was written as a visiting scholar in the Philosophy Faculty, University of Cambridge. The author would like to thank Pembroke College, Cambridge, for providing the necessary support.

1 In fact, the terms left- and right-wing find their origins in 1789, when the French National Assembly was created. In this new assembly, the Third Estate (representatives of the revolutionaries, who accounted for more than 95 per cent of the population) sat on the chamber's Left and the First Estate (the nobles) sat on its Right.
2 Kiyoshi Miki sought to overcome the Left–Right schema through the establishment of an 'Asian' political principle that could not be grasped by the individualist West. Kiyoshi Miki, 'The China Affair and Japanese Thought,' in *Contemporary Japan*, March 1938 – Miki is talking about the phenomenon of *tenkō*.
3 Recent exceptions to this might include Curtis Gayle (*Marxist History and Postwar Japanese Nationalism*, London: RoutledgeCurzon, 2003) and also (to some extent) H. D. Harootunian (*Overcome by Modernity*, Princeton: Princeton University Press, 2000).
4 Gayle, op. cit., p. 22.
5 Masao Maruyama, 'Theory and Psychology of Ultranationalism,' and 'Thought and Behaviour Patterns of Japan's Wartime Leaders,' in Masao Maruyama, *Thought and Behaviour in Modern Japanese Politics*, Oxford: Oxford University Press, 1963.
6 For an excellent account of Maruyama's ideas, see Rikki Kersten, *Democracy in Postwar Japan: Maruyama Masao and the Search for Autonomy*, London: Routledge, 1996.
7 Umemoto was a wartime idealist – trained by Tetsurō Watsuji and influenced by the Kyoto School. He made the transition to Marxism in the immediate postwar, publishing his controversial book, *Yuibutsuron to dōtoku*, in 1949 (reprinted Tokyo: Kobushi shobō, 1995).
8 Miki was charged with harbouring and assisting Teru Takakura, a known Communist.
9 Masao Maruyama, *Studies in the Intellectual History of Tokugawa Japan*, Princeton: University of Tokyo, 1974, p. xxiii.
10 Kawakami was the first to begin a translation of *Das Kapital* into Japanese, in 1915. Further details on Kawakami: Hikaru Furuta, *Kawakami Hajime*, Tokyo: Tokyo daigaku shuppansha, 1959; Gail Berstein, *Japanese Marxist: A Portrait of Kawakami Hajime*, Cambridge, Mass: Harvard University Press, 1976.
11 Originally serialised in the influential and respected newspaper, *Osaka Asahi*, bringing it to the attention of a wide audience.
12 Duus and Scheiner suggest that this approach was also a feature of the very earliest socialist thinkers in Japanese history, such as the late-Meiji activists Shūsui Kōtoku (1871–1911) and Sen Katayama (1859–1933), who were involved in the foundation of the Socialist Party in 1900: 'even while following Marx's analysis of capitalism, they could not accept his moral agnosticism.' Peter Duus and Irwin Scheiner, 'Socialism, Liberalism, and Marxism, 1901–31,' in Bob Tadashi

Wakabayashi (ed.), *Modern Japanese Thought*, Cambridge: Cambridge University Press, 1998, p. 153.

13 See J. Victor Koschmann, *Revolution and Subjectivity in Postwar Japan*, Chicago: University of Chicago Press, 1996. The influence of Tetsurō Watsuji and Kitarō Nishida on Umemoto's conception of the essential integrity of the individual (as an *ideal*) is clear in his work of 1949. Interestingly, more 'orthodox' postwar Marxists such as Sekisuke Amakura (1906–75) would argue that the influence of Kyoto School conceptions of the individual had hobbled the wartime Left, and that it should not be permitted to continue in the postwar. See Sekisuke Amakura, *Gendai tetsugaku hihan*, Tokyo: Kobushi shobo, 1995.

14 Returning from several years of study in Germany, Fukumoto famously attacked the work of Kawakami in a public address at Kyoto Imperial University in 1924. Miki spent 1922–25 in Europe on an Iwanami scholarship. He studied with Heinrich Rickert in Heidelberg and Heidegger in Marburg. In 1924 he intended to go to Oxford, but instead moved to Paris, where he learned French and started work on Blaise Pascal. Tosaka never went to Europe.

15 In *Gendai nihon no shisōjō no shomondai* (TJZ II:227–35), Jun Tosaka argues that the revolution left an admixture of bureaucratic and military factions originating from the feudal past. He termed Taishō democracy an 'unbelievably distorted democracy.'

16 Duus and Scheiner, op cit., p. 201.

17 Germaine Hoston, *Marxism and the Crisis of Development in Prewar Japan*, Princeton: Princeton University Press, 1986, p. 52.

18 It is interesting to reflect, therefore, that the shift towards nationalism in the socio-political discourse was not merely the result of the influence of idealist philosophy but also a consequence of Moscow's assertion that Japan required a nationalist revolution before it would be ready for a socialist one.

19 Kevin Doak notes that this mirrors the strategy of Lenin, who encouraged A. M. Deborin's *Unter dem Banner des Marxismus* to open itself to non-Communist material in a joint war on religion. Kevin Doak, 'Under the Banner of the New Science: History, Science, and the Problem of Particularity in Early Twentieth-Century Japan,' *Philosophy East and West*, 48:2 (1998), pp. 232–57.

20 Cited in Doak, *ibid*. Doak also notes that this approach to the utility of Marxism as a method of social analysis (rather than an ideological commitment) raises the question of the salience of Marxism itself – could it be 'dispensed with when other scientific methods seemed either more accurate or appropriate'?

21 Miki and Nishida held two series of discussions in 1932. Miki's relationship with Nishida was always very close, since being his student in Kyoto. There is evidence to suggest that Miki (and others) felt he was Nishida's natural heir (for more detail, see the excellent Nobue Satō, *Nishida Kitarō to Miki Kiyoshi*, Tokyo: Chūōkōronsha, 1947). Nonetheless, Miki and Nishida would remain in close contact throughout the 1930s, and the dual influences of Nishida and Marx on Miki's work are mirrored by his collaborations with Nishida and Tosaka throughout this period. For his part, Tosaka would single out Nishida as the clearest representative of decadent, bourgeois philosophy in modern Japan, although recent research has documented some close connections between Nishida and the interwar Left in Japan (see Kenji Hattori, *Nishida tetsugaku to saha no hitotachi*, Tokyo: Kobushi shobō, 2000).

22 Gino Piovesana, 'Miki Kiyoshi: Representative Thinker of an Anguished Generation,' in Joseph Roggendorf (ed.), *Studies in Japanese Culture*, Tokyo: Sophia University Press, 1963, p. 150.

23 In fact, it seems plausible to argue that academic Marxists (rather than Marxist activists like Shūsui Kōtoku, 1871–1911) were most instrumental in the spread of Marxist ideas in Japan – indeed, Piovesana emphasises that 'the real spread of Marxism in Japan is due, not so much to the communist leaders, as to Kawakami

Hajime.' Later in the same volume, he adds: 'If Kawakami gave respectability to Marxism in academic circles . . . Miki Kiyoshi introduced Marxist thought among philosophers as well as a wide circle of students and the general public which avidly read his essays, written in a fairly clear and easy style.' Gino Piovesana, *Recent Japanese Philosophical Thought, 1862–1996, A Survey*, Surrey: Curzon Press, 1997, p. 170, p. 177.

24 Reproduced in MKC III. Perhaps the three most famous of these are: *Ningengaku no marukusuteki keitai* (pp. 1–38), *Marukusushugi to yuibutsuronshi* (pp. 39–74), and *Puragumachizumu no tetsugaku* (pp. 74–116).

25 Indeed, in a classic study, Shin'ichi Funayama includes Miki amongst the 'idealists' in Japan during this period. See Shin'ichi Funayama, *Nihon no kannenronsha*, Eiōsha, 1956.

26 This appeared under the title *Doitsu Ideologī* as part of the *Yuibutsuron kenkyūkai* series.

27 Reprinted in TJZ II.

28 Tosaka develops this critique in *Gendai nihon no shisōjō no shomondai*.

29 Lucien Sève, *Marxisme et théorie de la personanalité*, Paris: Editions sociales, 1974. Of course, Sève makes no mention of Japan or Miki.

30 Lucien Sève (trans. John McGreal), *Man in Marxist Theory and the Psychology of Personality*, New Jersey: Humanities Press, 1978, pp. 65–6 – emphasis in the original. Sève suggests that this view finds support in the works of the youthful Marx, such as the *1844 Manuscripts*.

31 Sève wonders why Marx would have left this 'lacuna' had it been so central to his concerns.

32 Sève, *Man in Marxist* . . . p. 69 – emphasis in the original.

33 Karl Marx and Friedrich Engels, *Selected Works*, Moscow: Progress Publishers, 1969, Vol.1, p. 336. Engels was talking about the *Thesis on Feuerbach* and the *German Ideology*.

34 Sève argues that the mature Marx never entirely abandoned his youthful humanism; he finds evidence of it in the classic statements of historical materialism, such as the *German Ideology* and *Das Capital* itself.

35 Nishida develops this important concept in his seminal debut, *Zen no kenkyū*, 1911, which now appears in NKZ I. Nishida himself acknowledged a debt of gratitude to Henri Bergson's *durée pure*.

36 Miki was accused of pragmatism rather than Marxism and defended himself in *Puragumachizumu no tetsugaku*.

37 William Fletcher, *The Search for a New Order: Intellectuals and Fascism in Prewar Japan*, Chapel Hill: University of North Carolina Press, 1982, p. 18. For Fletcher, this 'theoretical relativism' provides the seeds for a radical right-shift in Miki's work.

38 Kiyoshi Miki *Ningengaku no marukusuteki keitai*, MKC III:2, 3. This text dates from 1927, the same year as Heidegger released his *Sein und Zeit*.

39 Harootunian describes this as the 'profound adhesion of experience to "real life" and "everydayness".' HD Harootunian, op. cit., p. 361.

40 Tosaka develops this in *Gendai nihon no shisōjō no shomondai*.

41 For a discussion of progressive nationalisms and the differences between *kokumin* and *minzoku*, see Gale, op. cit.

42 Fletcher, op. cit., p. 19.

43 This process of negotiation is made very clear at the start of *Ningengaku no marukusuteki keitai*, MKC III. For example, p. 10: 'It is not that humans *oppose* this world [as an external object], rather they themselves always *negotiate* intimately with it . . . it is not a "world of objective existence" (*taishōteki sonzaikai*) but rather a "world of negotiative existence" (*kōshōteki sonzaikai*)' – emphasis in the original.

44 In *Gendai nihon no shisōjō no shomondai*, Tosaka also refers to the method as literaturism (*bunkengaku-shugi*).
45 Based on his formulation of basic experience, Miki would argue the exact opposite in *Rekishi tetsugaku*, 1932 (MKC VI).
46 Kiyoshi Miki, *Ningengaku no marukusuteki keitai*, MKC III:8.
47 Here Miki side-steps the emanationist critique of Kitarō Nishida. For the latter, 'pure experience' actually co-creates the individual and his/her world – they literally spring forth out of absolute nothingness (*zettai mu*). For Miki, on the other hand, the individual has an originary integrity but its personality is forged in the process of 'basic experience.' Hence, Miki leans closer to Bergson than Nishida in this respect.
48 Kiyoshi Miki, *Ningengaku no marukusuteki keitai*, MKC III:9 – emphasis in the original.
49 Ibid., MKC III:33.
50 Jun Tosaka, *'Mu no ronri' wa ronri dearu ka – Nishida tetsugaku no hōhō ni tsuite*, TJZ II:341.
51 Term quoted in H. D. Harootunian, op. cit., p. 362.
52 Miki would develop this further in his 1929 essay, *Kiki ni okeru rironteki imi*, MKC XII:3–16. Here Miki explains how the momentum of history (*rekishi no chikara*) would induce the emerging class (closest to basic experience) to produce a new type of thought. Miki laments, however, that 'class based' or partisan thought is not new at all, and that it too should be overcome. This is *before* he alleged *tenkō* in prison. Later, at the very end of an important essay from 1932, *Fuan no shisō to sono chōkoku* (MKC XIII:133–57), Miki argues that rather than focusing on the class struggle, 'philosophy must crisply and appropriately define a new kind of human being.'
53 As Tosaka pointed out, it is by no means certain that even *junsui keiken* led *logically* to rightist politics – see also Christopher S. Jones, 'Ethics and Politics in the Early Nishida,' *Philosophy East and West*, 53:4 (2003).
54 It is in *Fuan* . . . that Miki first publically renounces Marxism as over dependent on materialism and logos at the expense of humanist and social issues.
55 See, for example, the 1935 essay, *Jiyūshugi igo*, MKC XII:68–75, and then Miki's contributions to the *Shōwa kenkyūkai*, such as *Shina jiken no sekaishiteki igi*, in which Miki talked of the need for a new cooperativist principle to assist in the resolution of the contradictions of capitalist society in Japan and East Asia.
56 An interesting discussion of these debates is David Williams, 'Modernity, Harootunian and the Demands of Scholarship,' *Japan Forum*, 15:1 (2003).
57 Tosaka argues that it is a mistake to view liberalism and materialism as related (just because they are Western imports), when in fact materialism opposes liberalism, and liberalism is 'nothing but a preparation for Japanism' *Gendai nihon* . . . TJZ II:233.
58 Zeev Sternhell, *The Birth of Fascist Ideology: From Cultural Rebellion to Political Revolution*, Princeton: Princeton University Press, 1994, pp. 5–6 – emphasis in the original.
59 Ibid., pp. 23–4.
60 See, for example, Miki's notorious essay from 1938, *Shinnihon* MKZ XVII.
61 As late as 1936 Miki was asserting that 'the concept of personality is not individualistic, but rather a personality exists as a personality only in relation to others.' Kiyoshi Miki, *Shakai jihyō*, MKC XIV:76–7. The language of 'personality' is very similar to that used by Nishida.
62 Fletcher, op. cit., p. 105.
63 Ibid., p. 105.
64 Jun Tosaka, *Gendai nihon* . . . TJC II:234–5.

2 Painting the Emperor red

The Emperor and the socialists in the 1930s

Rikki Kersten

Introduction

The 1930s is not considered to be the high point for socialism in modern Japan. The sorry fate of a divided, weak and ultimately flawed movement is not usually regarded as sexy. Accordingly, scholars have not shown much interest in seeking to understand the deeper, long-term significance of this era. After all, by 1945, the 1930s was seen either as a dark valley, an aberration, or a purely historical tale of the weakness of an idea whose relevance ended with the triumph of postwar democracy. In general terms, the failure of interwar Japanese socialism has often been collapsed into a general treatment of the failure of the Left as a whole in the face of the wartime emperor system.

On the other hand, Japanese postwar readings of the 1930s have roamed between the jaundiced poles of literary criticism from a communist 'New Left' that regarded its token wartime resistance as a ticket to postwar leadership of revolution, to a liberal desire to lance the boil of the failure to resist in wartime. The study of transwar *tenkō* (apostasy),[1] for instance, was written from a place of relative complacency, with a view to explaining in deceptively scientific terms a lamentable lapse on the part of their colleagues. The complacency came not so much from a sense of security with postwar democracy, but from a feeling that in postwar it was possible to identify those historical errors for the edification of future generations, who could then act in time to avoid this kind of thing happening again. It becomes in fact a 'how not to' lesson in intellectual and political resistance . . . just in case it is ever required again. Those who delivered the assessment were often missing from the rendering of their own lived experience, securely divorced from the wartime objects of their postwar scrutiny. Part tribunal, part kangaroo court and part self-exemption, the notion of *tenkō* provided a lasso with which to bunch together the rabble who fell into the arms of the Emperor in the 1930s and 1940s.

Alternatively, the tale of 1930s Japan written in the postwar era is a story about power, and analysis has tended to focus on explaining the mechanics of power in terms of the 'emperor system', the apparatus of state repression, and the popular seduction of emperor-centred patriotism. Here the implication of history repeating itself is frequently invoked, though curiously devoid of conviction all the same. In the end, the saga of the socialists in 1930s Japan is, in essence, assumed to be a contemporary irrelevance.

Yet this perception of irrelevance itself fails to value patterns of thought and discourse that represent a vital component of modern Japanese thought, patterns that continue to resonate in the intellectual life of contemporary Japan. Following the logic of socialism and socialists in a time of great national trauma and re-evaluation has much more to offer scholars of modern Japanese political thought than has been delivered to date. One might feel emboldened to trumpet the demise of socialism in a post-Cold War, unipolar world, but just as the end of the Cold War is a premature declaration in the Asian context, so too is it too hasty in another sense. The logic of socialist thought in crisis during the 1930s did not simply evaporate in 1945; it was neither an aberration nor a product of circumstances beyond anyone's control.

We begin this preliminary re-assessment of 1930s socialism with the obvious, big question: why did many leading scholars and activists of socialism in the 1920s, turn to embrace the ideology of the emperor system in the 1930s? The question becomes more intriguing when we realise that in many cases, those who ran rampant across this ideological landscape began at the feet of Japan's great proponent of liberal democracy – Sakuzō Yoshino (1878–1933) – and ended in the engine room of the Greater East Asia Co-Prosperity Sphere a decade later, seated at the table with Prince Fumimaro Konoe (1891–1945). The journey from the radical, free-thinking Shinjinkai[2] of the 1920s to the totalistic embrace of the Imperial Rule Assistance Association in the 1930s cries out for an explanation.

A second catalyst for re-examining the 1930s from a socialist point of view is the simple comparison of reactions on the Left, particularly amongst socialists, to the Manchurian Incident of 1931, and to the outbreak of war with China in 1937. How can it be that the despised imperialist war of 1931 could, by 1937, be metamorphosed into a national emergency requiring the unity of the people in the name of the imperial state? At the same time, how could those who regarded 1931 with a more positive outlook, feel uncomfortable with the clarification and consolidation of Japan's position in China from 1937?

A third hook to re-examine 1930s socialism is that of the curious, seemingly unholy alliance between sections of the army and the leaders of the 'legal', non-communist Left (notably the Socialist Masses Party). How could the enemy be transmogrified into a saviour? How could the state, once destined to disappear with the advent of socialist revolution, become the happy companion of renovation in the name of the propertyless classes? How did ethnicity (*minzoku*) supplant class as the core component of revolutionary idealism?

The urge to seek out intellectual and ideological flaws or inconsistencies in interwar socialism can begin quite productively if we acknowledge that for

the socialists who actually experienced this dramatic shift, this was a conscious and deliberate exercise in contemporary self-revisionism. They were
not 'tricked'; they walked into it with their eyes wide open. What did they see,
and how did they rationalise it? How did socialists come to believe that they
could paint the Emperor red?

This study will examine these questions through the eyes, words and
actions of a central figure in these tumultuous times, Hisashi Asō (1891–1940).
Asō was literally one of 'Yoshino's children', having studied under Yoshino
in the post-World War I era. More than this, Asō was a major catalyst for
Yoshino's political activism in the heady days of post-World War I Wilsonian
idealism, and a driving force behind the formation of the progressive Shinjinkai and Reimeikai in December 1918. Earlier in that year, Asō had acted as
a bodyguard for Yoshino in his triumphant debate with the ultranationalist
thugs in the Rōninkai,[3] carrying Yoshino out of the Kanda Nammei Hall on
his shoulders amidst crowds of students who were destined to lead the radical
activism of the 1920s. Many of them were to follow in Asō's footsteps over a
decade later, when he led the legal Left into the oblivion of the Imperial Rule
Assistance Association. The Shinjinkai was in some respects just as much a
breeding ground for adherents to the emperor system state as it was a hotbed
for labour, socialist and communist activism.

Asō's trajectory

Asō's story has been written by his supporters[4] and colourfully fictionalised
by Asō himself in his autobiographical novel *Dakuryū ni Oyogu* (Swimming
in Muddy Waters, 1923). The portrait that emerges from these works is that
of a dynamic, romantic and charismatic activist, who was categorised as an
'intellectual' because of his elite education (Third Higher High School and
Tokyo Imperial University's Department of French Law), but whose main
political and social contribution was undeniably in the realm of labour and
socialist party organization. The historical conjunctures that mark Asō's life
seem to provide a ready explanation for his radical trajectory after graduation. If context makes the man, then Asō's life is an open book. Asō was
radicalised by the High Treason Incident of 1911 in high school, but it was
the inspiration of the Russian Revolutions of 1917 that inflamed his social
conscience. He and his biographers, including himself, would also have us
believe that Asō was motivated by disgust at his father, whose quest for
property and wealth revolted the young Asō.[5]

If we search for clues to Asō's eventual intellectual flexibility, we can perhaps find ample argumentation in his overwhelming love for Russian literature, particularly for the works of Tolstoy and Turgenev. Indeed, the impact
of Russia in the early to mid-twentieth century in Japan was one of the
defining influences of Asō's generation.[6] It is tempting to try to trace the
ideological flaws of the 1930s back to the high blown, romantic idealism that
blossomed in the aftermath of 1917 amongst Asō's cohort of firebrand

activists. An examination of the work produced by Asō and his peers at this time creates the impression of utterly unrealistic populism (along the lines of *v'narod*), a dedicated but ill-defined humanism (Turgenev's *Virgin Soil* transposed), and a passionate but confused embrace of the humanistic symbolism and historical significance of Russia's October Revolution.[7] If intellectual *naïveté* and a somewhat distorted appreciation of revolution is to be mobilised as an explanation for the ideological failings of socialists in the 1930s, there is no shortage of material here to support that reading. Indeed, the impulse to adjust tactics towards a more populist direction was also embraced in 1922 by Hitoshi Yamakawa (1880–1958), as expressed in his famous essay 'The Change of Direction of the Propertyless Classes'.[8] This was to become the dominant line in the communist Left between 1922 and 1925, and was reinforced in the Sōdōmei's own '*hōkō tenkan*' (change of direction) statement of 1924.

However, such a causal, unilinear and contextual analysis would not do justice to other factors, notably those of subjective intent on the part of socialists, and their real-world desire to find particularistic pathways to revolution. Despite all of the froth and bubble of Russian humanism in the imaginations of Asō and his peers, they wanted social justice for the dispossessed of Japan, and their circumstances required considerable fleetness of foot and determination to keep this social goal within reach in the charged atmosphere of interwar Japan.

The passion inspired by Turgenev was not merely dreamed but lived by Asō. He moved from journalism to become a leader of the Yūaikai and its successor organization, Sōdōmei, and was instrumental in turning its labour union leadership and membership into a more radical, confrontational and political direction. After a successful career in labour activism, Asō turned to proletarian politics. Biographers concur that Asō was absolutely committed to the creation of a united socialist movement for the sake of 'the propertyless classes'.[9] Asō subsequently underwent what appears to observers as a long series of disappointments, as ideological divisions amongst labour fed into politics, and the Peace Preservation Laws challenged the viability of unity amongst a Left that enjoyed different levels of legality. An array of failed mergers, alliances and opportunistic couplings amongst the various players in proletarian politics and labour litter Asō's life during the 1920s and 1930s.[10] Asō's first attempt at unifying a divided movement was the creation of the Sōdōmei-backed Shakai Minshutō on 5 December 1926. Thereafter, Asō went on to be involved in many exercises in uncomfortable political cohabitation. His crowning moment was the creation on 24 July 1932 of the Shakai Taishutō (Socialist Masses Party),[11] the first unified body representing all proletarian political parties,[12] where Asō performed the pivotal role of Secretary-General. Their unprecedented electoral success in the February 1936 general election certainly underscored in Asō's mind the possibility of working within the system to achieve the liberation of the propertyless classes.

It is here that we see another defining element that Asō's biographers and apologists highlight as their implied explanation for Asō's lapse in the 1930s. Asō is painted as a die-hard pragmatist and realist, who recognised the limitations of his socio-political environment and chose the path of the possible over that of 'the nobility of failure'. For instance, Ōno writes that Asō adopted collaboration with the state 'as a mere tactic, not as a belief system', something far removed from the notorious 'Leftist imperial death syndrome' (*sayoku gyokusaishugi*).[13] This explanation has not convinced the postwar judges of wartime intellectual ethics, as Asō's inclusion in the first volume of the *Tenkō* study clearly demonstrates. There he is regarded as one who 'sold-out', and worse, as someone who led others down that dark path of wartime complicity and collaboration with the emperor system state.

> The Shakai Taishutō (Socialist Masses Party) led by Asō, at the decisive moment for the fate of the Japanese people known as the China Incident which began in 1937, did not fight as representatives of those masses who opposed the war, and without reflecting on the fact that this road led straight to hell, transformed themselves into fellow travellers of those who prosecuted that war.[14]

Was Asō guilty of active collaboration, or was collaboration more an expression of brutal realism on Asō's part? In choosing the path of complicity, did Asō perpetuate the ideas that formed the rationale of his own oppression? Large suggests that at least in the mid-1920s through to the early 1930s, Asō was not interested in the Emperor in more than a 'perfunctory' manner, and that his Nichirōkei peers were not closed to indirect collaboration with the communists.[15] Yet in July 1940, Asō actively and openly led his party and its adherents to voluntarily disband, in order to join the united enterprise of Konoe's New Order and the Imperial Rule Assistance Association. Asō died on 6 September 1940, before the weaknesses of Konoe's vision became evident.

Whether it was because of intellectual *naïveté*, historical circumstances, pragmatism unhampered by ethics, or a combination of all three, between 1932 and 1940 Asō had undertaken a journey from what could simplistically be framed as from the Left to the Right. However, Asō's fundamental consistency of ethical ambition not only persisted throughout his journey, it actually drove his tactical gymnastics. As with many other so-called *tenkō-sha* (apostates), comprehending the complexities of Asō's logic must go beyond a *tenkō*-type tale of betrayal and the deceptive neatness of the Left–Right paradigm. What did Asō think he was doing at the time? If we take him at his word, we would lean towards the pragmatism explanation:

> If we continue to oppose this war we will be murdered for sure. I have already resolved to be killed, however instead of adopting a lousy

strategy and being killed for nothing, I'd rather die having done something that can garner some understanding.[16]

Asō and Manchuria

Like many of his generation, Manchuria represented for Asō exactly what he wanted it to, and performed various roles in his political and social imagination to fit the extraordinary twists and turns of the era. The opportunistic employment of the Manchurian symbol does not detract from its usefulness as an analytical tool of the political mood of the day, even though Manchuria fulfilled disparate and often contradictory meanings even within the thought of a single individual such as Asō. Add to this the about-turn that assailed Asō and many of his contemporaries in the dwindling progressive sector of opinion between 1931 and 1937,[17] and it becomes clear that Manchuria[18] was a mirror for 1930s Japan, a depository of hope, and an unlikely intellectual vehicle for *gaiatsu* (external pressure) in a society that was desperate for certainty.

Asō opposed Japan's imperialistic activities in China as early as 1927, and as part of the Labour-Farmer Mass Party leadership, opposed the September 1931 Manchurian Incident, condemning it as evidence of shameless imperialism on Japan's part. At the time, Asō declared that this was also a capitalistic push to integrate China into Japan's orbit. Furthermore, this would escalate into a bigger conflict that would impact on the world.[19] Accordingly, the Labor-Farmer Mass Party structured its platform as a triple negative, declaring anti-imperialism, anti-communism and anti-fascism to be its cause. At the heart of it though, was the persistent emotional and intellectual appeal of Manchuria as a crucible for anti-capitalism. Asō projected this onto the blank screen that was Manchuria, making it the thread that represented the only continuity in his thought from that time onwards.

Once Manchuria was transformed into the 'independent' state of Manchukuo in March 1932, the era of assassination entered a new, active phase with the assassination of Prime Minister Inukai on 15 May 1932 (5.15) at the hands of young naval officers. In the exciting and excited aftermath of the Army Pamphlet Incident of October 1934 (which we will discuss in detail below), Asō employed the anti-capitalist lever to try to draw together, even unify, the scattered eruptions in Japanese society. In the process, Manchuria assumed a new significance in his thinking.

Asō's series of articles on Manchuria that appeared in late 1934 and early 1935, continued to condemn the 1931 Manchurian Incident. However, his condemnation became selective. This event would still lead to a world war and cause an anti-Japanese movement in China, but it revealed a vital new element in Japan's domestic scene: a split between the capitalists and the military.[20] Asō's logic commenced with the 5.15 Incident: 'the 5.15 Incident did not target the Socialists or the Communists, instead it targeted the *zaibatsu* (conglomerates) and their representatives, the bourgeois political parties'. According to Asō, the anti-capitalist intent of the 5.15 assassins set Japan apart from the fascist trend becoming increasingly evident in Germany and Italy.[21] Indeed, Asō regarded the 5.15 Incident as the catalyst for unstoppable momentum towards internal reform, one that admittedly marginalised and transcended the political sphere, but one that would nonetheless precipitate significant change within Japanese society in favour of the propertyless classes. Taken together, the 'twin crises' of 1931 and 5.15 presented a chance for reform that Asō believed would not be led by the propertyless classes, but would be conducted on their behalf. The anti-capitalist impulse of the army that emerged during and after the two crises reinforced Asō's idealism.

This anti-capitalist revulsion within the army was born in Manchuria. In Asō's view, the army went into Manchuria with an essentially feudal objective in mind: territorial acquisition. The capitalists, to the contrary, were pursuing profit and development, something that incensed the Chinese and eventually the Japanese army itself. For Asō, this revulsion was naturally part of the global response to the crisis of capitalism that had erupted after World War I.[22] But the Manchurian experience also brought out the latent anti-capitalist inclination of the army that had co-existed with the feudal impulse within the army's *raison d'être*. Asō noted that the army was quite separate from the capitalists and the bourgeois political parties who represented them. They were, in fact, directly linked to the Emperor. For Asō, this meant 'they are the Emperor's army, not the capitalists' army'.[23] Consisting of a majority of enlisted men from rural families, the rising poverty of soldiers' families in the late 1920s and early 1930s highlighted the contradictions of the Manchurian affair.[24] For soldiers, argued Asō, they could 'differentiate between doing service for the country, and doing service for capitalists'. For the army leadership, they realised that unless they looked after the interests and livelihood of their allies (the propertyless classes) within, they would have no chance in a protracted war against an external foe.[25] Asō believed that even Army Minister Araki had realised, through the Manchurian Incident, how important it was for there to be stability within the army and that real national security could only be achieved if the stability of Japanese workers' and farmers' lives was assured. For Asō, this indicated a promising sign that the army was moving away from fascism, towards a more enlightened alliance with the propertyless classes.[26]

The latent anti-capitalism of 1931 was made blatant by the events of 5.15. This logic led Asō to regard these two incidents as intrinsically connected. However, the coupling of 1931 and 5.15 was driven by other kinds of structural logic. Many scholars have noted the almost organic nature of the assumed interconnectivity of events in Manchuria, and events in Japan, in the eyes of Asō and his contemporaries in the 1930s.[27] This link was understood to be substantive and reciprocally causal, and was selectively invoked by different entities. In Asō's case, the anti-capitalist imperative made the link between Manchuria and domestic reform in Japan attractive, even essential.

Asō states how, in the early 1930s in Japan, two schools of thought were evident. One gave precedence to domestic reform before resolving the Manchurian question; the other assumed that 'domestic reform is unachievable now, so first provoke a situation in Manchuria, create an ideal state, and use it to stimulate reform within Japan'.[28] Asō not only subscribed to the second viewpoint, but he assumed that the failure of reform in Manchuria would lead to the failure of reform in Japan. The anti-capitalist tendencies within the army had to be championed at home as well as in foreign policy, for reform in favour of the property-less classes in Japan to succeed:

> Japan now confronts an emergency situation internally and externally as a result of the two incidents, and in looking to the future, this has created an engine for reform as well as wielding a blow on the bourgeois administration, and thus these incidents have led to a step being taken towards real reform.[29]

Where others saw the weakening of parliamentary politics and the rise of militarism, Asō saw opportunity. The army was not merely an entity increasingly opposed to capitalism, it was part of the ruling authorities. Reform would occur from above, and from within the ruling elite: 'in the special circumstances that prevail in Japan, within the ruling classes it is the army that is able to develop the character of disintegrating the ruling class and becoming an anti-capitalist force'.[30]

The socialist embrace of the nation as a vehicle for change was not unknown by the mid-1930s, but Asō's variant requires more explanation. He did not see himself as part of a global move towards national socialism, and in his own mind, he did not beautify fascism. Asō's 'nation' comprised the triumvirate of sections of the army, sections of the bureaucracy, and the Emperor. A closer look at what each of these represented to Asō will reveal a more complex vision of national socialism in its Japanese manifestation, and a consistent if flawed adherence to socialist ideas. Elucidating Asō and his dreams, without dismissing them because of political *naïveté*, is our task. Yet we do so in the knowledge that, by 1935, Asō was willing to contemplate war as a vehicle for the reform of capitalism in Japan, and later elsewhere in Asia, and that he saw the army as a suitable ally in this quest because they had realised that 'war should be for the sake of all the people and for the entire nation, not for the benefit of one class'.[31]

Asō and the army

Asō was not blind to the reservations held by his fellow activists concerning the militarist and fascist trend in Japan after the Manchurian Incident, but his conviction that capitalism was the primary enemy fed his need to believe in the reformist elements of the army. Even though by 1934 patriotic societies and ultra-nationalist groups were on the rise, Asō believed that 'the army is engaged in the development of a more positive political movement', enthusing further:

> The calmness of the army these days is like the quiet before a new dawn, and results from their desire to engage in self-criticism concerning the unfortunate results of the two incidents that they triggered, to cleanse themselves, and to seek new plans before making a new start.[32]

The source of Asō's stubborn optimism was the pamphlet issued by the army in October 1934, entitled 'The Fundamental Principles of National Defence and A Proposal on How to Strengthen It'.[33] In its timing, its socio-political impact and its audacity, this pamphlet was a pivotal document in the seething political scene of the mid-1930s in Japan, one that decisively imposed a particular direction onto the disparate, desperate reform movements across the ideological spectrum. It was the single most important element in tipping Asō towards a commitment to a certain kind of imperial state, even at the expense of the very existence of the propertyless movement to which he had hitherto dedicated his considerable energy.

As Hashikawa notes, the underlying assumptions in this pamphlet were traceable to the perceived lessons learnt from World War I. The principal lesson was that future wars would be total wars, that is, wars that involved every sector of society in their prosecution.[34] In the uncertain climate following the Manchurian Incident, and acutely aware of Japan's international isolation following their withdrawal from the League of Nations in 1933 in protest over the League's position on Manchuria, the need to consolidate the nation's resources in the name of defence appeared acute. This pamphlet was the army's attempt to get the ball rolling, to articulate and popularise the idea of total war in Japan.

Issued by the army's news division, the pamphlet was work-shopped and approved up through the chain of command. Written by Sumihisa Ikeda and ultimately approved by the Army Minister Hayashi himself, it was a product of intense collaboration between young army officers and young bureaucrats.[35] In the wake of the 5.15 Incident, these groups were exerting more and more influence on politics behind the scenes, and the pamphlet provided them with a common platform, much in the way that the Manchurian project had done. Manchuria was a tangible, formative presence in the minds of the creators of the pamphlet. In Hashikawa's words, Manchuria accordingly 'became an inextricable part of the national defence state plan'.[36]

In its opening section, the pamphlet declared that Japan had entered a new and dangerous phase in its international life. The changing nature of war since World War I had combined with this environment of enhanced threat to create the need for new thinking on national defence, thinking that would incorporate 'the full force of life' from the spheres of economics, politics, ideas and military might.[37] Total war was implied in its ominous, oft-quoted line: 'battle is the father of creativity, and the mother of culture'.[38] As

Tatsukichi Minobe (1873–1948) indicated, this appropriated the very logic of peace, which in his view made 'the freedom of individuals the father of creativity and the mother of culture'.[39] Minobe accused the pamphlet of warmongering, and in social terms this was accurate. Yet in political terms, this subordination of all social life to the creative act of battle was not only an open affirmation of the virtue of total war; it was also a bold declaration on the army's part of their right to intervene in all spheres of national life, and by extension, to determine policy beyond the boundaries of military matters.

After enumerating the different sectors of society that together comprised the elements of a new national defence thinking, the pamphlet fleshed out the portrait of the international environment threatening Japan. Manchuria's resources were described as 'essential' to Japan, yet they were the object of intense international competition and jealousy. The world depression had made the Western powers ignore the mutual benefits accruing to Manchuria and Japan in their alliance. Japan was isolated from world diplomacy, having left the League, and facing a situation where its immigrants were denied entry by other powers. Anti-Japanese movements in China, the unequal level of Japan's naval strength, and the looming threat of the Red Army were the bogies trotted out as proof of Japan's precarious situation. Diplomacy could not be expected to resolve this situation:

> In these current extraordinary circumstances, it is unlikely that coopera-
> tive diplomacy alone will lessen the threat, and despite the cooperative
> efforts of the great powers after the last war, this extraordinary situation
> is the destiny of the world, moreover with the catalysts of the Manchurian
> Incident and Japan's withdrawal from the League of Nations, it is an
> extraordinary time when trials should be undertaken for the sake of the
> prosperity and happiness of the imperial nation.[40]

In short: war was both necessary and unavoidable.

Subsequently, the pamphlet turned its attention to the situation in Japan, in particular, to the dire situation confronting the farmers, fishermen and workers at the lower end of the economic spectrum. There is no doubt that it was this consideration that so enthused Asō. Noting that only one part of the community was experiencing prosperity while the rest slipped into poverty, the pamphlet warned that this would lead to class friction, dividing the community and thus weakening national defence: 'This problem is of course important for national policy, but it is even more significant for the economic and military perspectives of national defence.'[41] The realm of ideas was also part and parcel of this great enterprise of national defence. Indeed, in the pamphlet this dimension assumed fundamental importance, providing the foundation for all other pillars of the national defence system. The pamphlet opined that 'extreme ideas should be avoided', 'the spirit of sacrifice should be encouraged', and 'ideas of internationalism, selfishness and individualism should be abandoned'.[42] After noting that the inclusion of Manchuria into

Japan's sphere of national defence had stretched Japan's military resources, the pamphlet concluded with a siren call for the people to develop their resolve. People needed to declare their faith in national defence, 'for the sake of the fulfillment of the Japanese spirit, and to secure the peace of the world'.[43]

Asō's response to the pamphlet was recorded in the party organ, the *Socialist Masses News* on 28 October 1934. Asō celebrated the army's stated concern for the welfare of the masses, and saw this as acceptance on the army's part that they could not reform – and thus defend – Japan without the full cooperation and involvement of the propertyless classes: 'In Japan's current circumstances it is essential that the army and the propertyless classes form a rational union in order to overthrow capitalism.' Moreover, the concern for the welfare of the masses showed a 'progressive' attitude on the army's part that was

> not like the anti-citizen, dictatorial one of the past; rather it starts from an imperial perspective, calls for the unity of popular reformist political forces, and establishes the goal of assisting these forces, and is thus popular in nature.[44]

Tellingly, Asō now felt free to draw a distinction between the hotheads of 5.15, and the supporters of the pamphlet. But although cracks became visible in Asō's vision of army-socialist collaboration, Asō stuck to his anti-capitalist line. To this end, even an alliance between imperial and popular power was acceptable.

Asō and the Emperor

In retrospect, it seems painfully clear that Asō's embrace of the Emperor, however indirect, was the ultimate sell-out on the part of a leading socialist-labour activist. The weight of history is damning, as we look back at the misery that ensued in the Emperor's name between the outbreak of the China war in 1937, and the bombings of Hiroshima and Nagasaki in 1945. The tone of the Socialist Masses Party platform in 1937 conveyed all of the slavish rhetoric that we associate with an environment of thought control, including references to the '*kokutai*' (the national essence centred on the Emperor) and the sacred mission of the Japanese race. The core aim of stabilising the livelihoods of the labouring classes was retained, but alongside a commitment to the national polity (*kokutai*) and the Japanese race as a whole: 'Our party, on the basis of the fundamental principles of our national polity, plans for the advancement and development of the Japanese people, and in this way aims at the uplift of human culture.'[45] By December 1937, Asō was enjoying a thrilling trip to the front lines in Manchuria as part of a delegation from the homeland. There he met several military and bureaucratic luminaries, including Kanji Ishihara (1889–1949) and Naoki Hoshino (1892–1978). According to Large, this visit 'convinced Asō that Japan was on the side of right in prosecuting the war'.[46]

The voluntary disbandment of the Socialist Masses Party in 1940, and Asō's inclusion in the planning for the New Order Movement, seems difficult to mitigate. This was wilful collaboration, not *naïveté*. But in one of Asō's last writings, we can glimpse the workings of Asō's mind. In a letter to Prince Konoe, Asō noted the need for someone who represented the Emperor to lead reform in Japan, because it had become clear that the propertyless classes would not be able to do it on their own:

> Japan's renovation, not unlike the renovation of the Meiji restoration, cannot be achieved only from below. Unless the influence of the Emperor above and the propertyless classes below is joined together it won't be possible.[47]

This smacks more of blind pragmatism than it does of starry-eyed love of country. In order to fully appreciate Asō's embrace of the Emperor, we need to penetrate his pragmatism. For Asō the Emperor was not only a symbol of cultural and racial unity throughout history; the Emperor was an historical figure and institution that had proven his reformist credentials during the great Meiji Restoration of 1868. The renovation of 1937 had a precedent, and this precedent featured the Emperor. Why couldn't it happen again? Asō's turn to the Emperor was partly based on his individual reading of Japan's modern history, and his frequent invocation of the Meiji precedent in his writings from 1935 onwards underscores its importance in his thinking. This reading of history combined with an evolving interpretation of reform on Asō's part that saw him position himself firmly in the loyal centre of the emperor system. Yet it was pragmatism rather than ideology that led him there.

The first pillar of Aso's pragmatism, and his great inspiration, was his reading of the revolutionary dynamics of Bakumatsu Japan (1850s–1860s). Asō's grasp of history and his simplistic application of historical precedent to his contemporary circumstances has not been taken very seriously by scholars, one of whom dismissed Asō's invocation of the Meiji experience as 'a Meiji restoration complex'.[48] For our purposes though, understanding what motivated Asō in his accommodation of the Emperor with reform rescues his Bakumatsu and Meiji studies from the periphery of analysis. To the contrary, this is one key to comprehending Asō's logic of Emperor-centred reform.

Amidst the upheavals of 1931, Asō had already excitedly noted that 1931 could well be 'the equivalent of the black ships' for the 1930s, equating the Manchurian Incident with the arrival of Commodore Perry's bristling modern fleet in Edo in 1853.[49] Asō delivered his history lesson to his fellow activists in a three-part series of articles on the history of the end of the Tokugawa era published in 1935, and in most of his subsequent writings on reform up until his death in 1940. Ironically, it is the lack of 'history' in his historical tale that undermined its efficacy, and blinded him in turn to the uncomfortable fact that the imperial state was not necessarily above or separate from the workings of capitalism in the prosecution of its reform mission.

Asō's understanding of the Meiji restoration involved valuing the role of agency over that of beneficiary in historical change. Asō realised that through the restoration, Japan moved from feudalism towards capitalism, and that capitalists were the main beneficiaries of the reforms that accompanied Japan's opening to the West. What mattered in Asō's mind was that members of the ruling elite, namely the lower-ranking samurai in the southern domains, along with a number of intellectuals, separated themselves from the ruling Tokugawa house in order to facilitate and lead reform. The resulting transition from feudalism to capitalism was clearly beneficial to the capitalists, but at no time was this class the object or motivation for reform. Similarly, while capitalists were the chief beneficiaries of Meiji renovation, they were not the agents of these reforms.

> While the slogans of *sonnō jōi* [revere the Emperor, expel the barbarians] and *bummei kaika* [civilization and enlightenment] were politically significant and effectively led to the maturation of the restoration, in the end the Meiji Restoration did imply a reform of capitalism, however it was the ideologues, the lower ranking samurai and the Emperor, who achieved it.[50]

It is this historical experience of renovation by one class for the sake of another, that in Asō's view set Japan apart from Europe. In Europe, he argued, the bourgeoisie fought against feudal entities, including the monarchy, in order to seize power in their own right. They did so once their power and influence had advanced to the point where they could promote their own cause with a prospect of success.[51] But in Japan, national survival was the objective, and reform the means to that end. The bourgeoisie were not sufficiently developed to carry out reform for their own sakes; they did not even necessarily realise the full socio-economic implications of reform. For Asō, the significance of the historical example of Meiji was: first, that meaningful reform could arise as a result of an external catalyst and did not have to emanate from within; second, the non-ruling class did not have to be the agent of reform, as reformism in their interests could arise from within the ranks of a disintegrating ruling elite.[52]

At the apex of the disintegrating ruling elite was the Emperor. The imperial institution was, in Asō's view, above class interests and vested interest, performing the role of unifying force and facilitator of reform:

> Since the founding of the nation Japan's imperial house has been above the ups and downs of the actual economic and political classes, standing before the whole people (*minzoku*), and through this benevolent presence

it has become the central focus of popular faith. It is precisely because of this that even when one class temporarily rises to a position of economic and political influence and the political rights of the imperial house appear to be diluted, the imperial house remains at the centre of the people's spiritual faith; no-one has been able to desecrate the imperial house, and through the fact that Japan's imperial house is unparalleled in the world in its longevity and continuity of the imperial lineage and has been able to remain above the ups and downs of the economic and political class conflicts that accompany historical development, it exists spiritually as the centre of ethnic unity on the basis of benevolence towards all of the people.

This is why 'the imperial house does not have any inevitable dependence on capitalism, and possesses an eternal character that transcends the ups and downs of capitalism' and why 'the imperial house has been at the heart of reform and development of the people as the leader of reform, as the figurehead of reform'.[53]

In keeping with the sweeping assessments in his historical account of Meiji, Asō deduced fundamental relevance for Japan's position in the mid-1930s. The young officers in the army and their counterparts in the bureaucracy were the latter-day equivalent of the lower-ranking samurai; and the property-less classes were the equivalent of the ill-prepared, ill-positioned bourgeoisie of Bakumatsu Japan. Taken together, the Manchurian Incident, and the 5.15 Incident 'were declarations on the part of the army that they were opposing the orthodox bourgeois authorities and distancing themselves from those authorities', thus hastening the disintegration of the ruling elite.[54] They would be the agents of reform, and the property-less classes would be the beneficiaries. Likewise, Manchuria was now not the crucible of Japanese reform, it was the 'external catalyst' for Japan's reform. Despite the cringing language of Emperor-worship employed by Asō in his writing at this time, the Emperor's inclusion was conditional on his continued support for the agents of reform:

> Today, determining whether the *kokutai* (national essence centred on the Emperor) is part of the maintenance of the status quo or a force for reform, will depend on whether the current political phenomena are appreciated in terms of their reformist significance, and whether the *kokutai* can be mobilised to contribute to the disintegration of the bourgeois political forces or not.[55]

At this stage, we can see that Asō was looking at 1930s Japan through Meiji spectacles. Yet when we consider his attitude towards the Emperor and the imperial institution, it was far from unqualified. Beneath the references to the enduring imperial line, we sense an undercurrent of realism attached to the Emperor's role in the reform proceedings. In political terms, Asō was not swept-up in the rush to confirm the infallibility of the Emperor. At least, not yet.

Asō's utilitarian approach to the Emperor reflected his belief that the Emperor would facilitate reform led by progressive elements of the ruling elite, and that because of the Emperor's transcendence over capitalism, this reform would be in the interests of the propertyless classes. Asō's logic of imperial utility, hitherto contained by pragmatism, began to break down however when he introduced the notion of ethnicity into his concept of reform. Asō's turn to particularism was a logical extension of his reading of capitalism, but it opened the way for his pragmatism to be undermined from within, as ethnicity subsumed and obliterated class as a socio-political entity in Asō's thinking. In the environment of 1930s Japan, on the cusp of war in China and with ideologues polishing a myth of imperial and racial supremacy, this distorted Asō's logic of imperial utility to breaking point.

Asō's association of the Emperor with racial and cultural uniqueness (and by implication, supremacy) was an indirect and subordinate conclusion on Asō's part, not the driving force or even the starting point for his turn towards the emperor system state. We must return to the fundamental value that motivated Asō through the 1930s, namely that of anti-capitalism, to reconstruct his logic. First, for Asō capitalism was a system imported from the West, which relegated Japan to an inferior international status, and condemned Japan (and other Eastern nations) to pursue the historical task of catch-up and imitation.[56] The problem of foreign-origin systems and ideas was underscored not only in the social divisions and exploitation introduced by capitalism, but also in the weakening of the movements that arose against capitalism within Japan. Marxism and communism, like capitalism, were ideas imported from the West.

> Since the Meiji Restoration when Japan appeared on the world stage as an undeveloped country because the development of capitalism was not of its own making but instead was imported from the Western capitalist countries, the propertyless movement in its early phase also imported ideas and methods from the West, and could not deny that it was in effect an imitation.[57]

The failure of the Comintern's Second and Third Internationals, later underscored by Stalin's 'socialism in one country' policy, confirmed that socialism, like capitalism, was not 'international' or 'universal' at all.

> Today in all countries the move towards socialism is occurring on an ever increasing scale as people confront the naked reality of the inevitable collapse of capitalism, however this is not a uniform, public move, rather it is shaped by the situation particular to each country, as an independent phenomenon, and it is through this particularity that it advances.[58]

It is only now that we see Asō encounter the value totalism of ethnicity. Suddenly, the Meiji restoration appears in a new light, as an example of the triumph of ethnicity over class conflict. The fight against feudalism in 1868, and the fight against capitalism in 1935, was an expression of faith in ethnicity, as much as it was a quest for national survival. This led Asō to associate socio-political reform with identity, alongside systemic reform: 'It is especially within the historical development [of our nation] that the way towards social revolution can be ascertained.'[59]

The cause of the frustrations of the propertyless movement in the past, and the key to successful reform in the future, was to reposition and reconnect ethnic identity with the objective of reform.

> What is the greatest obstacle to communicating our proposals to the nation's masses? It is the problem of *minzoku* (the ethnic nation). Further if we speak logically it is the problem of patriotism. The failure to disconnect the capitalist war and patriotism in the consciousness of the nation's masses stems from our idealistic class-based internationalism.[60]

The time had come to ditch class, and embrace ethnicity, for the sake of capitalist reform. By 1938, Asō had realised that the ethnic imperative changed everything. In his pro-war pamphlet *The Significance of the Current War*, Asō declared that the propertyless movement had been mistaken in assuming that this was a war between capitalists, and thus, that the movement was obliged to stand beside the people in opposition to the state. Misled by Marxist thinking, the propertyless movement had assumed that class could incorporate and transcend ethnicity in the fight against capitalism. But now,

> the reform of capitalism does not follow the internationalist line of communism or social democracy and pit itself against the ethnic nation, to the contrary it demands a new approach of revitalizing the ethnic nation and protecting the state.[61]

Transmogrified as the ethnic nation, the state was no longer a class enemy. Instead, it was the embodiment of identity that would deliver the reform of capitalism. The Emperor appears in this formula as a kind of afterthought, or symbolic affirmation, of the essential enduring unity of the people as an ethnic collective. The 1937 China war 'was a war of significance for national reform because it will build an absolutist system where the reform of the capitalist system is based on the fundamental principles of the national polity'.[62] In one swoop, Japaneseness itself became neo-capitalist, namely an ethically cleansed version of the Western-origin import of Meiji times. The presence of the Emperor ensured that the liberation of Eastern peoples from Western capitalism would not be self-serving. The Greater East Asia Co-Prosperity Sphere logic was hereby complete, in the mind of the leading labour-socialist activist of modern Japan.

By the time Asō saw the army cabinets of the mid- to late 1930s in a more sober light, the momentum towards a wider war had grown beyond the reach of mere pragmatism. While it came far too late, there is evidence that Asō saw the darker side of the military cabinets, and although the dust kicked up by the heels of the bolting horses must have almost been visible, he tried to rein them back in. The shock of the Young Officers Rebellion of February 1936 was what first pushed Asō to declare that the 'transitory phase' of reform was over, and it was now time for the propertyless classes to take the lead.[63] After experiencing electoral success in the polls, Asō openly called for the baton of reform to be handed over:

> Not only is state renovation and capitalist reform an inevitable historical demand, but this must occur quite separate from the desires and hopes of the army, the bureaucracy and the ruling classes, and instead be promoted by the Socialist Masses Party.[64]

The problem, Asō conceded, was that the army was not exclusively comprised of selfless reformists. 'They have a tendency to lean towards dictatorial methods, and are increasingly being pressured by capitalist conglomerates into an anti-reformist direction.' Furthermore, without a popular base, the army and bureaucracy could do little more than act as a bridge to the new era. Now that the parties representing capital were out of power, the work of the army and bureaucrats was done, and 'whether they are aware of their historical role or not is another matter'. The best way for reform to move forward was 'centred on the parliament, and . . . through parliamentary means'.[65] Asō's hearty cry echoed in a chamber that was already largely devoid of democratic force. As he led his party into non-existence and assumed his place at the table preparing for one great patriotic party in July 1940, Asō no doubt clung to his idea that while history sometimes appeared to be going in an undesirable direction, in the end, reform in Japan would occur, because it was a historical inevitability.[66]

Conclusion

How do we assess the thoughts and words of Hisashi Asō? Dismissing him as naïve offers some satisfaction, but it does little to explain the embrace by the Left of the Emperor in the 1930s. Asō's poor grasp of the dynamics of power, represented by his firm belief that power could be reformed from within, was matched by his assumption that capitalists and their interests were somehow quarantined from society at large, including from the imperial institution. The incremental shift over the course of the 1930s on the part of the legal Left from a commitment to revolution, to an expectation that capitalism could be reformed, was as pragmatic as it was idealistic. After the apostasy of leading communists in 1933 and the mass recantation of communism on the part of the remaining membership, only a masochist would have chosen the path of gaol or death over activism. Yet labelling Asō as a 'naïve realist' does not enlighten us about our core question.

Asō's case demonstrates that stereotyping the Left of the 1930s as turning towards the Emperor system requires deeper elucidation and refinement. Ultimately, Asō embraced ethnicity and turned away from class as his motivating value-markers. The Emperor was significant only in that as an institution, he represented an anti- and supra-capitalist position and a concurrent affirmation of cultural and historical identity. As Itō has indicated, Asō realised that in the climate of post-1931 Japan, the propertyless movement was perceived by the people as either disconnected from, or antipathetic to, patriotism. They therefore needed the Emperor, or at least an association with the imperial institution, to legitimise their role in national reform.[67]

But underlying all of this is the essential issue of the failure of intellectual indigenization, a problem that lay at the root of the rejection of capitalism, Marxism, and internationalism in 1930s Japan. These ideas and values were not condemned only because of their foreign origin; they were condemned because of the widespread perception that they did not resonate in Japanese society. Defensive, exclusionist renderings of identity translated into a failure to facilitate the interpenetration of ideas and identity on the level of the nation, and of the self. In this sense, particularism was a failure to go beyond translation, to a stage where ideas were more than passively received, and identity more than imposed. The implications of this for postwar Japan, where the progressive forces in Japan associated with a kind of 'Left' struggle to champion the values of democracy, pacifism and anti-nuclear neutralism, are loud and clear.

Henceforth, we should resist giving a knowing nod when historians portray the 1930s Japanese Left as sidling up to the Emperor with paintbrush in hand. The Left were self-deceived, in that they came to believe that the Emperor would, in a fashion, represent their cause. The political utility of the Emperor made him a chameleon, and red was only one of the many colours he wore.

Notes

This article was made possible through the excellent research assistance provided by Mr Paul Wijsman, librarian of the Department of Japanese and Korean Studies at Leiden; Ms Higuchi, librarian of the International House of Japan; the library of Keio University (Mita campus); and Mr Torsten Weber, all of whom helped assemble the primary sources for this research.

1 Shisō no Kagaku Kenkyūkai (ed.), Kyōdō Kenkyū Tenkō, 3 vols, Tokyo, 1959–1962.
2 For background on the Shinjinkai, see Henry D. Smith, *Japan's First Student Radicals*, Cambridge, Mass: Harvard University Press, 1972.
3 This debate was sparked by the so-called White Rainbow Affair of 25 August 1918, when reference was made to 'a white rainbow piercing the sun', a metaphor

for revolution that the Right found unacceptable. Yoshino's debate with the Rōninkai was effectively a debate on free speech in imperial Japan.

4 Jōtarō Kawakami (ed.), *Asō Hisashi Den* (Biography of Hisashi Asō), Tokyo, Asō Hisashi Den Kankō Iinkai, 1958.

5 Hisashi Asō, *Dakuryū ni Oyogu* (Swimming in Muddy Waters), Tokyo, Shinkōsha, 1923, pp. 1–10.

6 Peter Berton, Paul F. Langer and George O. Totten, *The Russian Impact on Japan*, Los Angeles: University of Southern California Press, 1981, p. 3.

7 See Rikki Kersten, *The Russian Revolutions and the Predicament of the Intellectual in Taishō Japan: The Case of Asō Hisashi*. Unpublished Honours Thesis, University of Adelaide, 1984.

8 See Chikazo Okio (ed.), *Shakaishugi* (Socialism) Gendai Nihon Shisō Taikei Vol. 15, Tokyo, Chikuma Shobō, 1963, pp. 332–43.

9 See, for instance, Shōichi Miyake, 'Tanitsu musan seitō kakuritsu ni kaketa jōnetsu' (The fervour that contributed to the establishment of the only property-less political party), *Gekidōki no Nihon Shakai Undō Shi: Kagawa Toyohiko, Asō Hisashi, Asanuma Inejirō no Kiseki*, Tokyo: Gendai Hyōronsha, 1973, p. 214.

10 See Stephen S. Large, *Organised Workers and Socialist Politics in Interwar Japan*, Cambridge: Cambridge University Press, 1981, chapter 5.

11 See J. A. A. Stockwin *et al.*, *Political Parties of Asia and the Pacific*, Vol. 1, Westport: Greenwood Press, 1985, pp. 622–5, for an entry on the Socialist Masses Party.

12 Except the Labour-Farmer group.

13 Okio Ōno, 'Asō Hisashi: musan seitō no sensō kyōryoku sekininsha' (Hisashi Asō: the person responsible for the wartime collaboration of the Propertyless Party), *Gendai no Me*, Vol. 22, No. 1, January 1981, pp. 72–3.

14 Hiroshi Hanzawa and Sōetsu Saga, 'Zenko Shinjinkai-in – Akamatsu Katsumarō, Asō Hisashi' (Former Members of the Shinjinkai – Katsumarō Akamatsu, Hisashi Asō), in Shisō no Kagaku Kenkyūkai eds, *Kyōdō Kenkyū Tenkō*, Vol. 1, Tokyo: Heibonsha, p. 94.

15 Large, op. cit., pp. 113–16.

16 Asō in Hanzawa and Saga, op. cit., p. 100.

17 Andrew Gordon succinctly puts it like this: 'from 1935–1937 the Socialist Masses Party followed a tortured trajectory from the pacifist anti-imperialism of its pre-decessor parties before 1932 to a fervent embrace of the China War upon its outbreak in July 1937'. Andrew Gordon, *Labor and Imperial Democracy in Prewar Japan*, Berkeley: University of California Press, 1991, p. 312.

18 For a superb account of Manchuria in the Japanese mind, see Louise Young, *Japan's Total Empire*, Berkeley: University of California Press, 1998.

19 Hisashi Asō, 'Nihon wa dō naru' (What will happen to Japan), *Keizai Orai*, 1 April 1932, Special Issue on Manchuria (censored), 1932, pp. 22–36.

20 Hisashi Asō, 'Manshu jihen oyobi 5.15 jihen no hihan to kokka kaikaku no shidō seishin' (Criticism of the Manchurian Incident and the 5.15 Incident and the spirit leading national reform), Part 1, *Kaihō*, October 1934, p. 19; and 'Manshu jihen oyobi 5.15 jihen no hihan to kokka kaikaku no shidō seishin' (Criticism of the Manchurian Incident and the 5.15 Incident and the spirit leading national reform), Part 2, *Kaihō*, November 1934, p. 26.

21 Asō, 'Manshu jihen oyobi . . .' Part 1, op. cit., pp. 30–1.

22 Ibid., p. 19.

23 Asō, 'Manshu jihen oyobi . . .' Part 2, op. cit., p. 21.

24 A pioneering study on the connection between rural poverty and militarism in Japan is Richard Smethurst, *A Social Basis for Prewar Japanese Militarism*, Berkeley: University of California Press, 1978.

25 Asō, 'Manshu jihen oyobi . . .' Part 2, op. cit., p. 22.

26 Hisashi Asō, 'Ishin to Mito Han' (The Restoration and the Mito fief), *Kaihō*, February 1935, p. 17.
27 For instance, see Gordon, op. cit., p. 290.
28 Asō, 'Manshu jihen oyobi . . .' Part 2, op. cit., pp. 22–3.
29 Ibid., p. 23.
30 Ibid., p. 26.
31 Ibid., p. 31.
32 Asō, 'Manshu jihen oyobi . . .' Part 1, op. cit., p. 30.
33 The pamphlet was reproduced in full in *Shisō Geppō* No. 5 in November 1934, and can be accessed in its reissued form in *Shisō Geppō* No. 5, dated October 1972, pp. 305–50. An abridged version was published in the November issue of *Kaizō* in 1934, pp. 186–212, along with several critiques.
34 Bunsō Hashikawa, *Shōwa Nashonarizumu no shosō* (Aspects of Showa Nationalism), Nagoya: Nagoya Daigaku Shuppankai, 1994, p. 80.
35 Ibid., pp. 180–1.
36 Ibid., p. 100.
37 *Shisō Geppō*, 1972, p. 314.
38 Ibid., p. 306.
39 Tatsukichi Minobe, 'Rikugunho happyō no kokubōron o yomu' (Reading the army information division's announcement on national defence), *Chūō Kōron*, November 1934, p. 129.
40 *Shisō Geppō*, 1972, p. 334.
41 Ibid., pp. 336–8.
42 Ibid., pp. 338–42.
43 Ibid., p. 349.
44 See Asō, (1934:c) or Kawakami, op. cit., pp. 456–7.
45 Quoted in Ryusaku Tsunoda, Theodore Wm. De Bary and Donald Keene, *Sources of Japanese Tradition*, Vol. 2, New York: Columbia University Press, 1964, p. 321.
46 Large, op. cit., p. 207.
47 Quoted in Hanzawa and Saga, op. cit., p. 96.
48 See, for instance, William D. Wray, 'Asō Hisashi and the search for renovation in the 1930s', *Papers on Japan* Vol. 5, East Asia Research Centre, Harvard University, 1970, p. 82.
49 Asō, 'Manshu jihen oyobi . . .', Part.1, op. cit., p. 30.
50 Asō, 'Bakumatsushi kenkyū 1 – Peruri raikō yori Meiji gannen ni itaru gaikō, seiji, shakai nenpyō' (A Study of Bakumatsu History 1 – foreign relations, politics, and society from the arrival of Perry to the first year of Meiji), *Kaihō*, February 1932, p. 11.
51 Asō, 'Meiji Ishin to shakai shinka' (The Meiji Restoration and Social Advancement), *Kaihō*, June 1935, p. 17, p. 20.
52 Ibid., p. 21.
53 Asō, 'Manshu jihen oyobi 5.15 jihen no hihan to kokka kaikaku no shidō seishin' (Criticism of the Manchurian Incident and the 5.15 Incident and the spirit leading national reform), Part 3, *Kaihō*, January 1935, p. 18.
54 Asō, 'Kokka kakushin ni okeru genzai no dankai to musan undō no shimei' (The current stage of national reform and the mission of the propertyless movement), *Kaihō*, July 1935, p. 21.
55 Ibid., p. 26.
56 Asō, *Gendai sensō no igi* (The significance of the current war), Tokyo: Shakai Taishūtō Shuppanbu, 1938, pp. 21–2.
57 Asō, 'Kakushinki ni okeru sōkoku' (Conflict in an era of reform), *Kaizō*, April 1938, p. 342.
58 Asō, 'Manshu jihen oyobi . . .' Part 3, op. cit., p. 15.

59 Asō, 'Meiji Ishin to shakai shinka', op. cit., p. 26.
60 Asō, 'Bakumatsushi kenkyū 1', op. cit., p. 27.
61 Asō, *Gendai sensō no igi*, op. cit., pp. 10–11.
62 Ibid., p. 19.
63 Asō, 'Rekishi no hiyaku: 2.26 jihen no seijiteki hihan' (The leap of history – a political criticism of the 2.26 incident), *Kaihō*, April 1936, p. 30.
64 Asō, 'Kakushinki Nihon no tembō' (The outlook for Japan in an era of reform), *Kaizō*, June 1937, p. 249.
65 Ibid., pp. 250–2.
66 Hisashi Asō, 'Kakushinki ni okeru sōkoku' (Conflict in an era of reform), *Kaizō*, April 1938, p. 345.
67 Akira Itō, 'Asō Hisashi no shisō ni tsuite – senji tennōsei ni kansuru shiron' (Hisashi Asō's thought – an examination of the wartime Emperor system), *Chiba Kōgyō Daigaku Kenkyū Hōkoku – Jinbunhen*, No. 28, 1991, p. 18.

3 The Japanese evasion of sovereignty

Article 9 and the European canon – Hobbes, Carl Schmitt, Foucault

David Williams

> The Sovereign is he who decides on the exception.
> Carl Schmitt[1]

> There exists no norm that is applicable to chaos.
> ibid[2]

> You are afraid of the people unrestrained – how ridiculous!
> Marquis de Sade[3]

Introduction: Japanese pacifism and the European political canon

The Western canon of political reflection has been 25 centuries in the making. It is the richest and most profound tradition of political thought the world has ever known – or is likely ever to know. On this subject, Paul Valéry's dictum that 'in matters that can be taught, European culture is, in the strict sense, infinitely superior' carries conviction.[4] To bring the insights of Thomas Hobbes (1588–1679), Carl Schmitt (1888–1985) and Michel Foucault (1926–1984) to bear on the theoretical foundations of twentieth-century Japanese pacifism is to affirm this truth.

Confronted by this European tradition of unrivalled excellence, the Orientalist who takes the political as his sphere will seek, as his supreme ambition, to win a place for Asia in this canon. In this essay, I renew my claim that 'the European tradition of political theory, initiated by Thucydides and Plato, will remain incomplete without the ingestion of the Japanese experience of government'.[5] For this claim to be sustained, one must show that the Japanese experience speaks directly to the fundamental concerns of European political theory: 'the nature of sovereignty, the legitimacy of the state, the basis of constitutionality and its relation to the rights and obligations of the individual, the purpose and limits of political power'.[6]

The lessons of the recent Japanese struggle over constitutional authority will be examined to probe the soundness of this assertion. I hope to demonstrate that the postwar Japanese debate over sovereignty contributes another hour to the *très riches heures* of the European spirit, one that matches the theoretical provocation of the Japanese miracle for the political economist. Here, too, is another canonic opportunity for us to deposit something resistant and Oriental beneath the skin of the Western tradition of political thought.

With the goal of making such a deposit in mind, two tests are proposed. First, can the premises and assumptions that underpin the Japanese Left's defence of constitutional pacifism withstand exposure to the full weight of the Graeco-European tradition? This test assumes that the ancient idea of sovereignty as a political idea and legal concept offers the crucial point of engagement between European thought and Japanese experience. From this test, I conclude that the Japanese Left's concept of sovereignty is frequently incoherent. Nevertheless, it is also true that the six decades of Japanese pacific practice challenge some of the key assumptions of political hyperrealists such as Hobbes, Schmitt and Foucault. This is not a one-sided contest; all combatants leave the ring bruised.

In a similar vein, a second test or thought experiment is proposed. Does careful analysis of what might be called 'the politics of sadomasochism' generate a deeper, more compelling understanding of postwar pacifist practice in Japan by exploiting Foucault-inspired ideas such as subjective-less or 'negative' sovereignty? The key assumption underwriting such an analysis is that French theory, particularly the critical dissection or deconstruction of the idea of subjectivity, allows one to call into question the metaphysics of agency.

This branch of metaphysics (the contact point between Hegel and Weber) is pivotal, or should be seen to be, to the formation and consolidation of America's global hegemony. By criticising agency, the deconstructionist may propose a metaphysical justification for the supposed 'weakness' of the European Union and Japan as actors on the world stage. The broader conclusions that I draw from this second test confirm those of the first: the pre-eminence of Eurocentrism in political theory is left intact, but the Japanese experience of pacifism redefines its contours and clarifies European assumptions in uniquely powerful ways.

Footfalls in the empty Prime Minister's Residence

On 2 August 1990, Iraq invaded Kuwait, thus provoking Gulf War I (1990–91). As soon as he heard the news, Ichirō Ozawa, secretary-general of Japan's ruling Liberal Democratic Party (LDP), rushed to the Prime Minister's Residence only to find not a single member of staff on duty. Because of such indifference, Gulf War I would eventually cost Tokyo some $13 billion to pay for a struggle fought by others. The affair left Ozawa, one of Japan's most formidable politicians, in a fury. His footfalls in the empty Prime Minister's Residence that evening have been reverberating in Japanese thinking about their constitution ever since because the postwar pacifist consensus has never recovered from the shock waves produced by that summer of blitzkrieg in the Middle East.

To the degree that Ozawa has animated the campaign to revise Article 9 (and the reinforcing Preamble of the 1947 Constitution), the psychological blow inflicted on this occasion makes it one of the defining moments in the long struggle over the consequences of Japan's defeat in 1945. Ozawa's criticism of establishment complacency also gave headline profile to the issue of 'crisis management', thus anticipating subsequent public arguments over the official response to the Kōbe earthquake and the Aum cult's gas attack on the Tokyo underground.

The intense discussions provoked by these crises have focused on the more obvious of these policy failings. But deeper analysis of the theoretical foundations of the pacifist state has been rare. Perhaps it is time to bring this submerged Atlantis of unexamined political and legal assumptions to the surface by exposing the question of Japanese sovereignty to canonic scrutiny.

In this reconsideration of the role of the executive within the Japanese constitutional order, I reverse the logic of Ozawa's expectations, arguing that the Prime Minister's Residence was empty on the first night of Gulf War I for other than accidental reasons. It was more than just another example of the post-1945 Japanese neglect of the realities of *Realpolitik* (*heiwa boke*). Something more fundamental, and more Japanese, was also at work: the impact of traditional attitudes towards power, authority and the law. The Prime Minister's Residence was empty as a major crisis engulfed the region that supplies Japan with the bulk of her oil. Specifically left-wing pressures were, in part, to blame for this lack of preparedness. If pacifism represents not a break with the nation's political, moral and intellectual history but a subtle continuation and deepening of traditional attitudes, the consequences for Japan's future place in the world may be even more serious than Ozawa feared.

In other words, Ozawa's instincts on this decisive issue may have been as un-Japanese as they were sound. He sought to shatter the postwar taboo on proper debate concerning the relationship between the Japanese executive and Japanese sovereignty. His controversial effort to return Japan to its prewar status as a 'normal country' thrust onto the national agenda the question that the Japanese Left has assiduously sought to avoid answering during the past sixty years: Who is Japan's real sovereign? Here the issue will be put in a form that cannot be evaded by the Left or the Right.

Where is the sovereign in postwar Japan?

The sovereign is a power (a judicial 'person') exercising supreme authority. European political philosophy strongly favours the view that all polities have sovereigns. Schmitt, as we shall see, severely tightened the definition of the sovereign, thus clarifying the idea of sovereignty. In contrast, the pacific discourse of postwar Japan clouds this clarity by constricting the powers of any Japanese sovereign so severely that it becomes reasonable to ask whether anyone in Japan is sovereign. But how can a sovereign-less Japan be squared with the canonic dictum that all polities have sovereigns? Furthermore, how does one explain Japan's progressive commitment to popular sovereignty given the Left's objections to the exercise of genuine sovereignty by any Japanese executive however legitimate?

In postwar Japan, the sovereign is absent by intention: if the Western constitutional theorist insists that sovereignty always exists, the Japanese constitutional thinker, particularly but not exclusively on the Left, has embraced the contrasting assumption that Japanese sovereignty can be abolished. This is a radical departure from one of the axioms of European political thought. Application of the constitutional insights of Carl Schmitt to the problem demonstrates that the Japanese hope to evade sovereignty by abolishing it verges on the incoherent. Is Japanese pacifism therefore an illusion?

Without acceptance of the notion of agency – even if nothing more than some version of what I call 'the wounded sovereign' – the Japanese pacifist argument falls. How might it be salvaged? One answer would be to focus on the unsettling idea of subjective-less sovereignty, as pushed to its conceptual limits by Foucault. This provides a coherent framework for a pacifist theory of sovereignty, one that can also cope with the suggestion that Japan has a sovereign but he is not Japanese.

Subjective-less, or 'negative', sovereignty (the political equivalent of 'negative theology') remains an undeveloped notion. But as the most influential critic of the predatory subject after Heidegger, Foucault has laid the foundations for a compelling definition of 'negative' sovereignty by probing the sexual-psychological condition of 'post subjective' free fall. In an unexpected way, Foucault's sexual insights illuminate the psycho-metaphysics that underwrite the Japanese rejection of 'normal' sovereignty and subjectivity.

Sovereign or no sovereign?

The phenomenon of constitutional pacifism is rare, certainly among major states in the modern era. However unusual, state pacifism must imply some degree of sovereign power if it is a form of 'state' pacifism. In the case of Japan, the nature of state pacifism and sovereignty are constitutionally defined: the state is pacifist; the people are sovereign. But this widely accepted formula misstates the position. In fact, the Japanese state is pacifist at the expense of popular sovereignty. This is the jurisprudential conundrum and political scientific anomaly that must be addressed.

Let us begin in classic fashion. The sovereign occupies the locus of power in a political system. Political science was born from the controversial discovery that constitutional theory frequently misconstrues this locus. The true holder of power is often hidden in the constitutional theorist's web of words. So, if we assume that the European doctrine that all polities must have sovereigns is correct, where is the sovereign in Japan's postwar constitutional order?

The 1947 Peace Constitution holds that sovereignty resides with the Japanese people, just as the Meiji Constitution (1890–1947) confirmed the sovereignty of the Japanese emperor. In neither case is the matter straightforward. Under the Meiji Constitution, the emperor did not *normally* exercise the kind of absolute authority supposedly invested in him. The very few occasions when the Shōwa Emperor (Hirohito) exercised the powers of a sovereign – the crushing of the 1936 military coup, the decision to surrender in 1945, and a few battlefield orders apparently given during the later stages of the Pacific War – are all exceptions that beg the crucial question: who was sovereign for the rest of the time between 1868 and 1945?

Perhaps sovereignty is better understood not as a continuous condition but rather as an intermittent one. Such a notion appeals, for contrasting reasons, to both the Japanese pacifist and the Schmittian realist. But tradition holds that sovereignty is a continuous condition. The sovereign is always present whether sovereign power is exercised continuously or not.

If the dictionary definition of sovereignty – 'supreme and unrestricted power' – is applied to the facts of Japanese government between the Meiji Restoration of 1868 and the end of the Pacific War in 1945, it might appear that Japan has not had an absolute but a dispersed 'here-today, gone-tomorrow' type of sovereignty, in which a variety of potential sovereigns irregularly and temporarily occupied the seat of supreme power as if in a game of musical chairs. This theory, however arresting, is rejected here in favour of Schmitt's understanding that the sovereign is implicit in any constitutional order but only exercises its fullest powers during an exception.

The reason for this rejection may be found in the task of devising a rigorous definition not only of 'sovereignty' but also of 'the sovereign' in postwar Japan. Among left-wing commentators on the 1947 Constitution, the overwhelming temptation has been to believe that the doctrine of popular sovereignty stands as the conclusive and unchallengeable answer to the question of who is sovereign, thus precluding the necessity for the problem to be examined more closely. Many on the Left believe that to probe the notion that the Japanese people are not sovereign is to open a Pandora's box of uncomfortable, even dangerous, ideas and facts that could undermine the entire postwar constitutional settlement, including the ideal of state pacifism itself.

Because of such dangers, the conundrum of Japanese sovereignty must be stated clearly. If the sovereign is the exerciser of supreme and unrestricted power, the Japanese people have not exercised such power since 1947. They have not wanted to. This is why the severe restrictions on Japanese sovereignty contained in the 1947 constitution have not been eased, while the executive has been consistently prevented from acting as a sovereign agent even when the constitution offers no bar to the exercise of state authority.

The crucial test is the right of belligerency. This right was taken from Japan by the United States during the postwar occupation, and this decisive restriction on the exercise of Japanese sovereignty was subsequently imbedded in

Article 9. In neither of these decisions did the Japanese people have a say. But in general elections both during the Occupation and after 1952, when the Occupation ended, the Japanese electorate implicitly endorsed this foreign restriction on national sovereignty.

The option to revise Article 9 has, until very recently, not been popular with a majority of the Japanese electorate, suggesting that the would-be constitutional sovereign denies his own sovereignty. Furthermore, the political scientist, trained to uncover the true locus of power in a political system, might observe that even if the Japanese electorate does choose, in a referendum, to revise Article 9 and reassert its sovereign right of belligerency, the Japanese people would still not be sovereign because the locus of sovereign power is not to be found within the Japanese constitutional order. Revisionists such as Ozawa must seek not only to resurrect Japanese sovereignty but also to make the sovereign Japanese. Any definition of Japanese constitutional normality that fails to address the absent *Japanese* sovereign is fatally flawed.

Such clarity about the true locus of Japanese sovereignty raises three questions. The first is obvious: if no Japanese exercises supreme and unrestricted power, who is Japan's foreign sovereign? Second, if foreigners ceased exercising supreme power over Japan, could the Japanese people learn to exercise it for themselves? Third, and this potentially subverts all of the hopes for Japanese self-mastery implied in the second question, is the Japanese Left's support for Article 9 grounded in a muddled but hitherto effective rejection of the very idea of sovereignty itself?

Foreign sovereign or no sovereign? At first glance, this dichotomy appears to be a subtle if extreme version of the traditional Japanese strategy of separating the legitimating organ of power from, and thus denying legitimacy to, the ultimate holder of real power. But in the Western tradition of political reflection, the insistence that Japan must have a sovereign, even if the sovereign is a foreigner, is consistent with the classical view that Nature abhors a vacuum. This venerable doctrine holds that Japan must have a sovereign because, as Western theory insists, all polities have an exerciser of ultimate authority.

If Japan's foreign sovereign is also the global hegemon – the American hyper-power, for example – this exerciser of ultimate authority ensures that Japan poses no threat to the global order. Japan is also likely to do the bidding of the hegemon. Attractive as the reality of foreign sovereignty over Japan is to the global hegemon, surely the Japanese themselves find the idea of constitutional colonialism unpalatable; but this appears not to be the case with the Japanese Left. Despite unease with US policies, many on the Left prefer foreign suzerainty over full-blooded Japanese subjectivity. Almost all left-wing commentators, Japanese and non-Japanese alike, endorse the existing Japanese constitutional order. But this endorsement is couched in language that, as we have seen, obscures the reality of Japan's under-theorised sovereign-less condition. Here we have the silence of assent.

Foreigners have ruled many nations but postwar Japan's ambiguous welcome to foreign sovereignty is striking. Many Japanese, and not just on the Left, are pleased with the consequences of foreign sovereignty, especially when one can cultivate the illusion that the absence of a Japanese sovereign suggests that the nation has no sovereign, and therefore one has successfully evaded the dangers and temptations of sovereignty. However disguised, the fact that the sovereign of Japan resides abroad ensures that no Japanese wields ultimate authority, thus precluding any possibility that a Japanese leader might exercise tyrannical power. The very notion of a domestic tyrant is an idea that most Japanese find repellent regardless of their ideological standpoint or the depth of their nationalist feeling.

Japan has a sovereign but lacks sovereignty because the sovereign is a foreigner. Does this uncomfortable political condition secure a place for the law? Does it offer a solution to Schmitt's assertion that 'The connection of actual power with the legally highest concept of power is the fundamental problem of the concept of sovereignty'?[7] We have located the locus of power but how is the exercise of foreign sovereignty over Japan to be squared with Schmitt's insistence that raw power be linked with the legally highest concept of power? How does the law bind ultimate power in the relationship between Japan and its foreign sovereign? Article 9 prevents the abuse of sovereign power in the military sphere by the Japanese government. But what restrains the hegemon? Japanese pacifism and constitutional theory offer no convincing answers to such questions.

Carl Schmitt and Article 9

To understand the ambiguities and evasions that characterise the Japanese Left's approach to pacifist constitutionalism, one needs to address the issue from a perspective that breaks with the most important un-stated premise of pacifist thinking: peace is the normal condition of society. Heir to a line of realists – Machiavelli, Hobbes and Jean Bodin – Schmitt rejects the assumption of pacific normality, taking the emergency as the defining ground of constitutional theory and the definition of sovereignty. Such emergencies are what Schmitt calls 'the exception'. The exception by its very nature is unpredictable and therefore cannot be legislated for in advance, nor does it permit the luxury of extended legislative deliberation.

> The usual definition of sovereignty today rests on Bodin's recognition that it will always be necessary to make exceptions to the general rule in concrete circumstances, and that the sovereign is whoever decides what constitutes an exception.[8]

Schmitt's analysis of the true test of constitutional sovereignty fatally subverts the complacent notion that the 'people', named as 'sovereign' in the 1947 Constitution, exercise sovereignty except in a residual or post-emergency sense.[9] Only the executive can decide when an emergency exists or when it is over. The people could never effectively exercise supreme power in an emergency, nor can the determination of when an emergency exists be left to the popular will.

Despite the great variety of left-wing approaches on this controversial issue, there is a fairly consistent unity of opinion, from the 'Peace Issues Discussion Group' in the 1950s until *Asahi Shimbun*'s 1995 proposal for constitutional reform, on the need to hobble Japan's constitutional executive.[10] The exception that proves the rule may be the constitutional reforms proposed by the intellectual monthly journal *Sekai* (1993–94) which accepted the need for the prime minister to be recognised in the constitution as the person responsible for the 'minimum defence' of Japan, but this compromise proposal is undermined by woolly and unworldly thinking on the subject of the exception.[11]

Contrary to the left-wing consensus on this issue, the weak executive has been one of the more troubling features of Japanese central government. Periods of strong effective leadership from the centre – the early *bakufu*, Meiji until the Russo-Japanese War and the reign of Douglas MacArthur, Supreme Commander of the Allied Powers (SCAP), after World War II – contrast painfully with periods of drift or paralysis or divided leadership (the 1920s, the last years of the Pacific War, and the Heisei recession of the 1990s). Examples of strong but ineffective leadership – the beginning of the Pacific War and Kishi's premiership during the Security Pact riots of 1960 – are the exceptions that prove the rule. The Manchurian Incident of 1931 was the product of a weak executive: not merely the absence of civilian control but also the lack of an effective chain of command within the Army itself. It reflected a breakdown in military discipline, not the triumph of militarism. On this subject, Masao Maruyama's classic *Thought and Behaviour in Modern Japanese Politics* can be read to support both sides of the argument.[12]

Legitimacy is not sovereignty

Thus, although a foreign imposition, and although the 1947 Constitution may have been effectively legitimated by national elections, and Article 9 has been widely admired and supported in Japan, legitimacy is not sovereignty. Japanese pacifism undermines the exercise of sovereignty by privileging the legislative function (national debate and the imperative of popular legitimacy) at the expense of executive authority and effective policymaking. But any political scenario that plunges Japanese society into a state of siege might instantly and comprehensively sweep away all the self-imposed fetters on the exercise of national sovereignty. The pacifist lives on the edge of a precipice.

If one lives on a precipice, one must not slip over the edge. Any false step would threaten the normative realm crucial to the pacifist thinker. If, as Schmitt observed, 'there exists no norm that is applicable to chaos', then the supreme goal of the pacifist must be to avoid any political situation that risks unleashing chaos. The Japanese pacifist therefore seeks to abolish all scope for efficient action by any executive, however legitimate, in the military sphere. Such pacifism rejects the doctrine of the 'unity of decision' as classically set out, for example, in *The Federalist Papers*: 'Different opinions are useful and necessary in the legislative; but not in the executive, where especially in times of war and disturbance action must be energetic; to this belongs a unity of decision.'[13]

On this matter, the traditional Japanese preference for consensus melds seamlessly with the liberal doctrine of 'government by discussion' (Harold Laski's definition of parliamentary democracy) by decisively turning its face against the executive and its need for emergency powers in a crisis. In the justification and practice of the Japanese dilution of sovereign powers and responsibilities since 1945, the impact of the Left has been decisive.

What can Schmitt tell us about the constitutional ideas of the Left? Arguably the greatest legal and political thinker of Weimar Germany, he has been condemned by his liberal critics for serving Hitler's new government between 1933 and 1936, and for his anti-Semitic prejudices, common enough at the time, and not just in Germany, but despicable nevertheless. But, such criticism does not touch the substance of his thought, nor reduce the value of his ideas for explaining Japanese legal politics. Schmitt's supreme intervention in practical politics came before Hitler assumed power. Indeed, if Schmitt had had his way, the Nazis would never have taken over the German state, certainly not by the ballot box. *Pace* his *bien-pensant* antagonists, Schmitt committed his formidable mind to the service of the most fateful liberal cause of the twentieth century: the defence of the Weimar Republic.

Three ideas figured prominently in Schmitt's defence: his classic 'enemy-versus-friend' distinction, the related idea of electoral 'equal chance' and finally, perhaps Schmitt's most explosive and debated idea, that notion of the sovereign emergency or what he called 'the exception'. Schmitt's 'enemy-versus-friend' distinction first won prominence in the 1920s. One might also note, *en passant*, that one of Schmitt's most topical insights is contained in his theory that political ideas tend to be secularised versions of theological concepts. This notion has achieved just notoriety. Indeed, the distinction between enemy and friend and the Manichaean theology that animates it captures the essence of America's war on terrorism. Like Islamic terrorism itself, the war on terrorism is an example of the tendency to demonise political oppositions in contemporary society that Schmitt noted.

During the final years of the Weimar Republic, Schmitt exploited his 'enemy-versus-friend' distinction to devise a shield for the Weimar Republic that might have saved it from its mortal foes. Writing in 1932, Schmitt insisted that the German constitutional authorities clearly identify and act against their enemies. Schmitt reasonably argued that the principal dangers to Weimar democracy were the Communists on the Left and the National Socialists on the Right.

To prevent the destruction of the Weimar Republic at the hands of its adversaries, Schmitt called for a resolute defence of the constitutional order. To this end he devised the notion of 'equal chance': all parties committed to preserving the Weimar Constitution should have an equal chance to compete for seats in the Reichstag. The crucial qualification was that no party that sought to undermine the Weimar Constitution should be allowed to participate in national elections.

If Schmitt's caveat had been rigorously enforced, the Nazis would never have achieved their electoral breakthrough because they would have been banned from standing for parliamentary seats. Only a *putsch* would have allowed Hitler to seize power, and the chances of his succeeding were slim. It is just possible that Schmitt's legal defence of Weimar might have prevented the birth of the Third Reich and the horrors that followed.

Schmitt's fundamental insights into political emergencies informed his uncompromising stance on the Weimar Constitution. The 'exception' was the moment of decision-making forced on a political system by an unparalleled crisis that could not be constitutionally anticipated. As almost all constitutional guarantees of civic rights rest on the assumption of normality, they may be rendered impotent overnight by unforeseen circumstances. It is at such moments that the true location of sovereignty within the constitutional system is exposed because only the holder of 'supreme and unrestricted power' is able to act.

What does Schmitt's triad of ideas tell us about Article 9? First, the enemy-versus-friend distinction can be seen as central to the defence of Japanese pacifism because it takes the armed forces to be an inevitable and possibly fatal threat to the sane and safe government of the nation. A negative, indeed Hobbesian, view of human nature is at work in arguments on behalf of Article 9, but, in the hands of the Japanese pacifist, this dark interpretation of humanity has focused exclusively on the Japanese nation. Critics of Japanese militarism insist that the Japanese are, *by nature*, a martial people: no chrysanthemum without the sword.

The pacifist assumes that the Japanese people, if left to their own devices and desires, might easily turn once again to military expansion. That is why constitutional barriers, the stronger the better, must be erected against the existence of any form of military force. The militarist is the enemy. Failing a total ban, any military body must be conceded the very minimum of legitimacy, and kept on the tightest of constitutional reins. For the pacifist, those who advocate the scrapping of Article 9 come close to falling into the same camp as the militarists because they may, intentionally or otherwise, launch the nation down the perilous slope to war and destruction by easing the constraints on military action.

The Japanese pacifist is Hobbesian in a triple sense: (1) he holds that the Japanese people are evil by nature; (2) his greatest fear is of violent death; and (3) he appears to be resolved to sacrifice a significant portion of his liberty to a supreme power if the Leviathan in question can shield him from a violent death (one says 'appear' here because of the obscuring belief among many Japanese that Article 9 abolishes the sovereign and the possibility of belligerency).

Schmitt's notion of equal chance can strengthen arguments made by Western defenders of Article 9 such as Glenn Hook and Gavan McCormack that for Japanese conservative politicians to advocate the abandonment of constitutional pacifism is to subvert the constitutional order.[14] In the context, such critics can be seen to echo Schmitt's insistence that any political party that campaigns for fundamental constitutional revision – and the scrapping of Article 9 would constitute a revolutionary change in the 1947 Constitution – risks its status as a legitimate participant in the postwar parliamentary order.

Invidious comparisons

The moment of decision-making forced on a political system by an unparalleled crisis that cannot be constitutionally anticipated reveals who is sovereign because, as Schmitt insists, one of the fundamental attributes of the sovereign is the authority to declare a 'state of emergency' and to judge how long constitutional guarantees may need to be suspended. The anti-terror legislation introduced by the Bush and Blair governments in response to the struggle with al Qaeda are in perfect accord with Schmitt's fundamental insight.

By contrast, Japanese constitutional pacifism assumes that such moments of supreme emergency will never occur. This is why the Prime Minister's Residence was empty on the first night of Gulf War I. *Pace* Schmitt, the exception does not reveal the true locus of sovereignty in Japan, not only because there is no sovereign but also because the exceptional emergency will never occur. The exception has been constitutionally banned. This is the logic of the pacifist case.

The pacifist theorist rejects comparative constitutional analysis because such comparisons are rightly judged invidious. They threaten to expose, and thus subvert, the pacifist argument. But this ban on comparisons, this *Denkverbot* on reflection about the constitution itself, is intolerable. Take, for example, the contrast between Article 9 and Article 48 of the Weimar Constitution. Here is Article 9:

(1) Aspiring sincerely to an international peace based on justice and order, the Japanese people forever renounce war as a sovereign right of the nation and the threat or use of force as means of settling international disputes.
(2) In order to accomplish the aim of the preceding paragraph, land, sea, and air forces, as well as other war potential, will never be maintained. The right of belligerency of the state will not be recognized.

And this is Article 48:

> If, in the German Reich, public security and order are considerably dis-
> turbed or endangered, the Reichspräsident may undertake necessary
> measures to restore public security and order, and if necessary may inter-
> vene with the aid of the armed forces. For this purpose, he may suspend,
> temporarily, in part or entirely, the basic rights as provided in articles
> 114, 115, 117, 118, 123, 124 and 153.

There is no equivalent of Article 48 in the 1947 Constitution. There is no
provision, from the perspective of Bodin or Schmitt, for 'the exception'. The
moment of truth, of sovereign revelation, that is the first constitutional fruit
of a state of siege is not only precluded by the Japanese text, it cannot be
legally imagined. By contrast, the framers of the Weimar Constitution sought
to achieve the precise opposite by trying to legislate for a legal response to
an emergency that could not, by definition, be anticipated with precision.
Schmitt made his reputation by his relentless dissection of Article 48 in which
he argued that the second sentence had been redrafted to bind the powers of
the Reichspräsident. This was an attempt to anticipate the unforeseeable. It set
the liberal urge to restrain legal authority against the claims of democratic
sovereignty. This dilemma haunts postwar constitutional pacifism with equal
force.

Schmitt's notion of the exception encourages probing of the 'unrealism'
of Article 9. Exceptions do occur. Any constitutional order that assumes
that such exceptions will never happen is living on borrowed time. The
implications for Article 9 are obvious. If North Korea were to launch an
attack on Tokyo, for example, constitutional pacifism would be mortally
wounded.

> [Schmitt's] sovereign slumbers in normal things but suddenly awakens
> when a normal situation threatens to become an exception.[15]

But this reality only highlights what is the most extraordinary aspect of
Japan's postwar experiment in subject-less sovereignty: how has the country
managed to elude Schmitt's exception for over half a century?

If the moment of the exception, that is the state of siege or its equivalent,
unveils and sets in motion the sovereign actor, the nervous pacifist seeks to
prevent this sovereign revelation by skilful evasion of any circumstance in
which the state of the exception might occur. This involves a double strategy.
First, sovereignty is assigned to an agency which cannot effectively exercise it:
the Japanese people in an emergency, for example. Second, even this hobbled
would-be sovereign is bound by sweeping constitutional constraints lest the
people 'run amok'.

More important still, the pacifist seeks to evade any and all occasions when
tensions with a foreign country might invite a challenge to Article 9 from the

Japanese electorate. The ruling assumption is that if no emergency ever arises, the pacifist clause will remain secure, and so it has for almost 60 years until the missile threat from North Korea resurrected Japan's potential moment of the exception. The miracle of the case is that the exception has been postponed so long.

Is the American president Japan's sovereign?

The Japanese evasion of sovereignty cannot last forever. Some day realists such as Schmitt will have the final say. The moment of sovereign revelation will arrive. In the event of an imminent North Korean attack, Japanese eyes would turn to the Japanese executive rather than to the Diet. But in the no longer empty Prime Minister's Residence, attention would focus on Japan's true sovereign: the American president. Only the United States has the will and the might to ward off a North Korean assault on Japan, to respond militarily to such an attack, and to punish it comprehensively. It is Schmitt's analysis that makes clear the true import of this moment of revelation: 'Sovereign is he who decides on the exception.' In this critical moment, sovereign power reveals itself in its purest form. Subsumed under Schmitt's definition are, of course, the sovereign's ability to decide 'what must be done to eliminate' the exception and the ability to decide whether order and stability has been restored and normality regained.[16]

Norms are the key. This restoration is, according to Schmitt, the 'precondition for the restatement of norms' and 'for a legal system to make sense, a normal situation must exist, and he is sovereign who definitely decides whether this normal situation actually exists'.[17] Because the Japanese pacifist rejects the very possibility of an exception, he effectively prevents any Japanese executive from restoring such normality. The pacifist assumes that normality requires no restoration. To bury one's head in the sand is effectively to surrender national sovereignty to the American president. In the face of the exception, Schmitt's logic is irresistible.

The Japanese Left has embraced Article 9 but utterly altered its intent. The American authors of the 1947 Constitution sought to ensure that Japan never again threatened the security of the United States. The humiliation of Pearl Harbor and the horrors of the Bataan Death March were the events that fuelled the insertion of Article 9 into the postwar Constitution. This was the American motivation.

A very different history informed the imperatives of the pacifist. The heavy battlefield casualties that the Imperial Army and Navy suffered in the Pacific War appalled the Japanese Left. More influential still were vivid memories of the American war of annihilation against Japan's cities, notably the firebombing of Tokyo and the atomic destruction of Hiroshima and Nagasaki. Cast in the language of Carl Schmitt, the goal of the aware Japanese leftist after 1952 was to prevent the moment of sovereign revelation by ensuring that the exception never occurred.

Constitutional anticipations of a national emergency, the elaboration of who had the power to act in an emergency and the prediction of which freedoms might be suspended, all figure prominently in the thinking behind the Weimar Constitution. By contrast, the Japanese Left has refused to dwell on the practical implications of the exception. Far better, so it was judged, to keep this particular legal bugbear not only out of sight but also out of mind. Renouncing sovereignty and subjectivity, the Japanese Left helped Japan choose its master: the American president.

Foucault's Japan: neither sovereignty, nor subjectivity

Surveiller et punir

Schmitt's notion of the exception boldly exposes pacifist unrealism about global politics and the hyperrealism about the dark side of the Japanese national character. Perhaps only the European canon itself can provide a *Grund* for a positive and convincing theory of constitutional pacifism, one capable of resisting the force of Schmitt's ideas. The basis for such a theory may be found in Michel Foucault's critique of subjectivity. The notion developed here of the 'willing victim' is a meditated response to Foucault's philosophy.

In constitutional terms, pacifism is the denial of sovereignty. In metaphysical terms, pacifism is the rejection of subjectivity. Pacifism opposes action. Virtue manifests itself in a kind of a political paralysis, because inaction does not pose the moral dangers of agency. Pacifism is a wise passivity in the face of the temptations that accompany national action, the urge to leave a boot print on the world.

There is an implicit link between such moral-minded passivity and Foucault's visceral reaction to the horrors of unrestrained power that he witnessed during the Nazi occupation of France during World War II. The link between French theory and Japanese pacifism is as important as it has often been ignored. It reveals the obscure centre of the psychology and metaphysics that informs the postwar Japanese rejection of national agency.

Foucaultian analysis holds that nationality is a social construction. The nation does not represent an essence that can command ultimate loyalty. Therefore, the most troublesome dimension of non-coercive nationalism, such as Japanese pacifism, is the concept of nation itself. The nation as subject must be deconstructed, and thereby rendered harmless. No project looms larger in the Western study of Japan today.

The chief inspiration for the critique of subjectivity one finds in Foucault is Heidegger. Liberals and conservatives have taken Heidegger to task for his rejection of the Cartesian-Hegelian subject because it appears to call into doubt the very idea of democratic agency. But such censure misses the point. Heidegger's warning about the dangers of subjectivity (in political terms, the sovereign must possess subjectivity) applies to totalitarian and democratic regimes alike. This is the lesson of the carceral politics, the brutal panopticism, of Abu Ghraib Prison in Baghdad.

To possess the power to act on the world is to be constantly tempted to act against other polities that lack a comparable degree of subjectivity. America's global hegemony is the most important contemporary demonstration that Heidegger was right in his insistence that democracies are not immune to the temptations of subjective power. In the case of Japan, the title of Tetsuya Takahashi's essay '*Sensō Shutai toshite no Kokka to Kokumin*' (The State and the Nation as War-Making Subject) ranges over the relevant rubric.[18]

The latest phase in the postwar evasion of sovereignty among the left-wing intelligentsia is the struggle to deconstruct the Japanese state and its armour of traditional values (male supremacy, ethnic purity, heterosexualism and gerontocracy) in order to create a 'post-Japan'. The goal is to abolish any notion of national essence. This campaign represents, at numerous points, the fulfilment of Foucault's vision and promise of what life might be like if it were possible to enjoy the political 'free fall' that comes with a 'free state'. Foucault, as Derrida does in another key, equips the critic with the watchmaker tools to deconstruct 'Japan' and then to reassemble it in a manner that ensures that it never quite works again.

Foucault versus Said

The neglected tear in Foucault's *oeuvre* of experience is the occluded moment when he discovered the potential of what might be called the 'willing victim'. As such, the notion of a 'free state' figures as only a fragment or trace in his major works, although this momentary surrender to '*l'homme de désir*' may be the source of the principal rupture in the development of his ideas – the shift from the subject as perpetual victim of power relations to the subject as manipulator of power in the sexual nexus – that writers such as J. G. Merquior have identified in the late Foucault.[19]

Foucault prepared for this epiphany with a lifetime of reflection on Nietzsche. But this moment reflects the delayed impact of the Nietzsche that Foucault neglected earlier, the Nietzsche of stoic suffering but also of the final transcendence of the superman who is the willing victim. On the metaphorical level, this *Übermensch* served as Foucault's faithful guide and Vergil during his descent into the sexual hell of the bathhouses of San Francisco in the 1980s, where the French thinker first tasted the pleasures of sovereign-less 'free fall'. For our purposes, one may conclude that the psychology of the willing victim (the victim who wills) informs the Japanese longing for subjective-less subjectivity and sovereign-less sovereignty.

The substance of this idea, as it occurs in Foucault, is a product of a thought experiment, but it is an idea, and therefore the concept of the willing victim cannot be reduced to raw politics and perverse sex. Some of the most influential of Foucault's American admirers (not being Platonists) have sought to reduce his thought to psychological or ideological residues and nothing more. One such admirer is Edward Said.

In *Power, Politics and Culture*, he sets the scene for his attack on Foucault in the following manner. First, Said describes the temptation of empire, and how this temptation applied with equal force to British and French imperialism in the nineteenth century. His caveats may be applied with like conviction to the Japanese empire during its heyday or to America's global hegemony today:

> . . . the experience of empire is essentially repetitive but is never perceived as that. You know, there's this wonderful line I quote from Coetzee's *Waiting for the Barbarians*, where the new men of empire come and they just do the same thing as the old men did. This seems to me of extraordinary interest for people who live in this country [the United States], where we have this idea that we are going to do things differently or, to paraphrase Laurence Sterne, that they 'order this matter better' in Washington. The fact is, the imperialist impulse is exactly the same.[20]

Nevertheless, national resistance, the cure for imperialism that is always prey to the same subjectivist impulses, offers, according to Said, no satisfactory remedy.

> The opposition to imperialism is of course the emergence of nationalism. Nationalism is many, many things. Obviously one aspect of it is a reactive phenomenon. It's an assertion of identity, where the problematics of identity are supposed to carry the whole wave of the culture and of political work, which is the case in the early phases of nationalist struggle against European colonialism.[21]

Empire is the fault for which nationalist resistance is supposed the cure. But the remedy also is flawed.

> There is an emphasis upon forging a self-identity as a nation or a people that resists but has its own integrity (as in Césaire's *negritude*). But it does seem to me that despite the essential virtues there are great limitations to that intellectually as well as politically. The limitations have to do with the fetishization of the national identity. The national identity becomes not only a fetish, but it is also turned into a kind of idol, in the Baconian sense – an idol of the cave, and of the tribe.[22]

Foucault sought to break this cycle of imperialism and nationalist resistance to imperialism, of aggression, violent reaction and renewed aggression by dissolving any convincing idea of essence. Nazi Germany, militarist Japan and imperial America all qualify as imagined communities, the dangerous residues of what Said calls 'the fetishization of the national identity'.

These communities are imagined because there is no essence to identify with. The Hitler Youth, the kamikaze pilot and the democratic warrior in Iraq all fight and die for a social construction. In his rejection of such clanging idols, Foucault links the anti-subjective pacifist with the contemporary urge among people who live in Japan (the word 'Japanese' itself is suspect here) to deconstruct traditional oppressive notions of gender, sexual orientation and nationality. The deconstruction of Japan, that is the freeing of the people who live in the Japanese archipelago from the need to be Japanese (or, more subtly, *datsu-Nippon*), is the pacifist's trump card and final ploy.

So far, so good. But in an extraordinary thought experience, Foucault pushed the matter further by exploring, via an intense 'psycho-sexual' encounter, the character and risks of the subjective-less condition. This thought experiment defeats Said. Blaming sadomasochism, the Palestinian-American concludes incorrectly that Foucault aligns himself 'with Power'.

> He is like a scribe of a kind of irresistible, ineluctable power. And I was writing in order to oppose power, so it was written out of a political position.[23]

This line of criticism suggests that Said does not take the French thinker quite seriously enough. Yet, Foucault explains Said's political dilemma while Said seems blind to the importance for the 'worldly critic' of Foucault's experimentation with sadomasochism and the psychology of subjectivity.

Thus, Said claims in the quotation above that he opposes power and that he writes from a political position. But it is not only Israel which is an imagined community; the Palestinian nation is one, too. There is no essence for the Palestinian to defend. Said claims that the French thinker eliminates 'the site of resistance', but Foucault is denying nothing; he is merely elaborating the price that all resistance involves.[24] What he does claim is that political engagement of any kind will necessarily plunge the resister into the paradox of power, as the career of Yasir Arafat and the tragedy of the Palestinian people demonstrate.

Foucault is not 'the scribe of power'. Rather, as has been noted, this French philosopher asserts the larger truth that power and its effects are inescapable. This is true of all forms of identity politics including support for the Palestine Liberation Organization. It is not possible to know Foucault well and exploit his ideas, and then declare that one is 'opposed to power' and write 'out of political position' without some form of qualification and explanation. Said offers neither.

In citing the reasons why he became 'even more disillusioned with Foucault',[25] Said observes:

> I felt that Foucault had this initial idea based upon the notion of confinement – confinement and the challenge to the confinement, the breaking loose – which we now know has a lot to do with his own biographical

trajectory. A man named James Miller is doing a kind of revisionist biography of Foucault, and Miller's point is that Foucault was always dealing with sadomasochistic impulses, including an early attempt at suicide. So this idea of confinement was very important to sort of getting it down and then breaking it open, hence the early importance to him of figures like de Sade.[26]

Most of this assessment is a garbled and implausible reading of Foucault's work and life, his sexual identity and psychology. This lack of comprehension is compounded by a rooted obtuseness, something Said shares with many North American academics, when confronted by the fact that European thinkers *think* all of the time. Even their impulses become thoughts. Foucault was a European thinker in this mode. He was constantly engaged in meditating on the 'life phenomena' in front of him. In one sense, it matters not at all that something pivotal to Foucault's philosophy was discovered in the cubicles of a gay bathhouse. In philosophic terms, the cubicle was merely the contemporary version of Descartes' famous 'oven' or the Marquis de Sade's 'philosophy of the bedroom'.

Master and slave

What Foucault discovered with his limit-experiment should colour how we read him as a political thinker. First, it must be understand that sadomasochism is a psychological event, an exercise in power and the endurance of pain, that may or may not have a sexual dimension. Power is a political word. In such events, the masochist or slave sets the absolute limits. The first obligation of the master is the 'care' of his slave, a task defined by his scrupulous observance of the limits the slave himself has mandated.

In subjectivist terms, and this is what interested Foucault as a critic of subjectivism, the master is responsible for his slave, thus freeing the slave of any need to be responsible. In such circumstances, the slave trades his subjectivity for pleasure, just as Hobbes's citizen trades his liberty for the security of sovereign authority.

The relationship between master and slave is one of infinite attention on the part of the master. One aspect of this intense accord between two human beings, caught up in a power-political embrace, is captured in Joseph Losey's film *The Night Porter*. Put in this manner, it becomes apparent that Foucault's cubicle thought-experiment proceeds from, and is a subversive elaboration of, Hegel's famous meditation on masters and slaves in the *Phenomenology of Spirit*. Derrida's parallel text, a contrived dialogue or textual battle between Hegel and Jean Genet, is to be found in *Glas*.

In those California cubicles, Foucault discovered that one could temporarily abandon one's subjectivity and suspend one's sovereignty – in perfect confidence. It was only in the cubicle that Foucault was ever 'the scribe of power'. There, the French philosopher *experienced* the ideal of political weightlessness, in the Platonic or Weberian sense. This perfection hints at the supreme motive behind what the Japanese call '*amae*'. The cubicle returns the slave to the womb or, better still, to the breast. At his mother's breast, the child confidently refutes the claims and duties of the world. Only in this secure condition is one able to enjoy fully the relaxed pleasures of free fall.

The tear in this free state is the slave's 'escape word', the pre-agreed phrase or cry that allows the slave, *in extremis*, to bring this theatre of cruelty to an immediate and total halt. In the case of the Japanese pacifist, this escape word is 'Article 9'. The whole constitutional business is a fantastic exercise in total trust of the hegemon. Foucault, as a commentator on Hegel, makes clear that to achieve this free state, one query, above all, looms large in the decision to entrust one's fate to another: Who is to be my master? For anyone, or any society, that would surrender to the sovereign-less and subjective-less condition, no question matters more.

Pacifism is the rejection of the world and its grim responsibilities and bloody excesses; it is also the politics of total dependence. It reflects an evasion of the need to exercise sovereignty and to achieve self-mastery. In this state, the illusions of identity politics and national essence are banished, but at a price: the muscles go flabby and the habits of discipline, command and sacrifice are unlearned. Lying on the ground watching summer fireworks burst overhead, the willing victim thrills to the awesome display of the gigantic, all-powerful Other. Hobbes called it the 'Leviathan'. Today we call it 'American empire'. Who is to say that only the Japanese have yielded to it?

Notes

1 Carl Schmitt, *Political Theology: Four Chapters on the Concept of Sovereignty*, translated by George Schwab, Massachusetts and London: MIT Press, 1985, p. xviii.
2 Ibid., p. 13.
3 Marquis de Sade, *Philosophy in the Bedroom*, in Marquis de Sade, *Justine, Philosophy in the Bedroom and Other Writings*, London: Arrow Books, 1991, p. 302.
4 Paul Valéry, 'Introduction to a Dialogue', p. 339, quoted in William Kluback, *Paul Valéry: The Statesman of the Intellect*, New York: Peter Lang Publishing, 1999, p. 78.
5 David Williams, *Japan and the Enemies of Political Science*, London and New York: Routledge, 1994, pp. 3–4.
6 Thomas McCarthy, 'Series Editor's Foreword,' in Carl Schmitt, *Political Theology: Four Chapters on the Concept of Sovereignty*, p. viii.
7 Schmitt, *Political Theology*, op. cit., p. 18.
8 Carl Schmitt, *The Crisis of Parliamentary Democracy*, translated by Ellen Kennedy, Cambridge, Massachusetts: MIT Press, 1988, p. 43.
9 The word 'ultimate' may eventually have a place in this definition, but it can be convincingly evoked only after the Schmittian critique is complete.
10 On the Peace Discussion Group, see Rikki Kersten, *Democracy in Postwar Japan: Maruyama Masao and the Search for Autonomy*, London: Routledge, 1996; and Glenn D. Hook, *Militarization and Demilitarization in Contemporary Japan*, London: Routledge, 1996.

11 Translations of the *Asahi Shimbun* and *Sekai* proposals may be found in Glenn D. Hook and Gavan McCormack, *Japan's Contested Constitution: Documents and Analysis*, London and New York: Routledge, 2001. This is an invaluable English-language reference source on this subject.
12 Masao Maruyama, *Gendai Seiji no Shisō to Kōdō*, Tokyo: Mirai-sha, 1957. *Thought and Behaviour in Modern Japanese Politics*, edited by Ivan Morris, London: Oxford University Press, 1963.
13 Quoted in Carl Schmitt, *The Crisis of Parliamentary Democracy*, op. cit., p. 44.
14 Glenn D. Hook and Gavan McCormack, *Japan's Contested Constitution*, op. cit., p. 9.
15 George Schwab, 'Introduction', Carl Schmitt, *Political Theology*, op. cit., p. xviii.
16 Ibid.
17 Ibid.
18 Yōichi Komori (ed.), *Towareru Rekishi to Shutai, 1955 Nen-igo, 2* (The Subject and its Suspect History, 1955 and Afterwards, 2), *Iwanani Kōza Kindai Nihon no Bunka-shi* (Iwanami Course in the Cultural History of Modern Japan), Tokyo: Iwanani Shoten, 2003, pp. 177–193.
19 J. G. Merquior, *Foucault*, London: Fontana Press/Collins, 1985, p. 138.
20 Gauri Viswanathan (ed.), *Power, Politics and Culture: Interviews with Edward W. Said*, London: Bloomsbury, 2004, p. 196.
21 Ibid., p. 129.
22 Ibid.
23 Ibid., p. 170.
24 Ibid., p. 138.
25 Ibid., p. 167.
26 Ibid., pp. 166–167.

Part II

The metamorphosis of the Left in postwar Japan

4 The rise and fall of Nikkyōso

Classroom idealism, union power and the three phases of Japanese politics since 1955

Robert W. Aspinall

Introduction

Any discussion of the relationship between the fortunes of the Left and the development of democracy in Japan would be incomplete without an analysis of the role of teachers' unions. Not only were debates about education policy at the heart of the ideological cleavage that defined the '1955 System', but the main teachers' union, Nikkyōso, acted as a massive bedrock of support for the public sector union movement and the Japan Socialist Party (JSP). During the 1980s and 1990s decisive transformations occurred, both within Nikkyōso and with regard to its relationships with its political allies and enemies. These transformations were both affected by and had an effect on fundamental changes that were taking place within the world of Japanese politics. For the union and for other political actors, the main events that changed the landscape of Japanese politics occurred between 1989 and 1996. This chapter, therefore, proposes to divide its examination of Nikkyōso's role in the transformation of Japanese politics into three periods: the '1955 system'; the period 1989–96 during which that system clearly came to an end; and events and trends subsequent to 1996. Before looking at these periods in turn, we will first discuss the political and ideological terminology that will be used in this chapter.

Divisions between Left and Right over educational politics in Japan

What is meant by the terms 'Left' and 'Right' in Japanese educational politics? As a broad method for classifying organizations in postwar Japan, these terms are relatively unproblematic. Scholars who have examined the educational politics of the 1955 system have painted a very clear bipolar picture. On the Left there was the progressive camp consisting mainly of Nikkyōso, the JSP and the Japan Communist Party (JCP); and on the Right was the conservative camp consisting mainly of the Ministry of Education, the Liberal Democratic Party (LDP), business interests and local education administrators. This two-camp model is a useful way of classifying organizations and individuals, and is an essential starting point for an analysis of educational politics in Japan. However, a deeper analysis of divisions within these camps and also the evolution (both organizationally and ideologically) of the various members of the two camps requires a closer look at policy, discourse and organizational transformations that take the form of splits, mergers, defections, the collapse of old organizations and the creation of new ones. Before going on to this deeper analysis, we will first review the main features of the two-camp model as it applied during the years of the 1955 system.

Political scientist Leonard Schoppa based his model of educational policy making on the central importance of the antagonism between the progressive and the conservative camps, arguing that while conflict did occur *within* each camp, it was of quite a different nature from that occurring *between* the two camps. He notes, however, that in the 1980s some issues came to prominence that 'left both camps disoriented.'[1] (This was one sign of the imminent demise of the 1955 system that will be dealt with later in this chapter.) Historian Byron Marshall, in his study of modern Japanese political discourse on education, identified conflict between these two camps (in every important respect identical to the two categories described by Schoppa) as being the defining feature of education as a political issue in the 1950s and 1960s.[2] Because of the (methodologically speaking) uncontroversial nature of the two-camp model, the following clear picture of the basic ideological make-up of the two camps can be drawn.

The conservative camp under the 1955 system

Organizations and individuals within this camp were united by the following beliefs: (1) one of the main purposes of education is to instill patriotism into young minds; (2) a centralised education system under the authority of the Ministry of Education is the best method for ensuring uniform standards of educational provision throughout the nation; (3) one of the main purposes of education is to provide Japanese business and industry with the skilled, hard-working and conformist workers that they need to catch up with the advanced industrial nations of the West; (4) many of the education reforms during occupation were foreign impositions, not in keeping with Japanese traditions and culture; (5) at the international level the threat of international communism should be resisted and Japan's alliance with the USA should be supported.

The progressive camp under the 1955 system

Organizations and individuals within this camp were united by the following beliefs: (1) one of the main purposes of education is to teach children the evils of militarism and the horrors of war; (2) education should be strictly egalitarian with all children receiving the same content of instruction during compulsory education (6 years old to 15); (3) educational administration should be democratic, meaning that local boards of education should be elected and the powers of the Ministry of Education should be severely curtailed; (4) school management should also be democratic, meaning that important decisions should be made collectively by all the teachers at the school; (5) at the international level American imperialism should be opposed, and socialist movements in other countries should be supported.

Divisions within the progressive camp during the period of the 1955 system

Of course, serious differences arising from competing organizational interests and ideological programmes existed within both camps. However, because the main focus of this chapter (and this book) is the Left, it is divisions within the progressive camp that will be looked at more closely. When it came to educational politics, the most important member of the progressive camp was Nikkyōso. At the start of the period of the 1955 system it had a membership that comprised over 85 per cent of all school teachers in Japan.[3] It provided organizational support, finance and personnel for the JSP. It also was given a free hand to write the education policies of that party. Finally, it was one of the main public sector unions that formed the left-leaning Sōhyō union confederation.

Nikkyōso had since its formation in 1947 been weakened by serious political and ideological divisions. These divisions existed within the national union's Central Executive Council (*shikkōbu*), the various executives of the prefectural unions that were affiliated to Nikkyōso (but enjoyed a large degree of local autonomy), and at the level of the individual school. In the early years of the union, political struggle was most visible between the supporters of the JCP and JSP.[4] One of the main policies that JSP sympathisers were opposed to was the communist-supported tactic of direct confrontation. During the 1950s, this tactic, in the form of strikes, boycotts and mass demonstrations, led to violent clashes between union supporters and the police or right-wing gangs. Those prefectures where the violence was worse (Tochigi, Tokushima, Kagawa and Ehime) saw a drastic decline in union membership. This helped increase support for the socialist faction's policy of opposition through 'gradualism', a tactic that aimed at opposing government education policies through passive resistance, often taking the form of refusing to implement those policies at the school level, or *genba*.

By 1962 the JSP-supporting faction had taken control of the national executive of Nikkyōso, and became known as the mainstream faction (*shuryūha*) of the union. The next development was the emergence of splits *within* the mainstream faction. These splits mirrored the splits that existed within the JSP, and in the case of both organizations individual rivalries over power and influence became confused with ideological differences. In the case of educational politics, ideological differences mostly arose from disagreements over how to respond to changing social and economic pressures for

educational change. Japan's economic miracle was in the process of trans-
forming the nation's social and economic institutions. These changes placed
pressures on the postwar education system that forced would-be reformers of
all political persuasions to reconsider their ideas about what would be best for
Japan's schools and the children in their care. Ideas that did not change were
in danger of becoming irrelevant to new generations of children and parents.

Period one: the two sides face off during the trench warfare of the '1955 system' (1955–1959)

The political conflict between the two main camps during the period of the
'1955 system' has been described as 'trench warfare', a description that conjures up images of great armies bogged down in static but relentless conflict,
with little visible gain for either side. One intrinsic feature of trench warfare
is the attrition suffered by both sides. In such circumstances the side that
has greater resources and greater strength in depth will probably prevail over
the long term. It may come to the point where the weaker side has to sue for
peace in order to avoid complete destruction. Since the strength of trade
unions is usually measured by the number of members they have, any state of
affairs that leads to a continuous decline of members will cause a union
leadership to reconsider their strategy. Thus public sector unions that were
members of the progressive camp in the '1955 system' were forced to devise
strategies to cope with the losses they were suffering through opposition to
the governing conservative camp.

There were other reasons why military metaphors were appropriate for
describing the '1955 system'. The system was so named because 1955 was the
year in which the LDP was formed out of various competing conservative
parties, and the JSP was reunified (following a split in 1951). The division of
the political world into two great camps was not confined to political parties
but also applied to allies of the two sides, especially private business and
industry interests in the case of the LDP, and public sector unions in the
case of the JSP. This binary division was even extended into the international
sphere with US support (and CIA money) being provided for the LDP while
the JSP strengthened its links with socialist states and parties around the
world. These international links added another dimension to the pseudo-
military language used to describe relations between the two camps. The
linking of domestic politics with the international politics of the Cold War
led some people on both sides to see their enemies as literal military threats.
Thus, right-wing conservatives worried about communist subversion and the
role of the Left in Japan as an agent of Soviet or Chinese aggression. Meanwhile, left-wingers worried about Japan's role as an agent of American
imperialism and the danger of Japan being sucked into an American war
in Asia.

From the above it can be seen that, for some at least, the use of pseudo-
military language to describe the struggle between Left and Right in Japan

under the 1955 system was more than mere rhetorical flourish. Actual violence did take place on the streets – between the police and demonstrators – and on the floor of the main chamber of the Diet – between Socialist politicians and their opponents. But it was not this violence that gave the language of violent conflict real meaning to many people involved in political struggle. More real and more menacing for them was the overall ideological context of a Herculean struggle between Left and Right. It was the idea that the stakes that the two sides were playing for were extremely high. The Left feared a resurgence of fascism and militarism that would turn the clock back to the dark ages of 1930s Japan. The Right feared the destruction of Japan's centuries-old culture and traditions and the nation's enslavement by Soviet-style totalitarianism. However, as time went by, fears based on events in the 1930s and 1940s became less and less relevant to new generations of Japanese who had no direct experience of those times. For these people, other concerns about education and politics arose during the 1970s and 1980s.

Changes in the discourse on education that took place during the period of the 1955 system

As Japan's postwar economic miracle pulled its people out of an era of war and deprivation and into an era of increasing affluence and prosperity, political issues for many became more related to practical matters like the reduction of pollution, the increase in welfare provisions, improvements in infrastructure and so on. The LDP as the governing party had to busy itself with dealing with these kinds of issues. Challenges from new parties of the centre like Kōmeitō, made LDP leaders worry that if they did not address these issues they would lose votes and maybe one day even power.[5] For those in the progressive camp, however, permanently excluded from the reins of central power, the need to adapt to changing political trends was less pressing. There was the danger that ideological furor might persist among the politically active at the same time as it was becoming more irrelevant to the lives of ordinary voters and union members. Some saw within the progressive camp a dangerously complacent combination of ideological purity with a comfortable acceptance of the role of permanent opposition. The political scientist, Jirō Yamaguchi, for example, has argued that some JSP Diet members were content to stay in opposition, knowing that their party had sufficient numbers (before it was overtaken by electoral disaster in the 1990s) to block any review of the Japanese constitution by their conservative rivals.[6]

An examination of the case of the Japan Teachers' Union (Nikkyōso), a pillar of the progressive camp, will give us a clear illustration of what happened to an organization of the Left in political and ideological terms when it did (unlike the JSP) try seriously to adapt to changing times. We can also observe the union suffering the kind of attrition in its membership that makes the use of the analogy of 'trench warfare' entirely appropriate. According to government figures (which were never guilty of over-stating union membership) over 86 per cent of school teachers in Japan were members of unions affiliated with Nikkyōso in 1958. By 1987, this figure had declined to 48.5 per cent. The drop in union membership below the halfway line made front-page headlines in the national press. The decline was put down to anti-union pressure by the government and educational administrators and trainers, as well as the rise of an apolitical generation of teachers who found the political slogans of union leaders irrelevant to their life and work.[7]

Significant changes were also underway in educational thought and practice in Japan that had a bearing on the decline of Nikkyōso. Educators and politicians on the Left traditionally shared an ideology of egalitarianism. They wholeheartedly supported the uniformity of educational provision that took place in the compulsory sector of schooling (for all children from 6 years old to 15 in the postwar system). The postwar constitution of Japan, which they also supported, stipulated that this education had to be free of charge. The Left also regarded the streaming or setting of pupils as a form of discrimination that must be opposed.[8] Paradoxically, although they opposed the centralised control over education wielded by the Ministry of Education (Monbushō), they were in favour of a system that gave all of Japanese youth a standard, uniform educational experience. This meant that no child would be discriminated against due to social class or region.

Equality in the compulsory sector of education was one area where the Left, the Right and American reformers of the Occupation period had a lot in common.[9] It is therefore not surprising that it became an enduring feature of the postwar education system. By the 1980s, however, it was coming in for criticism from education experts, business leaders and the public at large. Critics argued that an overly uniform system stifled creativity and produced well-disciplined but inflexible workers. Education reform, it was argued, should aim at the twin goals of improving the educational experience of children as well as equipping them with the skills required by the changing economic circumstances of the late twentieth century. The most popular buzzwords adopted by the reformers were individuality (*kosei*), creativity (*sōzōsei*), internationalization (*kokusaika*), and liberalization (*jiyūka*).[10] For the conservative camp the best-known proponent of this wave of reform was Prime Minister Yasuhiro Nakasone. His *ad hoc* Council for Education Reform (Rinkyōshin) carried out a thorough review of the entire education system. Schoppa, when he analysed the politics of Rinkyōshin, found that they were unable to bring about the hoped-for reform because of internal disagreement in the conservative camp.[11] Although Nikkyōso as a member of the progressive camp was excluded from consultation on policy, the debate over Rinkyōshin's proposals prompted bitter disagreement within the union ranks. The JSP-supporting mainstream faction that dominated Nikkyōso was split into two: traditionalists on the Left wanted to resist all of the proposals because they emanated from the enemy camp and were seen as a threat to the egalitarianism of the postwar system; modernisers, on the other hand, believed that there were some good ideas among the proposals and that Nikkyōso should not adopt a totally negative attitude towards them.

For the modernisers in Nikkyōso, therefore, the debate over how to respond to Rinkyōshin's proposals signified a shift away from the previous policy of absolute opposition to government education reform. Before moving on to look at Nikkyōso's more flexible approach that resulted from this change of strategy, it is worth reviewing the significance of the role played by the teachers' union and its allies in resisting right-wing changes to the education system in the post-Occupation period. The main contribution of the Left to Japanese democracy in this period was the prevention of a right-wing reaction that may have turned the clock back in many vital areas to prewar authoritarianism and militarism. Thurston pointed this out in 1973 in the following summing up of Nikkyōso's achievement:

> The net result of the existence and activities of the JTU [Nikkyōso] on educational policy in postwar Japan has been positive. In fact, the existence of the JTU as an independent teachers' union has been indispensable to the democratization of Japanese education, a process that is by no means complete but that the JTU through its activities as a strong countervailing power to the hereto-fore absolute Ministry of Education has greatly assisted.[12]

Summing up Nikkyōso's contribution to Japanese democracy during the years of the 1955 system, we can agree with Thurston that, although largely confined to an oppositional role (at least at the national level), Nikkyōso was able to make a significant positive contribution to the development of postwar democracy. On top of this Nikkyōso made other contributions. In addition to its main function as a representative and independent organization for teachers helping them with professional development (such matters as pay and conditions at work), Nikkyōso was also a leading member of the public sector union confederation Sōhyō, and had yet another role as a main vote-gatherer and supporter of the JSP.

The chronic decline of Nikkyōso, combined with its rethinking of its policy of opposition to the government must have had a decisive effect on the whole progressive camp. Would this weakening of opposition have the effect of allowing the conservative camp to rule Japan unfettered? To answer this question we have to turn to the next period of Japanese politics, the period of realignment.

Period two: political realignment and the crisis of the Left (1989–1996)

In 1989 the transformation of global politics was marked by the collapse of the Berlin Wall, an event that heralded the end of the Cold War. In the same year, in Japanese domestic politics two significant developments took place.

At the House of Councillors election a surge of support for the JSP under its popular new leader Takako Doi helped to bring about the end to the LDP majority that had controlled that House up until then. Later that same year, Nikkyōso suffered a schism with about one third of its members leaving to form a new national teachers' union, the All Japan Teachers' Union (Zenkyō). In what ways are all of these significant events related, and how did they help bring about a period of uncertainty and change in Japanese politics?

The decline of the JSP and changes in public sector unionism

Electoral success for the JSP in 1989 led many on the Left to hope that the time had come at last for defeat of the LDP and the establishment of a progressive government. These hopes turned out to be unfounded. Voters abandoned the LDP not because of positive feelings towards the JSP, but in order to punish the LDP for the excesses of the Recruit corruption scandal, and also for introducing the very unpopular new consumption tax. With hindsight we can now see that the true state of the progressive camp in 1989 was better illustrated by the trials and tribulations of Nikkyōso rather than by the short-lived success of Takako Doi's JSP. The inability of the LDP to win back control of the Upper House, followed by its temporary loss of control of the Lower House, too, from 1993–4, was more indicative of the internal problems of the conservative camp, rather than of any resurgence of strength in the progressive camp. In fact, the LDP only lost power when three senior LDP politicians, Ichirō Ozawa, Tsutomu Hata and Masayoshi Takemura, broke away from the party to form two rival organizations that fielded candidates to stand against LDP candidates in the 1993 Lower House election. The strength of these two new organizations – the Japan Renewal Party and New Party Sakigake – combined with the Japan New Party led by another former LDP politician, Morihiro Hosokawa, was enough to force the LDP out of power.

Supporters of the Left celebrated the defeat of the LDP and were glad to see the JSP join the new non-LDP coalition government that was formed after the election under the prime minister-ship of Hosokawa. However, a look at the voting statistics of the 1993 election showed that actually it was the JSP that was the big loser, not the LDP. In the previous Lower House election, held in 1990, the JSP had won 136 seats, with 24.4 per cent of the popular vote. In 1993 it was able to win only 70 seats, with 15.4 per cent of the vote.[13] The fact had to be faced that in the new political system then in the process of formation, voters who wanted to punish an LDP-led government, were more likely to vote for a non-left-wing party if they had the opportunity. Because of its ideological devotion to the progressive principles of the postwar left-wing settlement, the leaders of the JSP were unable to face up to this fact before it was too late.

The deteriorating electoral performance of the JSP during the 1990s was not only due to the desertion of voters to the various new parties that were formed during that decade. Before 1989 the JSP had always relied on public sector unions for financial support and also for help in getting the vote out at election time. Unlike socialist and social democratic parties in other industrial democracies, the JSP had failed to build a mass membership support base of its own. Thus the party was seriously affected by the far-reaching changes that took place in the public sector union movement in Japan in the 1980s. In 1989 the public sector union confederation Sōhyō dissolved itself and its affiliated organizations joined with private sector unions to form the new confederation, Rengō. As one of the largest unions affiliated to Sōhyō, Nikkyōso's role in the formation of Rengō was decisive. The mainstream faction in control of Nikkyōso's executive had decided that the time had come to modernise their ideas and their organization, and to seek a policy of cooperation with the government and the Ministry of Education. They looked at how another giant of the public sector union movement, the railway workers' union Kokurō, had been almost destroyed in its confrontation with the government during the 1980s.[14]

Nikkyōso's executive's policy of cooperation was regarded as an act of betrayal by the anti-mainstream faction. When the decision to affiliate with Rengō was finally made many on the Left of the union decided they had to form a new organization that would uphold the original left-wing ideals of the teachers' union movement. That is why the new national teachers' union, Zenkyō, was formed in the same year as Nikkyōso and the other public sector unions joined Rengō. Also in the same year, Zenkyō and other left-wing unions formed the rival union confederation Zenrōren. Zenrōren's policy platform had a lot in common with that of the Japan Communist Party.[15]

Post-schism Nikkyōso continued, at first, to support the JSP. Some on the centre-Left saw the formation of Rengō as an opportunity to reunify the JSP and the Democratic Socialist Party (DSP). Before 1989, the DSP had been supported mostly by private sector unions affiliated to the union federation Dōmei, so the coming together of Dōmei and Sōhyō to form Rengō seemed to offer the chance of reconciliation between the two parties.[16] Before negotiations over possible reunification had got very far, however, Iraq's invasion of Kuwait and the subsequent debate about what Japan's role should be in the war that followed, brought to the fore an issue that was guaranteed to make reconciliation between the two parties impossible. A bill to allow Japanese SDF forces to take part in Peace Keeping Operations (PKO) in the Persian Gulf was supported by the DSP. The JSP, however, not only opposed the bill, but organised an infamous filibuster tactic known as the 'cow walk' which involved JSP Diet members walking through the voting lobbies extremely slowly. The JSP had used this tactic before in the 1960s. However, in the 1990s the combination of a changed ideological environment and the televising of Diet proceedings conspired to create a very damaging image that could only reduce the prestige of the party still further. The use of the 'cow walk' coincided with the collapse of efforts to engineer a reunion between the JSP and the DSP. The use of the tactic also showed how out of touch the JSP leadership was with changes in the political climate both inside and outside the Diet.

The JSP was in decline in the 1990s not only because its parliamentary tactics were out of touch and out of date, but also because it had consistently failed to address policy areas that were of concern to people who should have been natural supporters of the party. Kume makes the following point about the failure of the JSP to meet the expectations and needs of rank and file union members.

> It is telling that the Socialists were not interested in productive issues at the micro level (worker participation in production decision making) nor at the macro level (industrial policy). Rather they tried to appeal to ideological and foreign policy issues. By doing so, they missed a precious opportunity to develop an alternative to the LDP government.[17]

It can therefore be seen that although, in electoral terms, the decline of the JSP post-1990 was shocking and sudden, the reasons for that decline can be found in a long-term failure of the JSP leadership to address the practical concerns of union members (including teachers) and others who should have formed the natural constituency of support for a left-of-centre party.

Educational issues and political realignment 1989–1996

The decline of the JSP in the 1990s, going hand-in-hand with a less confrontational policy stance from a weakened Nikkyōso, removed a powerful force of opposition to the conservative camp. The Left had served a vital role in the period following the Occupation in stopping any drastic overhaul of the progressive reforms of that era. In the area of education, Nikkyōso's role in preventing the return of nationalistic and authoritarian educational practices was vital. Some observers worried, therefore, that with the decline of the Left as an oppositional force, the Right would be free to finally pursue the reactionary agenda that it had always favoured. The victory achieved by the LDP and Monbushō in the 1990s in one area – the forcing of compulsory respect for the national flag and anthem in school ceremonies – seemed to give credence to these fears. However, a closer look at the politics of education in the period following 1989 shows a more complex picture emerging.

In order to understand the period post-1989, it is first necessary to recognise one of the more enduring features of the postwar education system: that is the coexistence of high-profile conflict (between progressive and conservative camps) with the smooth functioning of the vast majority of Japan's educational institutions.[18] This can be explained by the fact that the overwhelming number of teachers and local level administrators went about their day-to-day jobs in an atmosphere of professional dedication and cooperation. Thomas Rohlen, in his ethnographic research, found that many teachers were as distrustful of union interference as they were of government interference in their professional lives.[19] Japan, whose teachers in general are held in high esteem and well paid, does not have the same problems of recruitment and retention that other countries have. The 'trench warfare' described in the previous section was really a feature of national-level relations in the educational world, and the breaking out of peace at that level, when it happened, brought all the levels of the education system into closer harmony than they had been before. This meant that the decline in power of Nikkyōso as a national-level organization would not have much effect on what went on at the *genba*: the level where education is actually delivered. During the years of the 1955 system it was at the *genba* that a range of educational problems came to the attention of the media and the public. Issues such as *juken jigoku* (exam hell), *ijime* (bullying), *tōkōkyohi* (truancy), and later *gakkyû hōkai* (classroom breakdown) became issues that signified that all was not well with the Japanese education system. During the prolonged economic recession of the 1990s these issues came to be linked with the alleged unsuitability of Japan's schools to provide the workforce necessary for the new economic needs. Reformers argued that schools should be improved to make them more intellectually stimulating and humane as well as economically relevant.

On the surface, the discussion about what to do about contemporary education problems seems to be a technical, non-political one – far removed from the ideological slogans of the 1940s and 1950s. However, a closer analysis of the educational discourse of the late 1980s and 1990s shows that it does have a political dimension – although one that is different from the early postwar period. For example, some education reforms have had serious implications for the postwar egalitarian consensus. Anthropologist Peter Cave has shown how the current wave of school reforms has led to concerns about increasing inequality.[20] Also, educational sociologist, Takehiko Kariya, has argued that the current relaxation of the compulsory school curriculum is leading to the reproduction of social divisions from one generation to the next.[21] Proposals to give parents more choice about where to send their children (although implemented in only a tiny number of cases at the time of writing) are another indication that the postwar egalitarian consensus is now a thing of the past. Arguments over the real meaning of 'equality' when applied to education have long been at the heart of disagreements between Left and Right in Japan as they have been in other nation states.[22] Since the 1980s, however, a growing discourse on education aimed at focusing on the child as an individual has forced both camps to reappraise their stance on egalitarian education. In this area, serious differences exist within the two camps as well as between them.

The adoption by Nikkyōso of a non-confrontational stance and the marginalization of Zenkyō means that unions are now just another set of interest groups in the education policy-making system. They may cooperate with MOE bureaucrats and LDP politicians over issues like tackling disruption and bullying in schools. In other areas, however, there are still clear and significant ideological differences. One such issue is the reform of the Fundamental Law of Education (FLE). This law was passed (or as some of those on the Right would have it 'imposed by the Americans') in 1947. In tandem with the constitution (that came into force in the same year) it is the main legal guarantee of a democratic, pacific and (for the compulsory years) free education for all the Japanese people. Traditionalists on the Right do not like the FLE because they believe it undermines 'Japanese' ideas of morality and values.[23] They also would prefer a basic law that stressed the importance of nurturing 'love of country' in young hearts and minds. When it comes to debates on traditional morality and patriotism the old divisions between Left and Right in education still endure.[24]

In general, it can be concluded that the disappearance of a united and strong union movement in the period following 1989 has not had the same effect that similar events might have had if they had taken place in the 1950s. As Stockwin points out, Japan's political economy has changed since then:

> Between the 1950s and the 1990s, the corporate sector grew enormously in size and wealth, and with the removal of many bureaucratic controls which had existed in the earlier post-war period, attained much greater independence. . . . This change did not mean the breakdown of relations between the corporate sector and government ministries, but the balance of power had certainly shifted.[25]

During the years of the '1955 system', the corporate sector, the LDP and the MOE were clearly on the same 'side' facing a common left-wing enemy. The removal of that enemy after 1989 meant that there was no longer any need for business interests to keep quiet about their dissatisfaction with the education system as it was run by the government and educational administrators. Calls from the corporate sector for more diversity and deregulation as well as more private sector input threaten the MOE's control over the national education system in ways that old Nikkyōso, for all its anti-government rhetoric and anger, never could.

Period three: the evolution of the '1996 system'

In 1994 a new election system was introduced for the House of Representatives. The old multi-member constituencies were replaced by a system that combined single member constituencies with eleven regional PR (Proportional Representation) constituencies. In 1996 the first election under this system took place. Subsequent elections took place in 2000 and 2003. The results showed a mixture of continuity and change with the old system that allows us to draw up a tentative list of the new system's main characteristics.

- The LDP continues to be the largest party in the Diet and the party in power.
- In order to form a working majority in both houses of the Diet the LDP needs to form a coalition government with other political parties.

- The 'Old Left' (Socialists and Communists) make up a small minority of Diet members who can have very limited impact on Diet business.
- Politicians trying to form a major opposition party or 'government in waiting' have so far been frustrated. The new parties, Shinshintō, collapsed because of internal disagreements. Minshutō (the Democratic Party of Japan) has, at the time of writing, had more success but still has serious problems with internal unity and discipline.
- Although Rengō and Minshutō have close (but not unproblematic) links, unions in general are no longer allied with national political parties the way they were in the '1955 system'. Union endorsement of politicians is now mostly a local matter.

The main continuity with the old system has been the retention of the reins of power by the LDP. Political scientist Gerald Curtis makes the point that this was not inevitable. If, during the period of transition, key political actors had behaved in different ways or made different choices the LDP might have broken up.[26] Especially during its traumatic period out of office from 1993 to 1994, the LDP was in a precarious state. However, it has adapted skilfully to changing times and is once again in firm control of the Diet.

What are the implications for the politics of education under the '1996 system'? I have already remarked that the fears expressed by some in the 1950s that the MOE wanted to turn the clock back to prewar style militarism and authoritarianism were no longer valid in the early part of the twenty-first century. That does not mean that the Monbukagakushō[27] and its allies in the LDP-controlled government were not pursuing a right-wing political agenda. Instead, it means that the nature of that agenda changed and contains – in the case of educational politics at least – certain contradictory impulses. Former members of the progressive camp have had to modify their ideas on the politics of education in order to take into account these changing circumstances.

The contradictory nature of the new government agenda on education was illustrated by events at one senior high school in the late 1990s. Government rhetoric on reform since the 1980s called for young people to adopt a more entrepreneurial spirit and to learn to act without waiting for orders from above. However, when students at Tokorozawa High School in Saitama prefecture decided in 1998 that they did not like the school ceremonies planned for them by the school principal, and that they would organise their own instead, education authorities instinctively tried to push the recalcitrant pupils back into line. The students objected to singing the national anthem and flying the national flag at the entrance and graduation ceremonies. For the school principal, backed up by the prefectural board of education and the Minister for Education, this was an area where the students were not supposed to be exercising freedom of choice.[28] Government reformers embraced the rhetoric of individualism, but when faced with students who genuinely were determined to 'think for themselves' local government and the Ministry soon retreated to an instinctive authoritarianism. In their criticism of the students the government and its supporters in the right-wing media argued that freedom and individualism taken too far were a threat to proper order in society. Those defending the students said that they were exercising their human rights that had been guaranteed by Japan's ratification in 1995 of the UN Convention on the Rights of the Child. Talking about educational problems in terms of children's rights was a recent development in Japan, as it was in many countries.[29]

The dispute at Tokorozawa High School was mostly a war of words and was settled by the holding of two consecutive ceremonies: the official one and the unofficial one. However, it illustrated very clearly the changing nature of conflict in the new circumstances of educational politics in the 1990s. The political significance of the fact that teacher unions did not play a major role in the dispute cannot be over-emphasised. Students and their parents who were in conflict with the educational authorities did not see themselves as taking part in a national struggle between giant political camps, but as individuals standing up for their rights. When threatened by the possibility of exclusion from the school for their resistance to the principal, they did not call for strike action or political demonstrations. Instead, they turned to lawyers to defend their legal rights as individuals with legitimate grievances.[30]

The Tokorozawa incident brought to light serious inconsistencies in the contemporary educational agenda of the Right. While business is calling for the production of workers who are more flexible and can think for themselves, the traditional authoritarianism of those in the educational bureaucracy stands as a barrier to this. The same kind of dilemma can be seen in foreign language education policy. Business interests are calling for workers who have a better command of foreign languages, especially English. However, traditionalists in the education establishment worry that if Japanese people become too good at English their identity as Japanese will be undermined.[31]

On the Left there are also divisions about how to respond to the challenges facing the contemporary education system. Nikkyōso, in the spirit of compromise, places emphasis on dealing with practical issues like bullying and classroom disruption. In the area of school management it has backtracked on its previous insistence that the teachers' meeting should be the ultimate decision-making body in the school, and now accepts a more powerful managerial role for the school principal. It also accepts the legitimacy of centrally decided course of study guidelines that it had previously opposed. One important difference with the Ministry of Education remains, however, and that is the union demand for more decentralization of educational administration. The ideologically charged rhetoric of the 1950s and 1960s has now gone from Nikkyōso's policies and slogans. The same cannot be said for its rival Zenkyō, whose published statements still insist that all educational problems are the fault of big business and an authoritarian central government. It calls on teachers to be politically active and to campaign against the government over various issues – not all educational. However, since Zenkyō only has a membership comprising about 10 per cent of school teachers in Japan its influence on this new phase of politics and education is marginal.

Conclusion

The plan, announced by the government in 2001, to go ahead with the rewriting of the Fundamental Law of Education in order to, among other things, insert a clause that calls for increasing patriotism in the nation's youth, seems to hark back to the political strife of the 1950s. On the other hand, other government plans to reduce the compulsory part of the junior high school curriculum and introduce 'integrated learning' periods into the timetable, are more concerned with introducing diversity and flexibility into the education system. The MOE seems to be involved in promoting an uncomfortable mix of centralised, authoritarian policies alongside measures designed to promote more decentralised, liberal school curricula.

In this new environment, the traditional Left as represented by Zenkyō, the JSP and the JCP, has been side-lined. The language of mass action and struggle that characterised postwar Japan has now been replaced on the mainstream Left by a more liberal, individual-based discourse. This may be in keeping with the transformation of Japan's economy and society from postwar, catchup industrialism to a twenty-first-century post-industrialism. Organizations of the traditional Left, like Nikkyōso, have found that they have had to adapt to this national (and international) transformation. Those that have failed to do so have been condemned to irrelevance by the reality of post-'1955 system' politics.

Notes

1 Leonard J. Schoppa, *Education Reform in Japan: A Case of Immobilist Politics*, London: Routledge, 1991, p. 52.
2 See Byron K. Marshall, *Learning to be Modern: Japanese Discourse on Education*, Boulder, Colorado: Westview Press, 1994, chapter 7.
3 See Robert Aspinall, *Teachers' Unions and the Politics of Education in Japan*, Albany: State University of New York Press, 2001, chapter 2, for an analysis of Nikkyōso under the 1955 system. See also Donald R. Thurston, *Teachers and Politics in Japan*, Princeton, NJ: Princeton University Press, 1973; and Benjamin Duke, *Japan's Militant Teachers*, Honolulu: University Press of Hawaii, 1973.
4 Although the JSP changed its name in the 1990s, for the sake of clarity the party will be referred to only as JSP in this chapter.
5 See Kent E. Calder, *Crisis and Compensation: Public Policy and Political Stability in Japan 1949–1986*, Princeton, NJ: Princeton University Press, 1988, for a detailed analysis of how the LDP was able to adopt policies that would appease and compensate various groups and sectors in order to retain their electoral support.
6 Jirō Yamaguchi, 'Why no Blair Revolution in Japan?', paper given at the Nissan Institute for Japanese Studies, Oxford University, 6 June 1997. So long as the JSP had more than one third of the seats of one or other of the two houses of the Diet, it could guarantee preventing any revision of the constitution.

7 Aspinall, op. cit., pp. 47–51, and Donald R. Thurston, 'The Decline of the Japan Teachers' Union', in *Journal of Contemporary Asia*, vol.19, no.2, 1989, pp. 186–205, look at the decline in Nikkyōso membership in more detail.

8 See Takehiko Kariya, *Kaisōka Nihon to Kyōiku Kiki* (Education in Crisis and Stratified Japan), Tokyo: Yushindo 2001, chapter 3, where it is argued that members of Nikkyōso during the 1950s and 1960s propounded the view that any setting of children by ability must be a form of discrimination.

9 Akito Okada, 'Secondary Education Reform and the Concept of Equality of Opportunity in Japan', in *Compare*, vol.29, no.2, 1999, pp. 171–189, shows how conservatives and progressives in Japan agreed on the basic idea of equality in compulsory education, but disagreed on whether the emphasis should be on a meritocratic equality of opportunity (the conservative position), or on encouraging a spirit of cooperation and solidarity among children and young adults (the progressive position).

10 See Roger Goodman, 'The Why, What and How of Educational Reform in Japan', in Roger Goodman and David Phillips (eds), *Can the Japanese Change Their Education System?* Oxford: Symposium Books, 2003, for an up-to-date overview of these concepts as applied to the education process in Japan; and Peter Cave, 'Educational Reform in Japan in the 1990s; "individuality" and other uncertainties', in *Comparative Education*, vol.37, no.2, pp. 173–191, for an analysis of reforms that focus on 'individuality'.

11 Schoppa, op. cit.

12 Thurston, *Teachers and Politics in Japan*, p. 265.

13 Through a combination of further loss of electoral support, defections, and an inability to cope with the introduction of a new election system, the JSP's strength in the Lower House continued to decline until it was reduced in the 2003 election to a total of six. After the 2001 Upper House election, JSP strength there was reduced to eight. Serious losses were also suffered in local elections during the same period.

14 During the privatization of Japan's national railways in the 1980s, government and management anti-union policies brought about the reduction in Kokurō's membership from 200,000 to 34,000.

15 For an account of Nikkyōso's schism, see Aspinall, op. cit., chapter 3. For two different versions of events from those involved, see Nikkyōso, *Nikkyōso Gojunenshi* (Nikkyōso's Fifty Year History), Nikkyōso: Tokyo, 1997, and Zenkyō, *Kyōshokuin Kumiai Undō no Rekishi* (The History of the Teachers' Union Movement), Tokyo: Zenkyō, 1997.

16 The DSP had been formed in 1959 by a group breaking away from the JSP. Since then, commentators had speculated from time to time about the possibility of re-unification.

17 Ikuo Kume, *Disparaged Success: Labor Politics in Postwar Japan*, New York: Cornell University Press, 1998, p. 228. Kume also makes the point that even JSP supporters were worried about its competence to govern if it ever got into power by itself.

18 The main exception to this trend was the outbreak of disturbances, sometimes violent, at universities during the period of student protest 1967–70.

19 See Thomas P. Rohlen, *Japan's High Schools*, Berkeley: University of California Press, 1983, and Thomas P. Rohlen, 'Conflict in Institutional Environments: Politics in Education', in Ellis S. Kraus, *et al.* (eds), *Conflict in Japan*, Honolulu: University of Hawaii Press, 1984.

20 Peter Cave, 'Japanese Educational Reform: Developments and Prospects at Primary and Secondary Level', in Roger Goodman and David Phillips, op. cit.

21 Kariya, op. cit.

22 See Okada, op. cit.

23 See Akito Okada, 'Education of whom, for whom, by whom? Revising the Fundamental Law of Education', in *Japan Forum*, vol.14, no.3, 2002, for an analysis of the revising of the Fundamental Law of Education.

24 This is not to suggest that people on the Left are unpatriotic. Schools in postwar Japan routinely performed the function of instilling ideas of national identity in young people. It was when patriotism was combined with militarism (for example, in whitewashing Japan's wartime aggression) or Emperor worship that they objected.

25 J. A. A. Stockwin, *Governing Japan: Divided Politics in a Major Economy*, Oxford: Blackwell Publishers, 1999, p. 100.

26 Gerald Curtis, *The Logic of Japanese Politics*, New York: Columbia University Press, 1999.

27 In January 2001, as part of a reorganization of the ministries, the Ministry of Education (Monbushō) was merged with the Science and Technology Agency. Its present title is Ministry of Education, Culture, Sports, Science and Technology, abbreviated to Monbukagakushō in Japanese.

28 See Robert Aspinall and Peter Cave, 'Lowering the Flag: Democracy, Authority and Rights at Tokorozawa High School', in *Social Science Japan Journal*, vol. 4, no. 1, April 2001, for a discussion of the issues surrounding events at this school.

29 Neary argues that 'the absence in the 1950s and 1960s of books linking children with rights is indicative of the way in which dissatisfaction with the way children were being treated in Japan was not conceived of in terms of rights until 1970.' See Ian Neary, *Human Rights in Japan, South Korea and Taiwan*, London: Routledge, 2002, p. 216.

30 The increasing use of lawyers by Japanese people is reflected by a government policy designed to triple, by 2010, the number who can pass the bar exam to about 3,000. To help with the training of this new army of lawyers, 66 new postgraduate law schools were created across Japan in April 2004.

31 See Robert Aspinall, 'Japanese Nationalism and the Reform of English Language Teaching', in Roger Goodman and David Phillips, op. cit., for more on the issue of the nationalist reaction to the spread of English language education in Japan.

5 'Democratic government' and the Left

Koichi Nakano

Introduction

Japanese politics from the 1990s on has been marked by the prominence of the issue of administrative reform (*gyōsei kaikaku* or *gyōkaku*) on the policy agenda. Coinciding with the advent of the era of coalition governments that began with the historical alternation in power of 1993 and with the rapidly deteriorating state of public finance following the burst of the bubble economy, countless cases of bureaucratic corruption, incompetence, and maladministration came to the surface and unleashed an unprecedented public distrust of the administrative elite. Party competition intensified as new parties were formed and old ones struggled to adapt (or merely to survive) in a fluid political context that followed after the collapse of the 1955 system. Administrative reform, combined with a good deal of bureaucrat-bashing, became everyone's fixation to the extent that the Lower House elections of 1996 were dubbed *gyōkaku* elections. No self-respecting party could do without having its own proposals for the reform of the state.

This competitive process in turn led to a new development: the emergence of 'democratic government' as a goal of administrative reform.[1] In earlier periods, 'simple and efficient government' (*kanso de kōritsutekina seifu*) has held *de facto* monopoly sway over the agenda of administrative reform. Changes in party politics placed political actors who advocate enhanced 'democratic control of government' within the framework of coalition politics, and thus, created a situation in which the very objective of administrative reform came to be contested. While the two policy goals are not necessarily mutually conflicting or contradictory, they represent distinct visions, priorities and emphases. A central element of 'democratic government' is the idea that the government should be kept in check from the *outside* through deconcentration of power to other branches of the state, local governments, or the civil society.[2] Thus, in the 1990s, such reform items as the enhancement of parliamentary power, decentralization, and government information disclosure, have been taken up in an attempt to reinforce democratic control of the government.[3]

In this chapter, I argue that the origins of such efforts to democratise the Japanese state can be traced back to the Left in opposition under the 1955 system. It was the Left that first articulated concerns for democratic government. In what follows, we shall first illustrate the Leftist proposals for enhanced democratic control of the government, with a focus on decentralization, and to a lesser extent, information disclosure and Diet reform, as well as account for the background of the Left's advocacy of such issues. Then, moving on to the 1990s, an analysis of the party-political conditions that finally propelled these hitherto much neglected policies on the political agenda, ironically at a time when the Left as we knew it was on its terminal decline, will be presented. In the process, we also seek to explore the abrupt transformation of the Left in the 1990s, and to shed a light on the connection between the Old Left and the New Left.

The Left in opposition: the origins of 'democratic government'

At first glance, administrative reform may seem to be an unlikely policy area for the Left to make a significant contribution. In general, the Left has commonly been associated with 'big government', and even though the Japanese Left cannot be said to have played much of a direct role in the growth of the state in the postwar (be it real or perceived) as it has been almost perpetually consigned to opposition, it is widely known that the Japanese Socialist Party (JSP) drew much of its organised support as well as many of its parliamentary candidates from the public-sector union, *Sōhyō*, and as a result, was highly sympathetic to the vested interests of the latter. Looked at from this perspective, the Left has been typically portrayed as the defender of the status quo, providing resistance to administrative reform efforts. Indeed, to the extent to which the LDP government controlled the policy agenda and focused on 'simple and efficient government', it is true that the Left invariably took an essentially negative stance against administrative reform.

In terms of ideological affinity, there is nothing inherently Leftist even in the policy goal of 'democratic government' either. If anything, even without going to the extremes of communist dictatorships, the Left in general has often been perceived to side with the overbearing, unaccountable bureaucratic machineries that claimed to know better than ordinary citizens. Put another way, leftist thinking usually sought to use the state to ameliorate or reconstruct society, with the underlying assumption that the state should control society and not vice versa, and this often led to its defence of autonomous, powerful, and centralised government. In that respect, it is interesting to consider why the Japanese Left came around to embrace the idea of 'democratic government'.

It is a central argument of this chapter that the Left in Japan became vocal proponents of enhanced democratic control of government, not because of any inherently *ideological* reasons, but because of its peculiar *situational* position in the 1955 system as a 'perennial opposition' (*mannen yatō*). Decentralization, information disclosure, and parliamentary accountability are all essentially policies of the opposition.

To put it the other way round from the standpoint of the governing party, the idea that the government should be kept in check from the outside through the deconcentration of power to the other branches of the state (e.g. legislature and judiciary), local governments (i.e. decentralization), or the civil society (e.g. legislation to encourage NGO activities, or information disclosure) would not be given top priority as long as it remained securely in power. Even in countries where alternations in power are a common occurrence, policy instruments that aim to reinforce the legislature's power to keep the executive in check, or to devolve power closer to the people at the local level, tend to be more eagerly advocated by political parties while in opposition. In Japan, where the LDP became coterminous with the government, and the Left with opposition, this tendency was arguably even more pronounced: the LDP, with repeated electoral mandates that allowed it to stay in power, felt no particular need to rush into the introduction of measures that are going to subject government to intrusive external control, whereas the opposition parties grew keen to pry open the iron grip of the LDP and the elite bureaucrats over the affairs of the state as the (self-appointed) representatives of the people and society.

Ironically, these 'oppositional' policies for the democratization of the Japanese state did not go anywhere as long as their advocates were consigned to perennial opposition. It was only in the fluid party-political context of the 1990s that these issues finally came to the fore. It is important to note, however, that the seeds were sown well before some of these policies bore fruit in a radically different political situation. The Left articulated concerns for democratic government while it was still in the political wilderness, including the *Rinchō* years.

Yasuo Maruyama, deputy chair of *Sōhyō*, who became the Left's representative in *Rinchō* upon the recommendation of the JSP, best captures the basic thinking of the Left on 'democratic government' in the *Rinchō* era. Identifying himself as 'the people's representative',[4] Maruyama issued a statement outlining his three fundamental principles at the first meeting of *Rinchō*.[5] First, he contended that administrative reform should not just be limited to institutional reforms of administrative organs or fiscal reconstruction, but should extend to 'political reform as democratic reform of politics'.[6] Second, the objective of the reforms should be the realization of 'fair, effective, and democratic administration' rather than 'cheap government' or 'small government'. He went on to argue, 'the principal theme of administrative reform today is the transition to an administration that enables popular control (participation)'.[7] Third, Maruyama, who was also the chairman of *Jichirō* (Local Government Workers Unions), claimed that the most fundamental task in this regard was 'the realization of transparent government through decentralization'.[8] Furthermore, and somewhat more concretely, he proposed that *Rinchō* should deliberate on such issues as reinforcing the legislature's power to effectively control the government, devolution to local governments, and the setting-up of a system of government information disclosure, instead of focusing narrowly on means to cut public expenditure.[9] In the remainder of this section, we shall take a look at the Leftist origins of decentralization in more detail, and more briefly, also information disclosure and Diet reform.

Decentralization[10]

The persistent centralization despite the Occupation reforms was seriously challenged first by an increasing number of Progressive Local Governments (*kakushin jichitai*) in the mid-1960s, and in a number of ways, it was the political upheaval caused by the revision process of the US-Japan Security Treaty in 1960 that served as a turning point that took Japan in the direction of this phenomenon.

On the one hand, the JSP was forced to renew efforts to regain its lost ground at the local level, after a sizable bunch of right-wing lawmakers, led by Suehiro Nishio, defected and formed the Democratic Socialist Party during the turmoil over Treaty revision.[11] On the other, the JSP's renewed interest in local politics was also due to an important reconsideration of its political strategy, following the widespread sense of failure and frustration among its members in the aftermath of Treaty revision. According to Ichio Asukata, who first gained national prominence as a sharp debater in the Diet over *Anpo*, but who later became a standard-bearer of PLGs as the high-profile JSP Mayor of Yokohama, it was his disappointment with parliamentary democracy over the issue of Treaty revision that prompted him to become candidate for Yokohama Mayor and pursue 'direct democracy'.[12]

In a similar vein, a 1961 JSP party document on its struggles over local government conceded, 'hitherto the emphasis of our activities were too much centred on national politics',[13] and asserted the importance of fighting for peace and democracy on the local front. In other words, it was the failure and frustration of the Left at the national level that forced it to reassess its policy stance and 'discover' the value of local government and decentralization. At the same time, the rapid industrialization and urbanization that accompanied the high-speed growth also brought to the fore both a new set of voters (i.e. urban workers) and political issues (e.g. pollution, traffic congestion, and the housing shortage) that presented an opportunity for the Left. These political as well as socio-economic factors combined to bring about an unprecedented success of PLGs from the mid-1960s to the late 1970s.[14]

At the municipal level, the advent of the era of the progressives was announced in 1963 when Asukata captured the Mayorship of Yokohama.[15] Among the nine designated cities at that time, six of them were in the progressives' hands after the elections in 1973.[16] With regard to cities more generally, the membership of the National Association of Progressive Mayors, which Asukata headed, peaked in 1974 with 142 members – close to 40 per cent of the city population nationwide resided in cities with progressive mayors then. This included, for instance, Kōzō Igarashi, who was then Mayor of Asahikawa in Hokkaidō, and who was later to have some crucial impact on the decentralization process of the 1990s as the Chief Cabinet Secretary of the Murayama government. At the prefectural level, Ryōkichi Minobe captured the most coveted prize for the progressives – the Governorship of Tokyo – in 1967. The number of progressive governors reached its high in 1975 at 9 out of 47 – namely, Tokyo, Osaka, Kyoto, Saitama, Kanagawa (whose Governor, Kazuji Nagasu, was later to become a member of the Decentralization Commission in the 1990s), Shiga, Okayama, Kagawa, and Okinawa.

The PLGs peaked in the mid-1970s, and already by the late 1970s, they were in full retreat. In fact, the demise of PLGs was even faster than their rise. Symbolically, Asukata resigned from the Mayorship of Yokohama in 1978 and Minobe retired in 1979. The PLGs did make some significant contribution to the development of local government in Japan. It might even be argued that it was the PLGs that truly established the principle that localities can also be arenas of *political* contention, as opposed to mere *administrative* units. Not least, the PLGs gave currency to the idea that local governments belong to the people, should be open to civic participation, and should serve the interest of the citizens.

Having said that, it is also true that PLGs did little by way of pressing the case of decentralization. For a great part, this stems from the fact that the leaders of PLGs conceived of their fight, not as an attempt to devolve more power and freedom to localities from the central government in Tokyo, but more as a part of a wider, nationwide (if not worldwide) ideological struggle against reactionary conservatism. In other words, the question whether local governments should be given more weight was ultimately not very relevant, for the important fight was taking place at the national level and PLGs were simply taking part in the same battle.

A page was being turned and the PLGs were on their way to the exit. The commitment of the Left to the renewal of local governments endured, however, in a different form. The new slogan of the time was 'from PLGs to the reform of local governments' (*kakushin jichitai kara jichitai no kakushin e*), and instead of the ideological battle of socialism against reactionary conservatism, the Left put an emphasis on decentralization itself as it analysed the ultimate failure of the PLGs in the light of the heavy and arbitrary constraints placed on local governments by the central state. For instance, it was generally perceived by the Left that the progressive chief executives were often 'bullied' by overtly hostile and uncooperative national government bureaucrats, especially on fiscal matters or when requesting administrative permissions, and it is in this context that Maruyama's (and the Local Government Workers Unions') concern for 'the realization of transparent government through decentralization' should be understood.

It was during this period, the *Rinchō* years of the early 1980s, that the Left articulated concrete decentralization measures, which were then completely ignored, but which were later to be enacted in the 1990s. The JSP issued a policy proposal entitled 'Towards an Administrative and Fiscal Reform for the People' in June 1982 in reaction to the successive *Rinchō* reports, and advocated the abolition of the system of 'agency delegation' (*kikan inin jimu*),[17] 'local administrators' (*chihō jimukan*),[18] and 'compulsory setting' (*hitchi kisei*),[19] among other things.[20] Similarly, the Left's sole representative in *Rinchō*'s main commission, Maruyama, presented a statement in the government council entitled 'Distribution of Competence between the State and the Local Governments as a Fundamental Issue of Administrative Reform' in December of the same year, and called for the rationalization of subsidies, devolution of competence (including the abolition of agency delegation in principle), reform of state field services, and abolition of local administrators.[21]

Information disclosure

The institutionalization of a system of public disclosure of government information is another 'oppositional' policy issue that the LDP government was reluctant to act upon. Indeed, local governments first took the initiative well before anything was done at the national level.[22] PLGs were among the keenest to institutionalise information disclosure,[23] and indeed, Nagasu's Kanagawa was the first prefecture to do so in October 1982.

At the national level, opposition parties submitted a series of bills in the 1980s, but none of them was even deliberated upon in the Diet before they were made void: the Public Documents Disclosure Bill of the Democratic Socialist Party (DSP) in 1980, the Bill concerning the Disclosure of Public Documents of Administrative Organs of the Japanese Communist Party (JCP) in 1981, the Information Disclosure Bill of the JSP also in 1981, the Public Documents Disclosure Bill of the Kōmeitō, DSP, New Liberal Club, and Social Democratic League in the same year, again the Information Disclosure Bill of the JSP in 1985, and the Bill concerning the Disclosure of Administrative Information of the Kōmeitō in 1989.[24]

In *Rinchō*, Maruyama presented his 'Opinion on Information Disclosure and Administrative Procedure' in May 1982,[25] and again in December he urged *Rinchō* to present some concrete proposal for the institutionalization of an information disclosure system in his 'Measures to Reinforce Democratization in Administration',[26] but all that *Rinchō* recommended in its final report in 1983 was to consider the eventual establishment of such a system and to set up a body of experts to study such systems and practices abroad and at the local level, and this study group issued an interim report in 1990 pointing out the need for further consideration of the matter from wider perspectives.[27]

Reinforcing parliamentary control of the executive

On this front, Maruyama made the point in his initial statement at *Rinchō* that, in order to enhance parliamentary accountability, such measures as the reinforcement of Diet staff, the reorganization of standing committees, as well as the reduction of the scope of legislative delegation to ordinances (*seirei*), at the same time as making the latter subject to parliamentary examination, should be given priority consideration, and reiterated the exact same points later when it was obvious that his argument had been ignored.[28]

In its policy proposal on administrative reform in 1982, the JSP too contended that 'in view of the executive dominance today despite the principle of separation of three powers, it is important to establish the leadership of the Diet, stipulated the supreme organ of state powers in our governing structure based on the representative system. While this is also a task for the political parties themselves, it is necessary to reinforce the administrative control function of the Diet, including its investigative power'.[29] As the JSP was in opposition, this too went unnoticed.

Thus, in spite of the Left's advocacy, the proposals for an enhanced democratic control of the state had virtually no impact at all on the actual political agenda.[30] The LDP and the elite bureaucracy defined the *Rinchō* administrative reform first and foremost in terms of 'simple and efficient government', and the call for 'democratic government' was safely marginalised. Although the LDP was going through a relatively rough phase of its continuous rule at that time,[31] it was rather successful in promoting its own version of cost-cutting administrative reform, and as a result, even the Left itself was in fact reacting to the agenda set by the government most of the time, rather than further elaborating its own policy initiatives (those would have gone nowhere in any case). In other words, the Left articulated concerns for strengthening democratic control over the government, but they were at best feeble counterproposals that were swiftly and quietly brushed aside in the political context of the 1980s.

From the Old Left to the New Left: the salience of 'democratic government'

Ironically, the Left's 'oppositional' agenda for the democratization of the Japanese state finally made some advances in the 1990s, particularly in the LDP-JSP-Sakigake coalition, when it was no longer in opposition but in terminal decline.

Thirty-eight years of continuous one-party rule by the LDP came to an end in 1993, and with it ended the near monopoly over policy agenda that it had together with the elite bureaucracy. It now became possible for administrative reform to mean something more than just 'simple and efficient government'. One has to be reminded, however, that the general elections of 1993 that resulted in the LDP's downfall from power simultaneously brought the biggest electoral losses yet to the JSP, which saw the number of its Lower House parliamentarians almost halved from 137 to 77 overnight. As if this was not sufficient, the JSP had no choice but to join the 'victory' of non-LDP parties, enter the Hosokawa seven-party coalition government, and get pushed around by its Centre-Right coalition partners (many of whom only recently defected from the LDP) to swallow difficult policy compromises. When the bullying became too much, it was forced out of the coalition with the non-LDP parties, and in a move that surprised all political observers, it returned to power (and allowed the LDP to return to power) with its party leader, Tomiichi Murayama, as premier in summer 1994, in a previously unthinkable coalition with the LDP (and the small liberal Sakigake).

A spent force, but a perennial opposition finally in power with a prime minister from its own ranks for the first time in 46 years, the JSP by then threw away virtually all of its core Leftist policies, including its opposition to the Japan–US Security Treaty, the Self-Defense Force, and the 'national' flag and anthem, in order to appear a 'responsible' and 'realistic' governing party in basic agreement with its coalition partners. Crucially, this also meant at the same time that all that the JSP was left with were 'oppositional' policies, which were developed primarily for *situational* reasons of a perennial opposition party rather than anything based on inherently *ideological* convictions of the Left, and among them was the advocacy of 'democratic government'. At a time when the JSP was rapidly losing its own identity, this at least was not an alien policy forced on it by the others.

It has to be pointed out at the same time that, while 'democratic government' was indeed a familiar concept for the JSP because of its long experience in the political wilderness, it also made partisan sense for it to promote the further democratization of Japanese government in the context of post-1993 politics. Even though the LDP no longer had a majority on its own, it remained by far the biggest party and a formidable force to be reckoned with especially now that it was brought back to power. In such a situation, it was doubly important for the JSP to rebuild a clear and distinct identity of its own, on the one hand because it was unceremoniously discarding its long-held leftist ideology and policy stance, and on the other because it had to justify its coalition with its former arch enemy to a suspicious electorate. Thus, facing a still dominant LDP in the context of rapidly declining ideological divide, the advocacy of democratic government allowed the Socialists (as well as Sakigake) to differentiate themselves from the LDP and present themselves as the true voice of the people. In this context, one also has to note the important role played by Sakigake as a key ally of the JSP then, and leading the latter in the advocacy of reinforced democratic control of the state.[32] It is arguably not a coincidence that some of Sakigake's leaders were associated with the leftist opposition under the 1955 system: for instance, Masayoshi Takemura was a former progressive Governor of Shiga, and Naoto Kan belonged for many years to the tiny Social Democratic League in the Diet.

Indeed, a focus on the politics of 'democratic government' in the 1990s helps us make sense of the apparent schism that exists between the Old Left (i.e. JSP), on the one hand, and the New Left that succeeded it (i.e. the Democratic Party of Japan or DPJ), on the other. It is a core argument of this chapter that the policies of 'democratic government' served as a bridge between the old, 'opposition-oriented', socialist Left, and the new, 'government-oriented', liberal Left that made the transition from the former to the latter possible in policy terms. Put simply, the agenda of 'democratic government' was 'old' and familiar enough for the disappearing Old Left that had to suddenly dispense with its long-held socialist ideology, but 'new' and exciting enough for the fledgling New Left that was rallying around the more viable principles of democracy and liberalism. It is this dual nature of 'democratic government' that helps account for the seemingly disruptive transformation of the Left that took place in the 1990s.

The following subsections outline the three cases of decentralization, information disclosure, and the parliamentary control of the executive in the 1990s. The Old Left played a crucial role as a chief architect of the reform in the case of decentralization. With regard to information disclosure, the Left in transition forced the LDP to react and enact the bill at long last. The agenda to reinforce the power of the parliament to check the executive was the least successful, but served as an initial rallying cry around which the New Left was constituted.

Decentralization: the last service of the Old Left[33]

The transformation of party politics in the 1990s placed an unusual number of decentralist politicians, including those from the Left, in key government positions. These political leaders provided general support for the decentralization efforts, and intervened at certain critical junctures to keep the process moving forward. Without them the reform would have been stymied somewhere along the line, as were past attempts at decentralization.

In terms of time sequence, the Hosokawa government placed decentralization on the legislative agenda by committing his Cabinet (and thereby also subsequent ones) to the reform with a clear timetable. Following a two-month interlude under the Hata minority government, the Murayama government made the crucial Cabinet decision to approve the government programme for decentralization and set up the Decentralization Commission accordingly. Alongside key LDP or ex-LDP politicians, such as Hosokawa, Takemura and Nonaka, socialist ministers, including Murayama, Igarashi and Yamaguchi, played vital roles in promoting decentralization.

Prime Minister Tomiichi Murayama originally comes from a background in the trade unions of local government workers (*Jichirō*), and served as a local councillor in Ōita prefecture. He was thoroughly unprepared to become premier, but when he was elected as Japan's second socialist prime minister in almost fifty years (supported by the LDP, of all parties), he decided that if he had to do the job, he would want to achieve two things that only his Cabinet could: decentralization and reconciliation with Asian neighbours over Japan's wartime past.[34]

Tsuruo Yamaguchi was made Director-General of the Management and Coordination Agency (MCA). This post was important, for it was not the MOHA but the MCA that was the agency in charge of coordinating various different ministerial interests in this particular decentralization process. Yamaguchi had a good understanding of local government, having served many years in the Local Administration Committee of the Lower House.

More than Murayama or Yamaguchi, however, it was Kōzō Igarashi, formerly Minister of Construction under Hosokawa and now assisting Murayama as his Chief Cabinet Secretary, who embodied the socialist commitment to local autonomy. As was mentioned earlier, Igarashi was the progressive Mayor of Asahikawa, Hokkaidō, before he entered national politics. Based on this experience, he was the 'Shadow Minister of Home Affairs' of the Socialist Party since 1991, and as such, he drew up his party's policy on decentralization that, in fact, proposed the abolition of *kikan inin jimu* in principle, the enactment of a Decentralization Promotion Law, as well as the setting up of a Decentralization Commission.[35] This initiative sparked a number of similar proposals from other parties and various think tanks, and in order to keep up the momentum, it was he who masterminded the unprecedented Diet resolution for the promotion of decentralization that was passed unanimously by both houses in 1993 a couple of months before Hosokawa took office.[36] As the Chief Cabinet Secretary, he played a key role in the appointment of the members of the Decentralization Commission.[37] For Igarashi who considers decentralization as his 'lifework',[38] the reforms of the 1990s are a project that follows in the footsteps of the battles he fought together with his comrades, such as Ichio Asukata, in the heydays of Progressive Local Governments.[39]

According to several accounts, these Cabinet ministers made a significant difference at a critical juncture in the decentralization process:[40] The draft for the government programme for the promotion of decentralization was being stalled because of the opposition from the central ministries and the *zoku* politicians before it had a chance to reach the Cabinet for approval, which would bind the Cabinet to proceed to legislation of the Decentralization Promotion Law. In a Cabinet meeting in December 1994, Nonaka expressed his irritation that the government programme had not been submitted to the Cabinet yet for its approval. Both Murayama and Igarashi agreed and Yamaguchi, who was the minister in charge of the issue, complained that he himself had been urging on the bureaucrats but to no avail. At this point, Takemura suggested that the Cabinet should confirm its position to approve the programme without further delay. Kōno, the then LDP President, Deputy Prime Minister, and Foreign Minister, agreed. Igarashi asked if any minister disagreed, and nobody did. It was then for Ishihara to tell the reluctant senior bureaucrats of the MCA to submit the government programme to the next Cabinet meeting, and also to tell all the administrative vice-ministers that should anyone oppose the programme, despite the Cabinet agreement on its prompt submission, they should come to see him to explain their objection in person by the next Conference of Administrative Vice-Ministers. Nobody came, and the government programme was finally approved in the following Cabinet meeting. The bureaucratic roadblock was thus surmounted.

Thus, the historical alternation in power of 1993 was significant in that it fundamentally transformed the dynamics of party politics, and brought different types of political leaders and their associates to the forefront of the policy process, who in turn placed hitherto neglected policy goals on the agenda. There were, however, apparent limits to the political leadership at the same time. Three weaknesses merit particular mention.

First, the perennial problem of frequent turnover of governments continued to haunt Japan. The Hosokawa government lasted only for eight months; Hata held the premiership for a mere two months; the Murayama government did somewhat better with a year and seven months; Hashimoto even better with two years and a half. But by the time the Decentralization Law was enacted under the Obuchi government, Japan had its fifth prime minister in six years, and indeed, Murayama, Igarashi, and Yamaguchi were already retired from politics, Takemura was a marginal figure in a dying party, and only Nonaka was at his peak of political power as the Chief Cabinet Secretary. The lack of steady political leadership is even worse when one looks at ministerial turnovers. Conforming to conventional practice, Murayama reshuffled his Cabinet during his premiership, which resulted in changes in such key posts as the Chief Cabinet Secretary and the Minister of Home Affairs. Hashimoto reshuffled his Cabinet twice, as did Obuchi.

Second, even though the fierce inter-party competition of the 1990s also had the positive effect of sustaining pressure for reform, it cannot be ignored that tension among the coalition partners, and the related frequent changes of coalition framework, added further to the destabilization of political leadership.

Third, related to the above two points was a glaring lack of party unity and discipline on all fronts. The 1990s saw a number of new parties form and disappear. Shifting party affiliation back and forth was not uncommon. This was particularly damaging to the democratic legitimacy of the politicians because proportional representation based on party lists was introduced for two-fifths of the seats in Lower House elections with the electoral reform of 1994.

Considering these limits, it was no mean achievement that the system of 'agency delegation' was abolished at long last, although the new system that replaced it left a way for the state to continue to intervene in local public administration. Similarly, regulations of 'compulsory setting' were somewhat alleviated. In spite of very real limitations, the decentralization of the 1990s is rightly considered the first substantial reform since the postwar reform under the Occupation, and the Old Left was instrumental in its success.

Information disclosure: enactment by a reactive LDP

The three-party (JSP-LDP-Sakigake) agreement that gave birth to the Murayama government included the swift enactment of an Information

Disclosure Law. The Information Disclosure Section of the Administrative Reform Commission, set up in March 1995, agreed upon the principle that the new Information Disclosure Law be based on the people's right to demand information disclosure, with a right to appeal to the court in case the government refused to comply. As deliberation of this Section began, the three governing parties also initiated the public disclosure of the minutes of government deliberative councils.

By the time the Final Report of the Administrative Reform Commission was submitted in December 1996, both the JSP and Sakigake were only supporting the LDP government from outside the Cabinet, and it was in March 1998 that Prime Minister Hashimoto finally put forward the bill for Diet deliberation. By then, the Old Left was all but gone, and a New Left was taking shape in the opposition in the form of the DPJ. The bill was carried over for several Diet sessions, and after a few compromise deals (including the LDP's concession to opposition parties' demand that the law be revised four years after its implementation), was finally enacted in May 1999 and took effect two years later in April 2001.

Thus, nearly two decades elapsed since the first local governments instituted their information disclosure systems, but this 'oppositional' policy was finally placed on the political agenda when the LDP had to listen to the JSP and Sakigake, and was finally enacted by the LDP government when a New Left was emerging as a possible alternative.

Parliamentary accountability and the emergence of the New Left

The enhancement of the Diet's power to keep the executive in check was the least well articulated by the Old Left in the 1980s and also the least successful in the 1990s, but it served as a crucial issue around which the New Left reconstituted itself by defining itself as the representative of the citizens.

Crucial party realignment in the Centre-Left took place in the run-up to the Lower House elections in October 1996. Important segments from both Sakigake and the JSP left their parties and joined forces to form the new Democratic Party of Japan under the joint leadership of Yukio Hatoyama and Naoto Kan. The DPJ as well as what was left of Sakigake promised the creation of an Administration Supervision Organization in the Diet during the electoral campaign. The LDP included this item in the post-election three-party (LDP-JSP-Sakigake) agreement, in part to satisfy Sakigake, and in part in order to retain the possibility of future cooperation with the DPJ.

In December 1996, the fledgling DPJ submitted an Administration Supervision Authority (the Japanese GAO) Bill that stipulated the establishment of a supervisory organ in the Diet, with full powers to assess and supervise the government. The proposed authority was to consist of three commissioners appointed by the speakers of both houses from outside the bureaucracy, and to have an administrative staff of eight hundred officials transferred from the Management and Coordination Agency by abolishing its Administrative

Inspection Bureau. The LDP delayed its final decision until spring 1997, but since the DPJ chose to place itself fully in the opposition camp by then, the bill was void. All that happened in the end was a minor reorganization of the standing committees in both houses by the LDP government in 1998.

Concluding remarks

In this chapter, we first pointed out the origins of the policies of 'democratic government' in the oppositional Left under the 1955 system. It was argued that such policies as decentralization, information disclosure, and the reinforced parliamentary control of the executive were articulated and espoused by the Left not so much for inherently *ideological* reasons of a socialist party, but primarily for the *situational* reasons of a perennial opposition party. 'Democratic administrative reform' was advocated by the Left as a counterproposal during the *Rinchō* years of the 1980s, but the LDP, as the perennial governing party, had no incentive to pursue these essentially 'oppositional' policies as long as the Left remained safely marginalised in the policy process in the opposition. Indeed, even in the Left, the calls for boosted democratic control of government were given less prominence than the more urgent need to resist the cost-cutting offensive of the LDP government that largely monopolised the policy agenda and effectively promoted the case for 'simple and efficient government'.

Ironically for the Left, the policies of 'democratic government' finally made some advances in the 1990s, when it was no longer consigned to perpetual opposition but rapidly losing ground as a political force. The Old Left, that is the JSP, turned out to be among the biggest victims of the new, incomparably more fluid, and considerably less ideologically polarised era of coalition politics that emerged in the 1990s. The perpetual opposition of the Left had to quickly throw away most of its cherished socialist policies when it entered coalition governments, first with non-LDP parties and later with the LDP itself. When it did so, the 'oppositional' policies of 'democratic government' that were not particularly leftist in nature came to the fore, in part because they were less ideologically divisive, and in part because they helped the Left start redefining itself as truly representative of the people and justify its coalition deal with its former nemesis.

At a critical juncture in Japanese politics, when the old, opposition-oriented, socialist Left was rapidly declining, and the new, government-oriented, liberal Left was struggling to emerge, the cause of 'democratic control of government' provided a focal point around which the Left grappled with its difficult renewal in policy terms. In the end, the Old Left continued its downward trend as a political force, and many of its key leaders either failed to be re-elected or retired by 2000. It may further be argued that the New Left initially rallied around the agenda of 'democratic government,' but that in its eagerness to prove that it was an alternative governing party, and not a perennial opposition, the DPJ gradually toned down its espousal of 'oppositional' policies, and increasingly turned to a neo-liberal economic policy agenda as a way to define itself against the Old Left as well as the LDP.

Notes

I would like to thank Arthur Stockwin, the editors and contributors of this book, the participants of the Japan Politics Colloquium at Sheffield University, and Mari Miura for comments, advice and criticisms.

1 See Koichi Nakano, 'The Politics of Administrative Reform in Japan, 1993–1998: Toward a More Accountable Government?', *Asian Survey*, vol. 38, no. 3, March 1998, pp. 291–309, and 'Gyōsei Kaikaku: yoha ka sanjiteki henka ka?', in Nobuhiro Hiwatari and Mari Miura (eds), *Ryūdōki no Nihon Seiji*, Tokyo: Tokyo Daigaku Shuppankai, 2002, pp. 137–54.
2 Its other important aspect concerns the control of the career bureaucracy by democratically elected representatives of the people *inside* the executive.
3 Of course, this does not preclude these reforms at the same time contributing to the goal of 'simple and efficient government' as well.
4 Yasuo Maruyama, *Shōgen: Dai 2-ji Rinchō*, Tokyo: Shinchi Shobō, 1984, pp. 12–21.
5 Yasuo Maruyama, 'Dai 2-ji Rinchō ni Nozomu Kihontekina Kangaekata' (March 16, 1981) in Zen Nihon Jichi Dantai Rōdō Kumiai and Chihō Jichi Sōgō Kenkyūjo (eds), *Gyōsei Kaikaku e no Teigen: Maruyama Yasuo Ikenshū*, Tokyo: Nihon Hyōronsha, 1983, pp. 20–6.
6 Ibid., p. 21.
7 Ibid., pp. 21–2.
8 Ibid., pp. 22–3.
9 Ibid., pp. 23–4.
10 This subsection draws partly on my PhD dissertation, *Democratizing Policy Communities?: the Politics of Decentralization in France and Japan*, Princeton University (November 2003).
11 Wataru Ōmori, ' "Kakushin" to Senkyo Rengō' in Wataru Ōmori and Seizaburō Satō (eds), *Nihon no Chihō Seifu*, Tokyo: Tokyo Daigaku Shuppankai, 1986, p. 214.
12 Ichio Asukata, *Asukata Ichio Kaisōroku*, Tokyo: Asahi Shinbunsha, 1987, p. 34.
13 JSP, 'Chihō Jichitai Kaikaku' in Zenkoku Kakushin Shichōkai and Chihō Jichi Sentā (eds), *Shiryō Kakushin Jichitai*, Tokyo: Nihon Hyōronsha, 1990, p. 34.
14 Progressive Local Governments usually refer to local governments whose chief executive is a 'progressive'. In turn, a chief executive is commonly regarded as a progressive, when backed by one or more of the opposition parties, notably the JSP and JCP. Crucially, however, when chief executives are also supported by the LDP at the same time, they are no longer considered to be progressives, but as *ainori* (joint-ride).
15 Among the designated cities, Osaka and Kitakyūshū, too, elected progressive mayors in the same year.
16 Yokohama, Kawasaki, Nagoya, Kyoto, Osaka, and Kōbe. The conservatives kept Sapporo, Kitakyūshū, and Fukuoka.
17 Under this system, the central government could use local governments, the prefectures in particular, as its 'agents', i.e. *de facto* field services, and delegate certain administrative tasks and supervise them.
18 This refers to the anomaly of prefectural officials in certain policy areas, such as social security, keeping the status of national public servants, and thus eluding the governor's personnel management authority.

19 These stipulations enabled the central ministries to order local governments to set up various administrative institutions and posts with minute regulations by law or by decree, and also restricted the local governments' right to manage their own affairs as they see fit.

20 Nihon Shakaitō Seisaku Shingikai (eds), *Nihon Shakaitō Seisaku Shiryō Shūsei*, Tokyo: Nihon Shakaitō Chūō Honbu Kikanshikyoku, 1990, pp. 864–907, especially, pp. 886–91.

21 Yasuo Maruyama, 'Gyōsei Kaikaku no Kihon Mondai toshite no Kuni to Chihō Jichitai no Kengen Haibun' (13 December 1982) in Zen Nihon Jichi Dantai Rōdō Kumiai and Chihō Jichi Sōgō Kenkyūjo, *Gyōsei Kaikaku e no Teigen*, pp. 324–38.

22 Shūichirō Itō, 'Gyōsei Tōsei: jōhō kōkai/gyōsei tetsuzuki kisei no taihi', in Hiwatari and Miura, *Ryūdoki no Nihon Seiji*, pp. 155–75. Itō also points out the 'oppositional' nature of information disclosure.

23 Ibid., pp.166–7.

24 Hiroshi Miyake, *Jōhō Kōkaihō no Tebiki*, Tokyo: Kadensha, 1999, pp. 12–13.

25 Yasuo Maruyama, 'Jōhō Kōkai to Gyōsei Tetsuzuki· ni kansuru Iken' (31 May 1982) in Zen Nihon Jichi Dantai Rōdō Kumiai and Chihō Jichi Sōgō Kenkyūjo, *Gyōsei Kaikaku eno Teigen*, pp. 228–31.

26 Yasuo Maruyama, 'Gyōsei ni okeru Minshuka no Tettei no tame no Hōsaku' in Zen Nihon Jichi Dantai Rōdō Kumiai and Chihō Jichi Sōgō Kenkyūjo, *Gyōsei Kaikaku e no Teigen*, pp. 339–45.

27 Motoaki Hatake, *Jōhō Kōkaihō no Kaisetsu to Kokkai Rongi*, Tokyo: Seirin Shoin, 1999, pp. 5–6.

28 Maruyama, 'Dai 2-ji Rinchō ni Nozomu Kihontekina Kangaekata,' pp. 23–4, and 'Gyōsei ni okeru Minshuka no Tettei no tame no Hōsaku,' p. 340.

29 Nihon Shakaitō Seisaku Shingikai, *Nihon Shakaitō Seisaku Shiryō Shūsei*, p. 867.

30 See also the observation of a leftist academic and theorist of 'democratic administrative reform', Tsutomu Muroi, 'Minshuteki Gyōsei Kaikaku no tame ni' in Zen Nihon Jichi Dantai Rōdō Kumiai and Chihō Jichi Sōgō Kenkyūjo, *Gyōsei Kaikaku e no Teigen*, pp. 9–14.

31 The LDP was in 'coalition' with the New Liberal Club, a tiny splinter group, which was later re-absorbed by the LDP.

32 See Nakano, 'The Politics of Administrative Reform in Japan, 1993–1998'.

33 This subsection draws largely on my PhD dissertation, *Democratizing Policy Communities?*

34 Tomiichi Murayama, interviewed by the author, Tokyo, 3 December 2002.

35 Masaru Nishio *et al.*, *Bunkengata Shakai wo Tsukuru: Sono Rekishi to Rinen to Seido*, Tokyo: Gyōsei, 2001, p. 5; and Kōzō Igarashi, *Kantei no Rasen Kaidan: Shiminha Kanbōchōkan Funtōki*, Tokyo: Gyōsei, 1997, pp. 198–200.

36 Nishio, *Bunkengata Shakai*, pp. 5–7 and p. 25; and Igarashi, *Kantei*, pp. 201–2.

37 Tomiichi Murayama, op. cit.

38 Katsuo Matsumoto *et al.*, *Daisan no Kaikaku wo Mezashite: Shōgen de Tadoru Bunken Kaikaku*, Tokyo: Gyōsei, 2000, p. 23.

39 Igarashi, *Kantei*, p. 209.

40 For instance, see Nobuo Ishihara's account in Hiroshi Shiono, Nobuo Ishihara, and Hideaki Matsumoto, *21- seiki no Chihō Jichi wo Kataru: Bunkengata Shakai wo Ninau Hitobito e*, Tokyo: Gyōsei, 2000, pp. 72–8. Ishihara was Deputy Cabinet Secretary (the highest-ranking position for a bureaucrat) at that time. It is unclear whether the recollection that follows is entirely accurate in its detail, but several other accounts, while somewhat different in the specific role played by each of the ministers, confirm the crucial intervention of the Cabinet. See Nonaka's account in Matsumoto, *Daisan no Kaikaku*, pp. 38–9; Igarashi's account in Igarashi, *Kantei*, pp. 206–7; and *Asahi Shimbun*, 16 December 1994.

6 The end-game of socialism

From the JSP to the DPJ

Sarah Hyde

Until 1993, the Japan Socialist Party (JSP) was the main opposition party in Japan, a position it had occupied since 1955. It formed the backbone of the 1955 system alongside the dominant Liberal Democratic Party (LDP). The 1955 system denotes the period between 1955 and 1993 when the LDP was the only party capable of forming a government in its own right, a time when the LDP was also permanently and successfully opposed by the JSP (and increasingly throughout that period, by other smaller opposition parties as well). But 1993 was a disastrous year for the JSP. It saw the number of seats it was usually able to win halve in the historic July Lower House election that also saw the LDP lose its majority for the first time in 38 years. While 1993 has become embedded in collective memory as the year of the LDP's collapse, little attention has been paid to the concurrent decline of the JSP, an event which has had a far greater impact on the face of Japanese parliamentary politics. This chapter shall attempt to show the extent and importance of these changes within the socialist opposition, and illuminate some of the differences between the pre-1993 led opposition party, the JSP, and the main opposition party that subsequently emerged, the Democratic Party of Japan (DPJ). The DPJ is proving to be an increasingly electable party, and while it does not yet have the power to win an election single-handedly, with each one it is moving steadily towards that goal. With each improvement in its performance, the possibility of the emergence of a two-party system of sorts becomes more likely, and with that, Japanese democracy acquires a more conventional structure.

At first, in the immediate aftermath of the 1993 election, the JSP managed to convince itself that the virtual halving of its Lower House seats from 136 to 70 was not a disaster.[1] After all, the party was still the largest party of the coalition government and collectively they managed to introduce electoral and political reform legislation in 1994. However, things began to unravel when they left the coalition in April after a disagreement with Ichirō Ozawa over his formation of a rival grouping within the Diet.[2] Once again, the JSP managed to find a solution that simultaneously seemed to improve their situation, yet with hindsight, was a move that delivered the final death-blow to the party. In June 1994 they formed a coalition government with their arch-rivals the LDP (and the small Sakigake Party) which lasted until September 1996 and gave to Tomiichi Murayama, the leader of the JSP, the coveted position of Prime Minister. Murayama resigned in January 1996, allowing the LDP faction leader Ryūtarō Hashimoto to take over until the election in October 1996. Throughout this period of coalition participation the JSP did realize that the party had identity problems and they tried to reform their party internally.[3] These attempts to strengthen the party came to little and resulted in the party splitting in September 1996, with its younger Diet members defecting to the new social democratic party, the Democratic Party of Japan. After the election in which further losses ensued, 48 party members remained in the JSP to fight the election, and the party managed to limp on, winning 15 seats. It continues to exist, yet in the November 2003 general election it only managed to take five seats. In comparison the DPJ grew, taking 55 seats in 1996 and 175 in November 2003. It eventually became the largest opposition party in Japan.

The DPJ had been formed by Naoto Kan, and Yukio and Kunio Hatoyama. Kan had been Minister of Health and Welfare in the JSP/LDP/Sakigake coalition. The Hatoyamas are the grandsons of the former Prime Minister Ichiro Hatoyama. Either Kan or Yukio has continued to hold the leadership of the party to date, but Kunio left the party in 1999 to rejoin the LDP. In April 1998, the DPJ expanded, absorbing members who had been left without a 'real' political party after the Shinshintō super-party split.[4] The DPJ at this point expanded to 94 members, not only increasing its size, but also widening its political orientation away from its initial Left of centre position. This party's name remained the same. The party expanded further, merging with Ichirō Ozawa's Jiyūtō Party in 2003. The 2003 Lower House election result, which further enhanced the party's representation by 38 seats, underpinned its claim to be the only postwar Japanese political party to have consistently grown since its formation, through mergers but also through elections. The DPJ is thus a party that represents 'the New Left' in Japan and has many similarities with and differences from the JSP, which represented 'the Old Left'. This new system of LDP coalition government, opposed by the increasingly powerful DPJ, can be described as the 1998 system, recognising the fact that the DPJ settled into being a coherent opposition facing a stable LDP-based coalition.

In this chapter, my intention is to examine the differences between the influence that the JSP had on policy-making prior to the break-up of the 1955 system, and the influence that the DPJ has had on the Diet since 1998. In order to gauge whether the growth of the DPJ will have any long-lasting impact on democracy in Japan, it is necessary to assess the degree to which the party has been able to turn its electoral growth into policy-formation potential. Utilising Minoru Nakano's analysis of the formation of the national pension legislation in 1985, we will first assess which factors seem to have contributed to the JSP's ability or inability to influence legislation.[5] Nakano has given us an extremely detailed account of how the bureaucrat

Shinichirō Yamaguchi was able to introduce pension reform. He micro-analysed the entire process, and through his account, it is possible to extrapolate which factors facilitated the opposition's influence on the final versions of legislation. In order to look at the impact of pacifism, the peace constitution and the 'cultural cleavage'[6] on policy formation, we shall also examine the 1991–1992 bill on United Nations Peacekeeping Operations (UNPKO). We shall use the factors identified by Nakano to guide us in answering two main questions:

- Does the DPJ have any influence on policy-making in the 1998 system?
- If it does have influence, what factors account for it?

It seems as if little has changed within the Japanese Diet since 1985 when it comes to the institutional factors that impact upon opposition influence on policy. Individual politicians mattered greatly in 1985 and still mattered in 2003, although probably not to the extent that they did in the 1955 system. However, other factors also matter, notably the opposition's relationship with the labour unions, institutional factors such as the power and electoral support of the party in power in relation to that of the opposition forces, and finally the nature of the bill being debated. It is this last point that seems to have undergone the most change since the 1955 system. It is at the level of pacifist policy, the maintenance of the constitution and other issues that have traditionally been incorporated into this debate, such as the legalization of the national flag and anthem, that there has been the greatest change in policy. In the final section, we shall analyse why this has happened. Furthermore, we will question whether or not there has been a move away from concentrating on pacifist policies towards a more pragmatic concentration on economic and fiscal policy.

Why was the JSP able to impose its will on policy?

Ideological pragmatism might be a good way to describe the JSP's approach to policy. While being ideologically committed to workers' rights, and a solid social security provision, they were prepared to compromise certain ideals as long as it did not involve the issues of the constitution or defence. Therefore for the JSP, the necessary question is to establish what impacted on their ability to extract concessions from the LDP in areas of policy where the JSP *was* prepared to compromise. From Nakano's account, the following factors seem to be important indicators of the opposition's ability to negotiate a compromise.

Number of seats in the House of Representatives

The number of seats held by the opposition in the Lower House obviously matters. In the case of the Pensions Bill of 1985, the JSP had more leverage than it normally would because 1983–1986 was virtually a hung parliament, had it not been for the cooperation of the small New Liberal Club with the LDP. This was why the JSP was able to get two members on the Diet Social and Labour Affairs Committee and *Seidoshin*, the Consultative Council for the Social Security System, which gave them greater influence over the final policy outcome. However, more generally, the number of seats won in the Lower House is obviously a factor that always affects the power of the Left to influence policy. More opposition seats in the Lower House means a better balance of government and opposition politicians on committees, and a greater number of chairs of those committees means the opposition is able to exercise the casting vote when the committee is unable to make a decision. Furthermore, greater numbers of Diet members means that a party is more able to seek concessions from the ruling party, through potential Diet coalitions with other parties and even the ability to win a majority on certain issues should individual members of the ruling party decide to vote against their party's position.

Balance between the Upper and Lower Houses

The balance of power between the Upper and Lower Houses represents a different yet related explanation. During the 1992 deliberations on the United Nations Peacekeeping Operations (UNPKO) Bill to allow Japanese Self Defence Forces (SDF) to participate in UN-led peacekeeping operations, it was necessary for the LDP to co-opt the Kōmeitō and the Democratic Socialist Party (DSP) in order for the bill to pass in the Upper House, where the LDP lacked a majority. The importance of the Upper House has traditionally been underestimated within the policy-making system. It was not until after 1989, when the LDP lost its majority in the house for the first time during the 1955 system, that the importance of a majority in both houses was fully understood by politicians and political commentators. Whilst it is possible to pass budget legislation in the Lower House even after it has been rejected in the Upper House, all other legislation needs to be passed within the Upper House without resorting to various extraordinary means.[7] This was a factor that remained salient in 2003 as the LDP continued to feel the after-effects of not having won an outright majority in the 1998 Upper House election, and this explains why they remained in coalition with the Kōmeitō from that time. However, to be able to take advantage of any possible weaknesses in the government camp, such as a lack of a majority in the Upper House, the opposition must be united. The relative strength of the JSP, as was the case in 1985, will do no good if the opposition parties are fragmented.

Fragmented nature of the opposition

According to Nakano, the fragmented nature of the opposition damaged the JSP's ability to influence policy. Johnson and Christensen have since discussed these electoral and Diet coalitions in detail and found them to have strengthened the LDP because the opposition parties were never prepared to compromise on policy preferences in order to fight on a combined front against the LDP.[8] However, Nakano makes another point concerning the effect that a fragmented opposition has on policy formation. He points out that were the opposition to propose one single set of amendments for Diet bills, without each party submitting their own amendments as occurred with pension reform, the LDP would try to avoid favouring any party and would, instead, adopt a section from each, thereby ensuring that no party was completely happy with the proposed legislation.

Influence of unions

Sōhyō (the General Council of Japanese Trade Unions) and Dōmei (the Japan Confederation of Labour), the two labour union umbrella groups who backed the JSP and the DSP respectively, were also influential in the policy process. In 1985 they both had representatives on the Welfare Pensions Subcommittee and the Social and Labor Affairs Committee (SLAC). With policies that were related to social policy, it was likely that the DSP and JSP had the benefit of the unions backing their arguments in consultative councils. However, as with the fragmented opposition, the fragmented union structure of Dōmei and Sōhyō also could have had a negative influence on policy-making, each attempting to push through mutually incompatible aims.[9]

Experience in the Diet

Experience counted, according to Nakano. Opposition Diet members with experience not only had more contacts within the Diet and the bureaucracy (thereby increasing their chances to influence policy); they also had more links with other politicians. 'Personal links between their respective "experts" can influence policy formation'.[10] Policy Tribes (*Zoku giin*) are also an important factor and their numbers increase as the cohort gains more experience. *Zoku giin* accumulate knowledge concerning one specific policy area partly as a means of finding a role within the party (particularly in the LDP) once their party no longer rewards them for experience with party posts. As Nakano has said, 'it is far from uncommon for the biggest leaps in the continuous policy process to be born of the informal actions of Diet members with power and rank'.[11]

Types of policy that the JSP tried to influence

The JSP's ability to extract compromise was very dependent on the policy area being targeted. The opposition has traditionally been able to influence social policy-related legislation, where they have a particular expertise and more backing from the labour unions. In these areas they have also had more *zoku giin* than in others. The presence of *zoku giin* in the JSP is less well analysed than those in the LDP, but their mere presence means that the government cannot ignore known experts when discussing legislation, thus giving the opposition a greater voice. This was the case with the pension legislation. Toru Ōhara and Shinnen Tagaya from the JSP were considered pension experts, as was Naoto Kan of the Shaminren, eventual leader of the DPJ.

The JSP was able to influence legislation in areas related to the pacifist constitution, defence policy and the Self Defence Forces (SDF). Unlike in areas of social policy, this influence is better understood as the party having an effective veto on policy decision-making relating to these issues. While any policy changes in this area are obviously subject to due process in the Diet, the JSP managed to maintain the sense that, by protecting the constitution from any changes, they were not only representing the views of the majority of the Japanese electorate but also taking the moral high ground. This was what Watanuki called 'cultural cleavage'.

Throughout the era of the 1955 system, there was gradual change in defence-related policy, as can be seen by comparing the protests outside the Diet in 1960 when Prime Minister Kishi wanted to revise the Japan–US Security Treaty, and the ability of the LDP to win Diet support from the DSP and the Kōmeitō to pass the United Nations Peacekeeping Operations Bill in 1992 against the wishes of the JSP. Whether the passing of the 1992 bill can be explained by a change in the electorate's attitude towards defence policy coupled with a growing realization that Japan had a global responsibility, or whether this change in policy was attributable to a strengthening LDP *vis à vis* a weakening JSP, it remained the central pillar of JSP-LDP policy differences. In many respects, it is this aspect of policy-making that represents the largest change in the ability of the left-of-centre parties to determine policy within the Japanese Diet, and we shall consider this area in detail below when examining the DPJ's impact on policy.

Policy and the DPJ – what types of policy have they attempted to implement and how has this affected their ability to influence policy?

In some respects, the DPJ's institutional ability to make their own mark as an opposition party has many parallels with the situation of the JSP discussed above. However, in other respects, factors such as the popularity of Prime Minister Junichirō Koizumi and the less polarised nature of the defence debate under the 1998 system, have meant that sometimes they have been more able to stamp their mark on policy. Yet in other areas, such as the July 2003 bill to send the SDF to postwar Iraq, they have been ignored. In some cases, such as the 1999 National Flag and Anthem debate, they even have allowed themselves to be ignored by being divided internally. Furthermore, the DPJ has shown significant change in the types of policies that it is formulating.

Below I outline the relevant legislation and attempt to show how the DPJ has changed during the course of the 1998 system.

1998 Non-Profit Organization (NPO) Bill

On 4 March 1998, the NPO legislation, which had been first mooted within the Diet in 1996, was passed. This was a bill in line with the liberal attitudes of the left-of-centre faction of the DPJ. Originally an LDP proposal, this private members' bill was eventually pushed through the Diet by the DPJ, who saw the strengthening of NPOs as an important facet of their new policy of creating networks with citizen groups. From 1996 the bill was stymied in permanent committees by questioning the definition of to whom it would apply (the DPJ wanted to limit it to the candidate but the JCP and the Kōmeitō wanted to limit all connections to politics), and what tax benefits would be given to those who were designated as NPOs. Eventually, the DPJ gave in to the other parties' demands, believing that by merely strengthening NPOs and allowing them the status of a limited company, it would amelior-ate any contact the party could have with citizen movements. This allowed the bill to be passed in the Upper House and it became law on 1 December 1998.

The bill to legalise the use of the National Flag and Anthem, August 1999; the SDF Dispatch Bill of November 2001; and the June 2003 Military Emergency Bill.

The National Flag and Anthem Bill was one of the most controversial bills to pass the Japanese Diet since the UNPKO Bill, passed in June 1992. It allowed for the Hinomaru Flag and Kimigayo national anthem to be legal-ised within Japanese law. This was a hugely contentious bill for the opposition parties and, in the 22 July 1999 vote in the Lower House, the DPJ made it a free vote for its members, as the party could not reach any consensus on how to vote. The bill split the party in two with 45 members voting for it and 46 against.[12] On the 9 August hearing in the Upper House, once again the DPJ made it a free vote for its members and, once again, some members voted for the bill, augmenting the numbers of government supporters and allowing the bill to pass the Upper House with ease. This support for the bill led a *Japan Times* columnist at the time to declare 'until last year, there was rationality in Japanese politics . . . But this year, things went awry'.[13]

The post-September 11 bill to send the Maritime SDF to lend logistical support in Afghanistan is an example of the DPJ becoming less concerned with pacifist views. Yukio Hatoyama stipulated that his party would support the bill and, when the faction centred on former JSP members led by Takahiro Yokomichi did not support the party in the Diet vote, he announced that they were to be punished by restricting their participation in the party's executive.

In June 2002, however, the DPJ once again changed its spots by calling for the resignation of the LDP's Chief Cabinet Secretary, Yasuo Fukuda, over his suggestion that the three non-nuclear principles should be dropped. While the party supported Koizumi's June 2003 War Contingencies Bill, which would allow the government to mobilise the SDF to cope with a 'military-attack situation', they began to question the extension of Japan's overseas presence and opposed Japanese troops being sent to help reconstruct postwar Iraq. However, they had previously agreed to the bill that sent the SDF to postwar Afghanistan in 2001–2. Furthermore, they agreed to the SDF being sent to Iraq in January 2004. The DPJ seems to have developed a haphazard policy formation process on matters relating to Japan's defence, the maintenance of the constitution and Japan's role in world security. At times, the policies that it follows have been dove-like and in line with the position the JSP would have taken during the 1955 system. At other times, they are much more hawkish and prepared to accept the traditional attitudes of the Japanese Right as defined by Watanuki's cultural cleavage, that is the need to change and react to a global era of mutual security.

Keddell has described changes to defence policy during the 1955 system as being incremental.[14] The same cannot really be said for the DPJ as they are responding in an *ad hoc* manner to defence policies. It seems to suggest a tendency of the DPJ to move towards a lessening of importance to the party of the issues which polarised around the constitution. Instead, they are moving to show their potential acumen against the LDP government and their ability to form a realistic government based on sound management.

The DPJ and economic policy

Whereas, under the 1955 system, the opposition parties were more likely to champion legislation that was connected to defence issues, it seems that the DPJ is changing the type of policy that it is opting to push for in the Diet. Since the normally dove-like Kan became party leader in December 2002, the party has made every effort to expose the weaknesses of the Koizumi administration's economic policies. The party's 2003 platform focused on the criticism that Koizumi had not stopped deflation or rising unemployment levels. In February 2003, the DPJ for the first time submitted a draft budget to oppose the LDP's budget. The main claim was that the DPJ's budget would generate one million more jobs than the budget put forward by the LDP. In their July 2003 no confidence motion in the government, (a frequently attempted tactic by the opposition), the DPJ questioned the responsibility of Financial Services Minister Heizō Takenaka for the failing economy, rather than the issue of the SDF being sent to Iraq, which was being debated in the same parliament.[15] We shall examine possible reasons for this change below, but first we will turn to an examination of the institutional factors that affected the DPJ's role in the Diet.

What institutional factors have impacted upon the DPJ's ability to influence legislation in the Diet?

Number of seats in the Diet and the balance between the Upper and Lower Houses

The DPJ has been severely constrained by the combined number of members they are competing against in the Diet. In the Lower House, the LDP has a majority in its own right and has had since 1997, when they finally managed to salvage a majority after their brief period of being completely out of government and relied on the JSP as a coalition partner. However, the DPJ's ability to influence policy has been further constrained because of the LDP's lack of an outright majority in the Upper House since 1998. This has resulted in the creation of LDP-led coalitions, combining since December 1998 the Liberal Party and Kōmeitō along with the LDP and, since April 2000, teaming with the Conservative Party and the Kōmeitō.[16]

In the Lower House, therefore, the LDP/Kōmeitō/Conservative Party coalition is an unnecessary coalition, and this is having a huge impact on the ability of the DPJ to push forward legislation in the Diet. As Aurelia George-Mulgan has said:

> Given the numerical realities, the opposition parties have neither the pulling power, nor the incentive to sustain a unified stance for long enough to pose a successful challenge to the Koizumi government[17]

In the example of the Pension Bill outlined above, the JSP managed to gain concessions because the LDP was in a weak position in the Lower House. At the time of writing (2003–2004), however, the LDP was in an invincible position in both Houses, and all that it needed to do was to make concessions to its coalition partners to guarantee getting a policy through the Diet. However, it must be acknowledged here that the DPJ may have some leverage against the LDP in cases where the coalition partners are trying to implement policies that are not in favour of the LDP or vice versa.

The nature of the opposition

In forming coalitions with first the Liberal Party and the Kōmeitō, and then the Kōmeitō and the Conservative Party, the LDP has managed to destroy any chances of truly effective electoral or Diet coalitions amongst the opposition parties, by effectively co-opting the opposition into the LDP. This strategy, which emerged out of the LDP's lack of an outright majority in the Upper House, has denied the opposition the opportunity to incorporate the Kōmeitō into some form of opposition coalition. Whilst the Kōmeitō are unwieldy and can be problematic as partners because of their own idiosyncratic style of campaigning, they are a useful middle-ground grouping within the Japanese party system and could be valuable coalition partners for the DPJ. Opposition electoral coalitions have had, to date, little success in Japan. In the late 1980s and early 1990s, despite this being the only potential means for the opposition to unseat the LDP, the parties were not successful in overcoming their differences to form stable, workable coalitions.[18] However, this lack of success during the 1955 system does not necessarily preclude the potential success of opposition-based electoral coalitions in the more coalition-viable period of the 1998 system.

Experience in the Diet

For the JSP, experience in the Diet was commensurate with the ability to influence policy. This was because, as politicians gained more experience, they would have more knowledge about particular issues, particularly if they had been part of a policy tribe (*zoku*). Experience also meant that an opposition politician would have more personal links with members of the government, which would mean they would be able to gain some leverage in policy decisions. Therefore, experience within the DPJ is also a factor which needs to be considered. The DPJ is a new party and as such has had many young politicians in its ranks, both in terms of their age and their political experience. The average age of the party in 2003 was 51 years and 6 months, in contrast to the LDP's 58 years 5 months. The average number of terms for the DPJ was 2.45 compared to the LDP's 4.38. Furthermore, as these DPJ politicians are younger in age, many of them opted directly for a political career and, unlike the LDP, had little experience of being a bureaucrat or a businessman before being a politician (which would have given them specialist knowledge in a certain area). In the old JSP, many members had been unionists before becoming politicians, which would have allowed them to garner expertise in certain aspects of policy. Younger politicians can be expected to have fresh perspectives on policy so this is not necessarily a major hindrance, but it has been a factor in the DPJ's potential ability to influence policy.

Unions

In the 1998 system, unions have bypassed parties and gained their own access directly to bureaucracy and government. This style of unionism was pioneered by Akira Yamagishi in his attempts to negotiate the privatization of NTT in the 1980s, and was to expand throughout the 1990s as a survival response to the situation that the unions found themselves in.[19] This is probably one of the most significant changes for the DPJ compared to the JSP. In the 1955 system, the links between the JSP and DSP and Sōhyō and Dōmei respectively, were a major influence on the policy directions that the opposition parties opted to take. The JSP and DSP gained financial aid and support during elections in exchange for the JSP and DSP representing their supporters' views in the Diet. In contrast to this, the DPJ has not had the same level of connections to the unions. During the 1990s, when the parties were in a constant state of flux, the unions had to gain their own access to government, as they did not have a party with which they had close ties, or which they could rely on to stay intact for more than a year or so. While the union–party relationship was reinstated, in a manner of speaking, by the Rengō/DPJ single partnership of the 2000 election, this relationship has been much weaker than it was during the 1955 system. Politicians and parties quite simply do not have the leverage in the Diet for unions to support them in the same manner as they did previously. Unions now have far more effective leverage by themselves.

In the June 2000 House of Representatives election in an unnamed prefecture, one of the DPJ candidates had to pay Rengō ¥6,000,000 in order to obtain their member databases, and for union manpower to help in the campaign office. During the 1955 system, it would have been the unions paying the JSP ¥6,000,000 to help them win an election. This example shows more than anything else the degree to which the relationship between the unions and the Left has changed, not to mention the low expectations that the unions now have of the DPJ's ability to implement union-friendly policy.[20]

Falling turn-out and the rise of the non-voter

An additional related issue is the continuing problem in Japan of falling voting rates and the rise of the non-aligned voter. These are separate yet interconnected problems. There is a general feeling in Japan that politicians are ineffective in dealing with problems such as the economy and corruption. Politicians are increasingly seen as remote and self-serving, with second and third generation politicians who inherit their support base (*jiban*)[21] reinforcing this impression. This, combined with a general belief that despite frequent elections and a huge amount of rhetoric little has changed, has made the non-aligned voter the largest identifiable group in the Japanese electorate. Occasionally, these non-aligned voters vote for a boom party such as in the 1989 Upper House election, and the New-Party boom of 1993, which indicates that a large non-aligned sector of the electorate does not necessarily lead to low voter turnout in elections.[22] As Doppelt and Shearer show, there can be many reasons for non-voting.[23] However, in Japan, particularly since 1995, when less than 50 per cent of the electorate voted in the House of Councillors election, the non-aligned voter has tended to stop voting altogether. Turnout was slightly higher in the 2000 and 2003 Lower House and 2001 Upper House elections, but this was partly explained by the institutional changes that the Japanese government introduced to counteract the low turnout. Polling station hours were increased, and it is now possible for anybody to vote before the election at the local city, town or village hall without having to prove that they will be absent on the day of the election.

Rules regarding the period of residence required before an elector is eligible to vote have also been relaxed. However, as long as the idea persists that people who oppose the LDP do not vote at all, rather than vote for the opposition as a protest vote, the opposition are not going to benefit from the public's feeling that the LDP is doing a bad job of running the country. As a result they garner insufficient seats in the Diet which means less influence, and this is a vicious circle that continues to limit the potential of the opposition.

Opposing Koizumi

We shall now turn to some factors that affect the DPJ's attempts to be an effective opposition against the Koizumi Administration in particular. Koizumi has benefited from unprecedented levels of support for an LDP Prime Minister. In 2001 when he took over from Mori, he had support levels of above 80 per cent. This dwindled somewhat in 2002 but he managed to recover when he went to North Korea in September 2002 and negotiated for the return of the abductees. His support levels subsequently shot back up to 65 per cent. Prior to the invasion of Iraq in March 2003 he once again lost support because of his pro-Bush stance, but even during this difficult period his support levels were 45 per cent, which would be high for any other LDP prime minister.[24] Koizumi has been seen by the electorate as being separate and different from the LDP, which is an image that Koizumi has created as a result of three main factors. First, throughout his long period before becoming prime minister he was in a small, non-mainstream faction and frequently campaigned unsuccessfully to become the LDP president; second, because of his criticism of the LDP in his campaign to be party president; and finally, because of policies such as the privatization of the postal industry, which is seen by the electorate as going against LDP core values.

Koizumi's high levels of support have made life very difficult for any opposition. This is because Koizumi is so popular and is able to win the electorate over to his viewpoint. He also has the LDP at his behest, because, without him, the party would not be in such a strong position. However, the main reason why Koizumi has made the position of the opposition difficult is because of his attempts to oppose traditional LDP policy and his maverick image as someone who 'goes it alone' with or without the party. Koizumi has effectively become a *de facto* opposition on his own, and this has left the DPJ with an identity crisis.

The image of the DPJ in comparison to the government

Koizumi has 'stolen' the opposition's policies, leaving the DPJ with little leeway to present itself as a reforming party. Koizumi has never been seen as a mainstream member of the LDP and now that he is the leader of the party, he appears simultaneously to be distant from it in some respects. During his campaign for the leadership of the LDP, he reinforced this maverick image by calling for deep-seated reforms of the system. This, coupled with his continuing popularity, meant that Koizumi was the one who could sport the label of 'reformer'. As George-Mulgan has noted:

> Because the prime minister himself acts like the leader of an anti-LDP opposition in advocating reforms that are contrary to the interests of his own party, he has usurped the role of the opposition and occupied their policy space.[25]

The DPJ's manifesto for the 2001 Upper House election, '7 Reforms, 21 Key policies', showed little contrast to Koizumi's structural reforms. The DPJ attempted to affirm that reforms need to take place, but in order for these reforms to succeed a change of government also needed to occur. Meanwhile, according to George-Mulgan, the DPJ accused Koizumi of being too cautious, impeded by his own party. But this then connects to the next problem that Koizumi presents to the DPJ and the opposition: their popularity in comparison to that of Koizumi and, by default, that of the LDP.

Issues relating to public opinion and image of the party

There are many dimensions to this question of the respective images of the LDP and the DJP. Crucially, there has been the perception that the DPJ would not be able to form an effective government because it lacks experience in managing the country. This is a perennial problem of opposition in Japan.

However, this aspect has been coupled with the amazing popularity of Koizumi. As noted above the approval ratings for Koizumi, even when he was being criticised for his pro-US approach, were at 45 per cent. In this political climate, the DPJ's line that Koizumi's reforms do not go far enough, appear little more than rhetoric and do little to convince the public that the DPJ would be a better choice. According to George-Mulgan, the DPJ have been refraining from openly attacking Koizumi in the Diet because being 'anti-Koizumi' could potentially lose them support. A DPJ party official was heard to say 'this is not normal ... We are in limbo because Koizumi's support rate with the public is so high'.[26]

The already estranged and difficult relationship between the DPJ and the labour unions has become more problematic since Koizumi has been prime minister. Within the DPJ there are politicians who are strongly supported by the unions and who manage to get re-elected mainly through union organization and finances. The unions organised around the former JSP politician Takahiro Yokomichi. He became the leader for the pro-union faction of the DPJ, which is itself mainly backed by former Sōhyō unions. According to George-Mulgan, Zentei, the Japan Postal Workers Union, is opposed to the reforms demanded by Koizumi for the postal industry. By default, as Zentei supports the Yokomichi faction, the faction also opposes these reforms.

There are also politicians and factions in the LDP who oppose these reforms. Yet, within the DPJ, there are members who agree with the reforms. So where does the party stand on issues like this where its factions and their traditional backers are divided? This is an example of how badly the party is responding to Koizumi. However, the DPJ is severely constrained by the different factions within the party because the party is an essential composite of many former parties and fundamental policy differences remain. We will analyse this issue further below.

Between December 2002 and July 2003, the DPJ was also stymied by their on-off decision to form a coalition, whether in the Diet or for the purposes of elections, with Ozawa's Liberal Party (Jiyūtō). Eventually, in late July 2003, this coalition was finally formalised. There are two reasons why this was problematic. First, the LDP/Kōmeitō/Conservative coalition was so large that even with its coalition partner, the DPJ barely had half of the combined seats of the government. But the situation is more complex than that because the DPJ, Liberal, SDPJ and JCP opposition parties no longer understood what each other stood for. As George-Mulgan has said in her assessment of the Koizumi government:

> At regular intervals fissures open up in the opposition camp when the DPJ decides to cooperate with the ruling coalition in order to 'normalise' Diet operations behind the backs of the Liberal and other opposition parties.[27]

Parties of the opposition no longer have an identifiable policy preference. This is partly because the DPJ is forced to enter into alliances with the government on policy issues which they might otherwise be against, such as the June 2003 Military Emergency Bill.

This problem leads us to the final constraint on the DPJ's ability to influence policy within the 1998 system. The party has no identifiable goal or cohesion. This is due to the factionalization of the party, and at times it has left the DPJ announcing decisions that cannot be reconciled with the beliefs of their supporters. That also has damaged party cohesion.

The factionalization and identity problems of the DPJ

So why does the DPJ lack any internal policy cohesion? This is because the party is a composite of politicians from various different party backgrounds. This affects the way in which they are financially backed (as we have seen above in the section on unions) and their basic policy stances. These different groups have in turn formed 'factions' within the DPJ. These are not as definite as those in the LDP, whose membership is published in *Kokkai Binran*, the Diet handbook. LDP factions also have their own headquarters. DPJ factions, on the other hand, are groupings that are important only within the party. A DPJ Diet member will know which 'faction' most of the other Diet members in the party belong to but, unlike the LDP, some younger members who have no prior party identification show no factional allegiance. DPJ faction membership has the potential to change.

Currently the party is considered to have six main identifiable factions:

1   Naoto Kan's faction which is based around the old Sakigake and Shaminren politicians and is moving towards economic policy emphasis over their traditional dovish stance.

2–3 Hatoyama and Tsutomu Hata's factions represent the former LDP members who are now in DPJ (although the ones who came via Shinshintō are in the Hata faction).

4   The former JSP members faction is led by Takahiro Yokomichi and, as we saw above, is heavily influenced by former public-sector unions.

5   The Yuai Kaigi faction is based around the former DSP members who are backed by former private sector unions.

6   The younger members, who have no prior party identification and are frustrated by the inability of the party to have a greater influence on events.

So what impact do these factions have on the LDP? There are two main issues here. First, they restrict any real party identity, which means that when the party is facing problems, such as in December 2002 when they were discussing a possible merger with the Liberal Party, the separate parts of the party become more important and inhibit strategic decision-making. Lack of unity may also result in the 'personality' faction-leader becoming more important than policy, though it must be recognised that factions have developed along broadly ideological lines. Second, and more importantly for the DPJ, they have no common policy, because their backgrounds are so disparate. As can be seen through the 1999 flag and national anthem legislation, the party would have split had it not allowed for free voting on the issue: 45 party members voted for the legislation, 46 against, thereby splitting the party into two identifiable opposing groups.

As long as the party is this divided, their impact on policy formation is limited because they are restricting themselves through their over-reliance on personality and former party identification, and they are not doing enough to reduce their former policy differences. It may be that their recent concentration on economic and budgetary policy over defence policy is a means of papering over these divisions, as well as being a shift in their method of 'opposition', that may lead to enhanced party unity.

Conclusion

In this chapter, we have seen that the DPJ are finding it more difficult to influence policy-making within the Japanese Diet than their predecessor, the JSP. The JSP, although they were limited by a highly formal and defined context of opposition that featured policies relating to social policy and defence, nonetheless had leverage on policy because of their experience in the Diet. For defence-related policy they also occupied the moral high ground, as their position coincided with that of the Japanese constitution. This situation resulted in a polarised and defined system of opposition-government relations.

The DPJ does not have the luxury of being in such a defined environment. Huge changes within the Japanese political system in the 1990s made the job of being the opposition party in the Diet more complicated and less predictable. The new party lacks the experience of its predecessor. The LDP has made life harder for the opposition by forming a coalition government. In particular, Koizumi's popularity made it difficult for the DPJ to define itself as being potentially 'better' than the government.

The DPJ has also made its own job of being the opposition party more complicated by being unable to overcome its own disunity. It is an amalgamation of other parties of mid-1990s origin, and these different backgrounds continue to be apparent within the party. This results in policy squabbling within the party. In 2003, however, the DPJ began to attempt to paper over these problems and create a new image for itself as a reform-minded, economically aware, capable, potential government. It stopped emphasising defence issues and opted to emphasise economic policy. Whether this was a cover for its inability to form a coherent policy on defence, or whether it was a genuine attempt to display its economic management potential, it seemed to be moving into a new era. Whilst the DPJ lost the moral high ground that the JSP used to occupy in defence policy, it was almost creating the image of having a sensible and moralistic policy on the economy in comparison to the LDP's policy of pumping money into public works.

In August 2003, the Democratic Party of Japan expanded further when they merged with Ozawa's Liberal Party. By doing this they further changed the political orientation of the party, as Ozawa is more conservative than even the right wing of the pre-August 2003 DPJ. It remains to be seen what will happen as a result of this merger. The party is larger and therefore should have more leverage. Furthermore, should the party continue to champion the economy over defence, Ozawa will be a useful member of the party. However, further party disunity could destroy the enlarged party.

At the Lower House election of November 2003, the DPJ faced yet another growth in party size tinged with potential problems which the party needs to resolve. Their growth from a pre-election 137 Lower House members (including the new Jiyūtō members) to 175 was phenomenal. However, they still face the problems described above which continue to limit their potential in the Diet to use this growth effectively. The dispatch of SDF troops to Iraq in January 2004 heightened awareness amongst the Japanese public of defence issues, and concurrently the DPJ's stance on defence. Whilst over 50 per cent of the Japanese electorate opposed the sending of troops, the DPJ have said they support the dispatch. Whether this will solidify the DPJ policy to move away from the Left's traditional stance on defence and move towards economic policy, or whether it will cause them to lose support as they contravene public opinion, remains to be seen. Nonetheless it is further evidence that the Japanese Left is in a process of redefinition of its policies which will be instrumental in shaping the future of democracy in Japan.

Notes

1 136 is the number of seats the JSP won in the 1990 Lower House election.
2 Within the Diet, the parliamentary process is carried out predominantly within groups called *kaiha*. *Kaiha* are as yet under-studied within English-language works on the Japanese political process. For explanation of the significance of the creation of *kaiha*, see Gerald L. Curtis, *The Logic of Japanese Politics*, Columbia Press, 1999, pp. 174–177.
3 This refers to what is known as *Shintō tsukuri* which coincided with the changing of the name of the party from *Nihon Shakaitō* to *Shakai Minshutō*. This brought the Japanese in line with the change of name they made to their official English translation in 1990 – changing it from Japan Socialist Party to Social Democratic Party of Japan. In this chapter, for reasons of clarity, I will consistently refer to the party as the Japan Socialist Party (JSP).
4 With the break-up of Shinshintō, the former Kōmeitō reformed itself as its own party, and Ozawa created the Liberal Party (Jiyūtō). This still left other groups who did not fall back into an identifiable party or viable number of politicians to create an effective party. Examples of such groups include those around former Prime Minister Tsutomu Hata who created the Taiyō Party (Sun Party) before merging with the enlarged DPJ and the former Democratic Socialist Party (DSP) grouping who formed a party of six people, called the Yuai Kaigi. This also joined the DPJ in April 1998.
5 Minoru Nakano, *The Policy-Making Process in Contemporary Japan*, translated by Jeremy Scott, Basingstoke: Macmillan, 1997.
6 The Cultural Cleavage is how Jōji Watanuki in Flanaghan, Scott *et al.*, *The Japanese Voter*, New Haven: Yale University Press, 1991, has described the central importance of the Japanese postwar constitution in party politics during the 1955 system.
7 Article 59 of the constitution allows for a joint conference committee of members of both houses if the Upper House does not pass a bill passed by the Lower House. If this conference agrees on the bill, it can be passed with a simple majority in both Houses. This is the method by which Prime Minister Hosokawa managed to pass the 1994 Election Reform Legislation.
8 Ray Christensen, *Ending the LDP Hegemony: Party Cooperation in Japan*, Honolulu: University of Hawaii Press, 2000, and Stephen Johnson, *Opposition Politics in Japan: Strategies under a One-party Dominant Regime*, Oxford: Routledge, 2000.
9 Nakano, op. cit., p. 54.
10 Ibid., p. 14.
11 Ibid.
12 *Asahi Shimbun*, 23 July 1999.
13 Minoru Tada, *The Japan Times*, 30 July 1999.
14 Joseph P. Keddell Jr., *The Politics of Defence in Japan*, New York: M. E. Sharpe, 1992.
15 *The Japan Times*, 10 July 2003.

16 The Conservative Party is a breakaway party from the Liberal Party. The Conservatives decided they wanted to stay in the coalition when Ozawa wanted to take the Liberals out of the coalition in April 2000, so they created a new party and remain in the coalition today.
17 Aurelia George-Mulgan, *Japan's Failed Revolution: Koizumi and the Politics of Economic Reform*, Asia-Pacific Press, 2002, p. 56.
18 See Christensen, op. cit., and Johnson, op. cit.
19 Ikuo Kume, *Disparaged Success*, Ithaca: Cornell University Press, 1998.
20 Confidential interview with the author, 5 August 2000.
21 For a good description of *jiban*, see Gerald L. Curtis, *Election Campaigning Japanese Style*, New York: Columbia University Press, 1971.
22 Steven R. Reed, 'Bu-mu no seiji. Shinyūkurabu kara Hosokawa renritsu seiken e' (A Story of Three Booms – From New Liberal Club to Hosokawa's Coalition Government), *Leviathan*, Vol. 18, special edition, Spring 1996.
23 Jack C. Doppelt and Ellen Shearer, *Nonvoters: America's No-Shows*, Thousand Oaks: Sage Publications, 1999.
24 *Asahi Shimbun*, 22 March 2003.
25 George-Mulgan, op. cit., p. 57.
26 Ibid., p. 56.
27 Ibid.

Part III

Settling accounts

Globalization, American empire and history's judgement

7 Neoliberal economic policy preferences of the 'New Left'

Home-grown or an Anglo-American import?

Leonard J. Schoppa

A political party supports the elimination of taxes on investment (such as the capital gains tax) and higher taxes on consumption. It favours aggressive deregulation aimed at introducing more competition into sheltered sectors of the economy. It supports free trade. It favors an aggressive approach to Japan's banking problems that would involve nationalizing most of the large banks, dividing them into 'good' and 'bad' parts, returning the good parts to the private sector, and disposing of the remaining assets at whatever price the market will bear. It favors the privatization of public corporations because of the role they play in propping up inefficient sectors of the economy. And it calls for the devolution of more powers to local governments, arguing that this will encourage localities to compete to make their communities attractive places to do business.

In any party system besides Japan's, a party that advocated positions like these would be considered a party of the Right. These are the policy positions of Thatcher, Reagan and Chirac. In Japan, however, they are advocated by the Democratic Party of Japan (DPJ), the leading opposition party competing with the long-ruling 'conservative' Liberal Democratic Party (LDP). Since the LDP is on the Right, the DPJ must be on the Left, right?

Once upon a time, during the extended period between 1955 and 1993 when the LDP faced the Japan Socialist Party (JSP) as its leading opponent, Left–Right labels based on economic policy made some sense. The LDP, like parties of the Right in most advanced industrialized countries, was in favor of capitalism and private ownership of the means of production. The JSP favored the nationalization of industry and redistribution of income from the rich to those in need. After the JSP imploded at the end of this period, however, Japan found itself with no party of significant size that fit the mould of a traditional party of the Left. After the Lower House election of 2000, the only parties that might have had a claim to this title, the Japan Communist Party (JCP) and Social Democratic Party of Japan (SDPJ), were left with only 20 and 19 seats, respectively. Only the DPJ, with 127 seats out of a total of 480 seats in the Lower House, was in any position to compete with the still-much-larger LDP. The Democrats were, arguably, the 'New Left' of Japan, and yet they were advocating neoliberal prescriptions endorsed by parties of the Right in most other political systems.

How did this happen? How did Japan end up without a significant traditional party of the Left after delivering 30 per cent of its votes to the socialist and communist parties for 40 years? Everywhere, the collapse of the Soviet Union and the end of the Cold War delivered body blows to parties of the Left, but in most political systems the traditional parties of the Left emerged with only slightly diluted versions of their social-democratic platforms. The Italian Communist Party helped form several governments in the 1990s after re-labelling itself the Democratic Party of the Left; the Socialists in France stuck stubbornly to a traditional left-wing agenda and still managed to win some elections; and even in Britain and Germany, where the Labour and Social Democratic Parties declared themselves 'new' and more market-oriented, party leaders advocated what they called a 'Third Way' that continued to place social justice and social welfare near the top of their agendas. Why is it that Japan doesn't even have a Third Way? And what does this tell us about the state of Japanese democracy today?

This chapter takes a close look at the economic policy prescriptions of the DPJ and the process that produced them, seeking to explain why Japan's New Left has ended up embracing such a neoliberal economic reform agenda. As suggested by the title, I consider two possible explanations for this puzzling outcome. The first is the possibility that the Democrats' turn toward neoliberalism was caused by years of trade pressure and 'markets-are-best' lecturing by foreign (especially Anglo-American) economic officials. In a previous paper, I argued that such pressure has played an important role in causing economic elites (economic officials, opinion leaders, and some politicians) to focus on neoliberal economic reforms as the primary alternative to status quo policies blamed for the nation's prolonged period of economic stagnation.[1] It could be that this 'learning' process accounts for the Democrats' embrace of neoliberal economic reforms. The second possibility is that positions taken by the Democrats reflect a more 'home-grown' process, including the incentives of the party and electoral systems. My answer is that foreign pressure alone cannot explain what is going on. We also need to look at the political incentives motivating those joining and leading the DPJ.

The transition from the Old Left to the 'New Left'

The Japan Socialist Party is the focus of many other papers in this volume, so I do not need to dwell in detail on the decades it spent as leading opposition party to the LDP. While the party was most passionate about its views on security policy, supporting unarmed neutralism and opposing constitutional revision, it long subscribed to similarly radical views on economic policy.[2] 'The Road to Socialism' (*Nihon ni okeru shakaishugi e no michi*), its core policy statement from 1964 to 1986, called for a 'peaceful revolution' and held up the Soviet model of socialism, rather than European social democracy, as its goal.[3] Socialist leaders such as Itsurō Sakisaka (1897–1984) spoke of 'the desirability of continued class struggle, a democratic dictatorship of the proletariat, as well as the need for a centralized state that would own land and large industry'.[4] On economic issues as well, therefore, the JSP was clearly a party of the Left.

While the party held tight to these views much longer than parties of the Left in most European countries, it began modifying its positions under Masashi Ishibashi in the mid-1980s and even enjoyed a brief renaissance under the leadership of Takako Doi later in that decade. The election of 1993 made it clear, however, that the JSP's best days were behind it. In that election, held after Kiichi Miyazawa's LDP cabinet collapsed over its failure to address public concerns over political corruption, the ruling party lost 52 seats, but the Socialists lost even more, falling from 136 to 70 (see Figure 1). The biggest beneficiaries of the LDP's troubles were a set of brand new centrist parties: the Japan New Party under Morihiro Hosokawa; Shinseitō under disgruntled LDP faction leader Ichirō Ozawa; and Shintō Sakigake, another LDP-breakaway group.

The election of 1993 ushered in a period of remarkable turmoil in the Japanese party system, with parties splitting, merging, and forming at a dizzying rate. For a brief period in the mid-1990s, it looked like Ozawa would succeed in welding together a disparate group of parties to make the New Frontier Party the new leading opposition party facing off against the LDP, but by the end of 1997 Ozawa's mega-party had collapsed, leaving another group of splinter parties in its wake. Shortly before the 1996 election a group of moderate Socialists joined a group of centrists from Shintō Sakigake to form the Democratic Party of Japan. This party was not big enough to contest elections in all parts of the country, but it came out of that election in a strong enough position to negotiate a merger with some of the NFP splinter groups in 1998, making the 'new' DPJ by far the largest opposition party. The party confirmed its claim to this role by winning 127 seats to the LDP's 233 in the 2000 election.

Because the Democrats were born out of this messy process, making sense of their strategies and public policy positions requires an understanding of where the disparate elements in the party came from. The original party, formed before the 1996 election, was made up of two distinct groups. The first was a group of young and urbane Diet members from Shintō Sakigake, led by Yukio Hatoyama and Naoto Kan. Sakigake had formed in 1993 around a nucleus of ten ex-LDP Diet members, including Hatoyama, who were later joined by various newcomers and party-switchers, including Kan (who came to the party from the small Social Democratic League). Relative to Ozawa and others who split from the LDP at the same time, this group of Diet members was moderate, especially on security issues, and derived much of their support from citizen activist groups. Kan, in particular, was

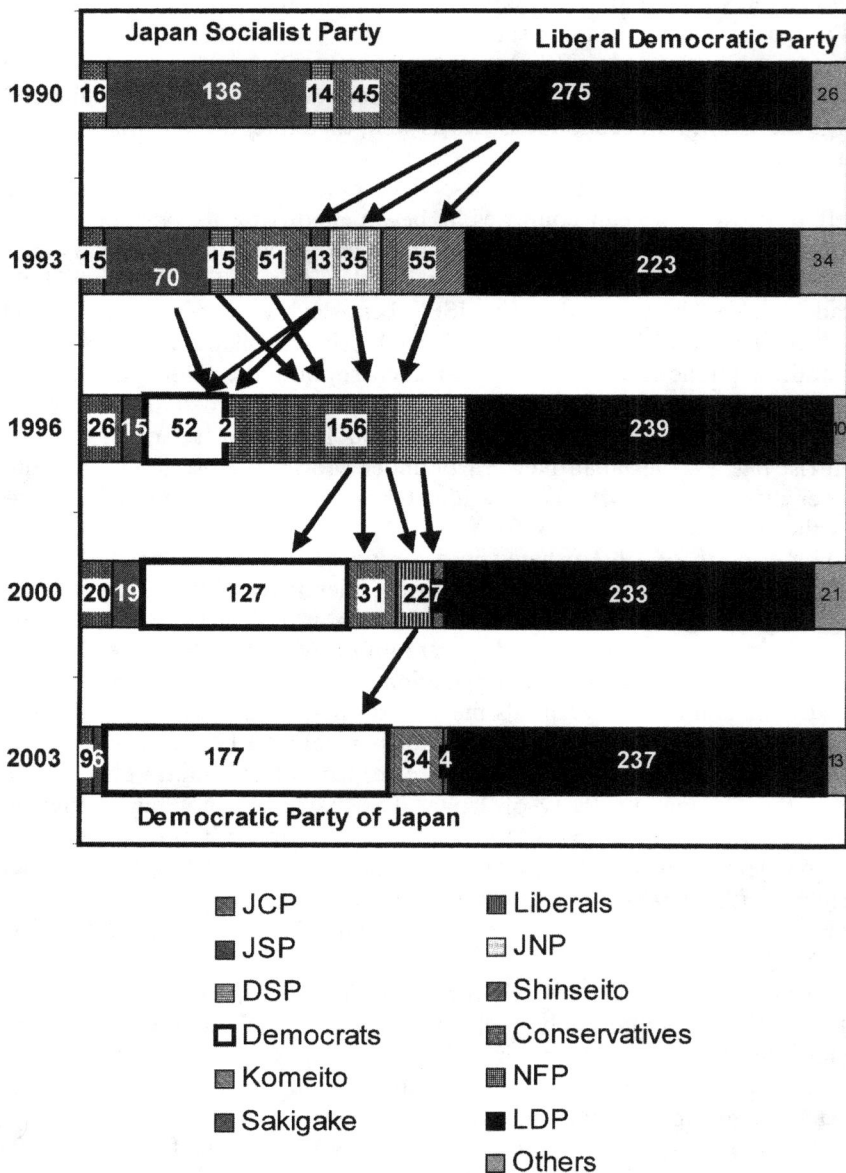

Figure 1 Lower House election results in seats, 1990–2003.

associated with this citizens' movement tradition and went on to make his name bucking Health Ministry bureaucrats who tried to cover up policy blunders that led to the spread of AIDS through blood transfusions. Hatoyama, the grandson of Ichirō Hatoyama, a former prime minister (1954–1956) and one of the founders of the LDP, brought a famous name and a large sum of money to the new party – which was known initially as the 'Hatoyama New Party'.[5]

The other component of the original DPJ was a group of moderate Socialists (the party was known by this time as the Social Democratic Party of Japan), led by former Hokkaidō governor Takahiro Yokomichi. The Socialists had entered a marriage-with-the-devil coalition with the LDP in 1994 under a deal that made their party leader Tomiichi Murayama prime minister (1994–1996) in exchange for his agreement to modify the party's long-standing opposition to the US-Japan alliance, the Self Defence Forces, and the use of the national flag and anthem in schools.[6] By 1996, the party had alienated its base with these concessions while discrediting itself with urban swing voters by joining an LDP-dominated coalition. Facing the prospect of going into the 1996 Lower House election under these conditions, Yokomichi's group of moderate Socialists bolted from the party and helped form the brand new Democratic Party of Japan, hoping it would become a moderate Left party that could compete with the LDP for the new single member district plurality seats created under electoral reforms being used for the first time that year.

Despite the desperate conditions that surrounded its birth, the DPJ formed in 1996 was surprisingly coherent. Looking back on these early years of the party, Yokomichi claims that the original DPJ had 'quite a clear vision of what it wanted in the area of economic and social policy. It wanted a much less powerful central government. It wanted a shift of powers from the central government to localities, citizens' groups, and the market.'[7] He explained that early priorities included decentralization of government functions, shifting more responsibilities to the local level, the privatization of some government activities, and social welfare reforms designed to draw on 'the vitality of the non-profit sector in the delivery of social services'. The agenda included elements that overlapped with neoliberal priorities, but its emphasis was on empowering *citizens*, not consumers or stockholders.

This original core of the DPJ was able to hold its own in the 1996 Lower House election, winning a total of 52 seats (20 seats for former socialists and 32 for centrists). That was not enough, however, to make the party the leading challenger to the LDP in the evolving party system. An opportunity to take up that role emerged only after Ozawa's New Frontier Party broke up at the end of 1997, leaving several splinter parties in its wake. DPJ co-leaders Hatoyama and Kan negotiated with leaders of these groups and relaunched the 'new' DPJ in 1998 with substantial additions that brought its seat totals in the Lower House to 95. The additions significantly changed the composition of the party, bringing in two more groups of politicians, some of them senior, and many of them with policy views quite different from those of the DPJ founders.

The first group was composed of relatively senior and conservative Diet members, led by former prime minister Tsutomu Hata, who had travelled a tortured path since 1993. Most had left the LDP that year with Ozawa, joining his Shinseitō and then following him into the NFP. Frustrated with Ozawa's personality and leadership style, however, a group of veteran politicians deserted him in late 1996 when they formed the Taiyōtō, which eventually combined with a larger group who left Ozawa when the NFP split in late 1997 to form a new party called Minseitō. Minseitō then merged with the Democrats in 1998. A measure of party system instability at the time was a campaign poster I saw in the Diet office of Tetsundo Iwakuni on a visit there in 2000. Iwakuni had been elected for the first time in 1996 as a member of Ozawa's NFP. After the NFP broke up, he could not leave up a campaign poster showing that party affiliation, so he placed a sticker over it showing his new party. By the time I saw it in 2000, the poster had four layers of stickers on it. Other new members of the DPJ who travelled similar routes had changed parties six times since 1993!

What distinguished this Minseitō group from the original DPJ were their more conservative views on security policy and economics. Some were strong supporters of constitutional revision and a larger security role for Japan. As we will see below, others were strongly committed to neoliberal economic reforms. Because of their seniority and willingness to leave the party if they did not get their way (these threats were quite credible since they had left so many already), they carried a great deal of weight in the 'new' DPJ.

The final faction joining the DPJ also came out of the NFP but was associated with the old Democratic Socialist Party (DSP) – the party long supported by private sector unions. Like Hata and his associates, the DSP had thrown their lot in with Ozawa, but after the NFP broke up they formed a separate group known as Shintō Yūai. Like the Minseitō group, these politicians tended to be more conservative on security issues than the original core of the DPJ. Their views on economics were mixed, favouring market forces in principle but frequently opposing liberalization measures that threatened the job security of their union member supporters.

Economic policy views of the Democrats

Not surprisingly given the diverse origins of the four DPJ factions, the party has not had an easy time coming to a consensus on its policy views. It has been plagued from the beginning, in particular, by public disagreements over the issue of constitutional revision and the deployment of Japanese troops overseas. In 2000, after party leader Hatoyama suggested the party might support constitutional revisions to make it clear that Japanese personnel could participate in United Nations 'peace-enforcement' activities, the leader of the ex-Socialist faction, Yokomichi, threatened to push for Hatoyama's resignation as party leader if he did not stop making such statements.[8] In the fall of 2001, when party leader Hatoyama backed Prime Minister Koizumi's plan to authorize the deployment of Japanese naval forces to the Indian Ocean, Yokomichi went even further. He and 27 DPJ compatriots voted against the Anti-Terrorism Law, abstained, or absented themselves from the vote, in open defiance of party discipline.[9] Such battles have contributed to the DPJ's image as a divided party, a reputation that has cost it votes at election time.

Although DPJ internal battles over economic issues have not been so heated, the party has developed a reputation for being divided over these issues as well. Steven Vogel, for example, points to the different support bases of the DPJ factions and argues that 'the new Democratic Party is just as riddled with internal contradictions as the [New Frontier Party], and even more ambivalent about deregulation'.[10] Citing DPJ leader Naoto Kan's assertion that his party needs to become 'the party of Thatcher and Blair', Gerald Curtis points out the contradictions inherent in such an undertaking.[11] I do not deny that such divisions exist, and I discuss some of them below. What I find more striking than the divisions, however, is the degree to which the party has staked out official party positions that are to the neoliberal *Right* of the LDP on a whole host of economic issues. That ex-Socialists sometimes object to these positions is not surprising. What is surprising is the degree to which they have ultimately gone along with a party strategy that has taken them not just closer to the LDP position (as is the case on security issues) but *to the other side* of the LDP on these economic issues.

The party has been most unified in its support for the neoliberal position on public spending. The DPJ opposes 'wasteful public spending' and favors measures to restore fiscal balance. Prior to the 2001 Upper House elections, for example, the party made 'reform of public finances' one of its top priorities in its manifesto, pledging to cut public works spending by 30 per cent and restore the budget to primary balance (no new borrowing beyond that needed to refinance old debt) in five years. It even went so far as to pledge to do away with the government tradition of adopting supplemental budgets whenever the economy showed signs of slowing. The DPJ would reserve such budgets, it said, for emergencies like natural disasters and financial crises.[12] The party had run on a similar promise prior to the 2000 Lower House election, when it pledged a 20 per cent reduction in public works and a reduction in the public debt to GDP ratio from 123 per cent to 60 per cent over the next decade.[13]

Needless to say, this policy is well to the right of the usual position of parties of the Left on fiscal policy. Rather than advocating the use of fiscal policy as a tool of Keynesian demand management, the DPJ has consistently argued that this tool needs to be discarded. Instead, it has called for the government to be put on strict timetables for public works spending cuts and debt reduction that virtually guarantee fiscal policy will exacerbate recessions and increase unemployment.

Closely related to the party's position on fiscal balance has been its support for a smaller central government, with its calls for the privatization of public corporations and decentralization of government functions. Let us look at each of these positions in turn. In contrast to the mainstream of the LDP, which has defended public corporations and the fiscal investment and loan plan (FILP) that has channelled postal savings, postal life insurance, and public pension money to these politically-connected institutions, the DPJ has campaigned for a clean up of this system since its founding. It has argued for transparency in the accounting systems used by the public corporations to make it clear exactly how large the annual public subsidies are, and in its party manifesto issued before the 2001 Upper House elections called for the government to sell its remaining shares in NTT along with its stakes in public and special corporations.[14] The following line from this manifesto is particularly striking: 'The DPJ will introduce appropriate private sector methodology and know-how to the public sector, to improve public sector efficiency and transparency, as was done successfully in the UK.' Margaret Thatcher's policies of the 1980s appear to be the model the DPJ has in mind!

Even where the public sector remains involved in providing services, the DPJ has argued, a much larger share of power should be devolved to regional and local levels of government. As discussed above, this emphasis on decentralization began with the original core of the party in 1996. Even Socialists like Yokomichi, who had experience dealing with heavy-handed central bureaucrats when he was governor of Hokkaido, were enthusiastic proponents of devolving power to the local level. By 2001, with the addition of the Minseitō and Shintō Yūai contingents to the party, views on this issue had coalesced to the point where the DPJ placed decentralization at the very top of its policy agenda. 'The DPJ believes that local services are best provided locally', the party manifesto reads. 'Issues that cannot be handled by individual prefectures are best handled at the regional level. Accordingly, a lean and more flexible central government should deal only with issues affecting Japan as a whole, such as diplomacy, defense, and monetary policy.'[15]

While decentralization advocated in these terms sounds admirably democratic, elaboration on the motives for this policy by Akira Nagatsuma, a newly elected DPJ member who was formerly a business journalist, makes it clear how it is connected to the neoliberal reform agenda:

> One of the party's top priorities is decentralization by reorganizing government into eleven states. This was our number one promise in the last election. These units should have taxing power and the power to decide regulations. The central government would be radically shrunk. It would set a 'civil minimum' (doing some redistribution across regions and setting up a safety net below which no one would be allowed to fall), but the rest would be up to the states. If one of them wanted to lower wages, reduce regulations, and lower taxes to attract business, it could. It could compete with China for manufacturing business. The problem in Japan is that everything is made uniform across prefectures, so local areas cannot develop the means to compete and attract jobs and industry.[16]

Decentralization, Nagatsuma explains, will create structural incentives that encourage localities to cut taxes, lower wages, and relax regulations to attract jobs and business. It will no longer be necessary to fight these issues out at the national level, where interest groups and bureaucrats block moves to remove regulations. By devolving responsibility to local governments, reformers will be able to rely on regulatory competition between localities – described by public choice scholars as 'market-preserving federalism' – to accelerate the pace of liberalization.

If the DPJ's advocacy of small government is somewhat surprising in view of positions traditionally taken by parties of the Left, the positions the DPJ has taken on tax policy make one wonder if the world has turned upside down. Tax policy was one area of economic policy where the old Socialists actually had an impact. Throughout the period of LDP dominance, they defended the progressive structure of the income tax system tooth and nail. Taxes on capital were preferred to taxes on labour, and they fought pitched battles against LDP efforts to introduce the regressive consumption tax. Given this history, the positions the DPJ has taken on tax policy are positively baffling.

Prior to the Lower House election in 2000, DPJ leader Hatoyama made the party's plan to lower the minimum threshold above which residents are required to pay income tax one of its top priorities. The Japanese income tax system at the time was quite progressive by international standards because of the high level of income one needed to earn before one was required to pay the tax. Hatoyama proposed lowering the threshold as a way of broadening the tax base to produce revenue he argued was needed to shrink the government's massive fiscal deficit. His advocacy of this policy meant, however, that the party was proposing to raise the bulk of this new revenue from moderate-income citizens. In response, Shizuka Kamei, the chair of the LDP Policy Affairs Research Council, pointed out the regressive character of the proposal and claimed '[the LDP] will never hike taxes, targeting the socially weak alone'.[17] Which of these parties is the party of the Left?

The party was more divided during the most recent debate over tax reform, begun after LDP Prime Minister Koizumi announced that this would be a priority of his administration. Because of these divisions, it failed to produce a coherent alternative package of reforms, but it nevertheless was able to come to an agreement on a set of tax cut proposals that were designed in a way that would have delivered most of their benefits to better-off segments of the Japanese citizenry. It proposed to eliminate the capital gains tax on stock dealings for a limited period of time and proposed to make interest payments on mortgage and educational loans deductible from income for the purposes of calculating income tax.[18]

Some of the tax reform plans backed by segments of the DPJ were even more regressive. The plan authored by Iwakuni called for a series of reductions in taxes collected primarily from wealthy citizens (the complete elimination of the capital gains tax; a reduction in the gift tax to 20 per cent for a period of two years; and a reduction in the land-holding tax), to be offset by a gradual *increase* in the consumption tax up to the level of 10 per cent. Iwakuni's plan was backed by 44 DPJ members of the Lower House, including Yokomichi and several other ex-Socialists.[19]

On most of the economic policy issues discussed up to this point, the DPJ has been able to stake out positions without actually having to put them into practice. It has not yet participated in any ruling coalition or cabinet, and sceptics will no doubt question whether the party would be able to retain unified party support for its 'tough' neoliberal positions were it to be faced with the prospect of actually implementing policies opposed by redundant workers and firms threatened with bankruptcy. Therefore the DPJ's policy on how to deal with the Japanese banking crisis is probably the best test of where the party stands on economic issues, for this is one area where it actually helped decide government policy.

The highpoint in the DPJ's participation in economic policymaking came shortly after the party won an unexpectedly large victory in the 1998 Upper House elections. Party leader Naoto Kan was riding on a wave of popular support after this impressive showing, and he took the lead in coordinating opinions of a block of opposition parties (including Kōmeitō and Ozawa's Liberal Party) that held the votes needed to block passage of legislation in the Upper House. While the DPJ was not invited to join the LDP-only cabinet that was in place at the time, the party's control of votes in the Upper House and the LDP's need to pass legislation of some kind to deal with the impending collapse of the Long-Term Credit Bank gave Kan and the DPJ more policymaking power than they had ever enjoyed – or have enjoyed since.

The party used its power to block legislation the LDP had proposed to deal with the weak condition of the Long-Term Credit Bank (LTCB) and other large financial institutions. Convinced that a collapse of mega-banks like these could be avoided, the LDP was proposing that the government continue propping up weak institutions by helping to arrange for mergers with stronger institutions – rewarding banks willing to take on weak partners with capital injections financed with public funds. Legislators in the DPJ were convinced the LTCB was too big and too broke to be dealt with in this fashion, and they worried that with many other mega-banks in similar straits, a collapse of the LTCB could trigger a system-wide financial crisis with implications for global markets.[20]

With these concerns in mind, they drafted an alternative non-cabinet bill that was designed to recapitalize the Japanese financial system with a massive sum of public money while imposing strict conditions on banks receiving this capital to assure that the problems in Japan's financial system would not reemerge at a later date. Strict audits were to be conducted to determine banks' actual capitalization levels after accounting for bad loans. Those institutions determined to have zero or negative capitalization levels were to be turned over to a Japanese equivalent of the American Resolution and Trust Corporation (RTC) – the body created to clean up the Savings and

Loans mess – which would dispose of bad loan assets and set up 'bridge banks' with the remaining assets that would be sold off to the highest bidder. Those banks in danger of failing, with low but positive capitalization levels, were to be forced to accept involuntary injections of capital through forced sales of bank shares to the government – 'temporary nationalization'. At that point, the government would again strip out the banks' bad loans before putting the now-healthy institution back on the market.[21]

DPJ leader Kan stood firm in his negotiations with the LDP and forced Prime Minister Obuchi to accept most of the terms of this bill, including agreement that the LTCB would be dealt with as a 'failed bank' with its assets sold off to another bank.[22] This package of legislation, known as the Financial Revitalization Law, was passed with DPJ support on 2 October 1998. In a last-minute manoeuvre, however, Obuchi was able to undercut much of the purpose of the DPJ-backed legislation by passing a second set of laws two weeks later – with the support of Ozawa's Liberal Party and Kōmeitō who abandoned the opposition coalition Kan had created to make a deal with the LDP that would eventually bring both of them into the cabinet. Under this Early Strengthening Law, weak banks that had not fallen below key capitalization thresholds were allowed to opt for 'voluntary recapitalization', making available public subsidies without the strict conditions of the DPJ-backed legislation. A key concession by the DPJ on its own law, allowing banks to avoid strict audits, combined with the provisions of the LDP's second set of bills to allow banks to take public money without strict conditions – guaranteeing that the banking problems would resurface at a later date.[23]

What is interesting about the position the DPJ took on banking legislation when it actually held the power to make policy is that it stuck to its guns and supported the neoliberal 'hard landing' approach to resolving the nation's financial problems. It was willing to force banks to write off bad loans even though it was clear this policy would lead to the bankruptcy of many firms and layoffs of workers. Alone among the major political parties, it opposed legislation designed to extend public money to banks in a way that would allow them to continue propping up struggling borrowers.

In the period since its brush with power, the DPJ has continued to call for this neoliberal solution to the nation's banking problems. In its 'Final Plan for Financial Reconstruction', issued in January 2002 after it became apparent the earlier rounds of recapitalization had not solved Japan's banking system troubles, the DPJ again calls for forced injections of public funds into weak banks to achieve temporary nationalization. It further proposes that 'big companies requiring monitoring and worse' be turned over to the Resolution and Collection Company (RCC), with the assets of the weakest of these firms sold off within a year.[24] These positions continue to put the DPJ to the neoliberal right of the LDP mainstream on banking reform, and probably to the right of Koizumi given his unwillingness to follow through on his rhetoric in this area.

While the party was united in 1998 when it pushed for a hard-landing approach to the nation's banking problems, the intervening years have revealed enough additional information about the likely impact of these policies to raise opposition within the party. The compromises the DPJ has had to make to accommodate these views can be seen in the provisions of the party's 'Final Plan' dealing with bad loans to small and medium-sized businesses. The RCC should distinguish between struggling large firms and struggling small ones, the DPJ advises, giving the smaller firms 'the opportunity for self-reconstruction, holding off on direct write-offs'.[25] Interviews with a number of DPJ Diet members in December 2002 confirmed that the party is split over how to deal with the nation's banking problems.

However, even those who oppose the hard-landing solution (such as Yokomichi and Iwakuni) support market-based solutions. The Iwakuni plan mentioned above calls for the banking problem to be dealt with through a system of convertible bonds designed to create a 'stockholder democracy'. They suggest that instead of recapitalizing banks with tax money and forcing them to write off bad loans immediately, the government should give banks cash in exchange for half of their holdings of stock (no picking and choosing, the government would take half of everything, at market prices). It would then raise this cash by turning around and selling principal-guaranteed convertible bonds to the public, including foreign investors. Five years later, investors could exchange these bonds for their face value, plus 1 per cent annual interest, or they could accept the underlying stock. The plan appeals to those worried about the hard-landing approach because it would give banks and firms five years to work things out, but its effectiveness rests on the hope that the bond sales would create a nascent 'stockholder democracy' that would demand that the banks and firms use this time to fix their problems: write off bad loans when this is necessary, forgive them when not.[26]

That even this last plan, put forward by the wing of the DPJ opposed to a hard landing approach to banks, puts its faith in 'stockholder democracy' and relies on convertible bonds to raise funds from investors is a measure of how far the Left has come since the socialist days. When placed alongside the DPJ plans for tax reform, fiscal reconstruction, decentralization, and privatization of public corporations, the party's plans for the banking system reveal the degree to which neoliberal ideas have penetrated this 'New Left' party's thinking about how to fix Japan's economic problems. Let us now consider the question of why this perplexing turn of events has come about.

Home-grown or an Anglo-American import?

On first glance, the overlap between DPJ positions on economic issues and the positions taken by American economic officials over many years of bilateral economic discussions suggests that there is a cause and effect relationship between the two. The DPJ's 1998 proposals for addressing the nation's banking problems, for example, echoed the suggestions of US Deputy

Treasury Secretary Larry Summers, who in May and June of that year had urged Japan not to prop up its weak banks. These proposals were also applauded, and abetted, by foreign financial firms in Tokyo.[27] There is similar overlap between foreign demands and DPJ positions favouring selling the state's remaining shares in NTT and privatizing other public corporations. A few DPJ positions not discussed above, including the party's support for 'competition in the area of public utilities in order to rectify the high-cost structure . . . and promoting more penetration of foreign capital into the Japanese market', are virtually verbatim repetitions of advice Japan has received from the OECD and US government officials.[28]

Overlap of this kind, however, does not necessarily mean foreign demands are the direct cause of the DPJ's neoliberalism. One reason to be sceptical comes from repeated party statements emphasizing that the DPJ does not want to bring 'American-style capitalism' to Japan. In a 2002 *Ronza* article, for example, four young DPJ members begin an article in which they advocate aggressive bank reform and tax cuts of the types summarized above with the following statement:

> The problems our nation faces today cannot be solved with a simple-minded notion of a 'small state'. We do not stand in favor of market fundamentalism, which says the state should do absolutely nothing. President Bush came to Japan and addressed the Diet by saying 'competition is fundamental', but this American-style market fundamentalism is exactly what we feel needs to be rethought.[29]

The policies they support in the article are mostly consistent with Anglo-American neoliberalism, but the DPJ politicians nevertheless are repelled by the example of US capitalism and do not seem to have been attracted to these policies by their respect for George Bush's advice.

I heard similar comments from DPJ politicians I interviewed, often without any prompting from me. Akira Nagatsuma, for example, brought up the subject of American pressure in his very first comments after I began asking him about his economic policy preferences. He emphasized that Japan needed to 'break from its dependence on American pressure' and 'needed to think for itself, decide for itself'.[30] Other Diet members pointed out that it was American pressure that got Japan in the fiscal mess it was now in. In 1998 when Japan's financial crisis threatened to disrupt the global economy, the United States had urged Japan to use fiscal policy to stimulate its economy. The result was an orgy of public works spending by the LDP that put Japan deeper into debt without fixing its economic problems.

These last comments point to a crucial area in which the DPJ's policy preferences do *not* overlap with the demands they have been facing from the United States, the IMF, and foreign capital. Whereas the DPJ has advocated spending cuts, debt-reduction targets, and increased taxes on income and consumption in order to reconstruct Japan's public finances, foreign pressure has consistently called on Japan to adopt stimulative fiscal policy, especially during its recent period of prolonged economic stagnation. Even the monetarist Reagan and Bush administrations have been surprisingly Keynesian when it comes to Japan's fiscal policy, urging tax cuts and public works spending increases on a regular basis since 1984. The fiscal conservatism of the DPJ, certainly, cannot have been caused by American pressure since the United States has been urging the opposite.

If we are to identify the roots of the New Left's neoliberalism, therefore, we need also to consider the domestic political context in which the DPJ has had to operate. The most fundamental feature of that context, which has shaped the way the DPJ was born and every move it has taken since, has been the dominance of the Liberal Democratic Party. The LDP was there first. It had superior numbers of incumbents, access to the resources that flow to the ruling party, and connections to many organized constituencies. The party had also staked out an established position in 'policy space', the terrain defined by the issues voters and politicians care about. The DPJ could not just move in and set up shop wherever it wanted. It had to work around this 800-pound gorilla.

Throughout the period of the '1955 Party System' (1955–1993), the policy space in which parties staked out positions was defined by the dominant cleavage over security policy. It was this issue that voters cared most about, and it was this one that defined the 'Left-Right' conflict between the Old Left and the LDP. Voters and politicians cared about economic issues as well, but over time the established parties of the Left and Right all came to support Japanese-style capitalism, with its extensive *informal* system of social protection. This system channelled public works spending to construction firms, which made sure contractors across the country stayed in business and provided jobs in job-poor rural areas. It propped up farm incomes through subsidies and protectionism. It upheld a lifetime employment system that protected a large proportion of workers, including many blue-collar workers, from the risk of layoffs. And it used regulations to manage supply and demand in industries ranging from retail to finance to provide firms with the support they needed to live up to their employment commitments and keep paying their small-business suppliers. Since this system was built under LDP rule, the party naturally supported it strongly. But the Old Left supported it too since it provided unionized workers with a fair measure of job protection and helped the small farmer and the small businessman. No party campaigned on a plan to dismantle this system.

This consensus on economic policy was disrupted by the collapse of the bubble, the banking crisis, and the government's deteriorating finances. Suddenly there was room to challenge the LDP on economic policy, and policy space was transformed into a two-dimensional arena. In this new policy space, the LDP maintained its position in support of Japanese-style capitalism, with its extensive system of informal social protection. Although few said it at the time, over the course of the decade more and more Japanese have come to identify the LDP as 'the Communist Party of Japan' because of its support for the weak sectors of the economy.[31] Since the dominant party had occupied this position in the debate, parties that wanted to take on the LDP had to stake out alternative positions from which to challenge it.

At this point the Japan Socialist Party was still the largest opposition party, and if it had been nimble enough, it might have been able to manoeuvre in such a way as to benefit from this opportunity. It could have defined the alternative to the LDP's Japanese-style capitalism as Swedish-style liberal social-democracy, with its *formal* system of social welfare programmes cushioning the impact of market forces that are allowed to operate much more freely than in Japan. Advocating this position would have required the JSP to support market-orientated liberalization (including labour market reform) along with a major expansion of social insurance programmes. Unfortunately, the JSP was not nimble enough to pull this off. It remained too obsessed with the security policy debate and too wedded to unions (that preferred lifetime employment to Swedish active labour market policies) to consider supporting this kind of programme. In 1992, as the economy began its long slide into stagnation, JSP legislators were taking a final stand against the LDP's *security* policy, cow-walking in futile protest against Miyazawa's plan to authorize sending Japanese personnel on United Nations peacekeeping missions.

The JSP's failure to redefine the economic policy debate in this way left the door open for new parties to step into the vacuum. Searching for a way to critique the LDP's economic policy, they naturally settled on the neoliberal line of argument, which had already established a track record in Japan under the patronage of LDP politicians who attempted to use it to advance their political careers. The ideology got its first tryout in the 1980s under Prime Minister Nakasone, who was impressed by the examples of Reagan and Thatcher and saw political opportunities in bringing this programme to Japan. Later in that decade, Ichirō Ozawa, then LDP Secretary General, again drew on this ideology when he wrote his 'Blueprint for a New Japan'. Both Nakasone and Ozawa were direct targets of many lectures by US economic negotiators, who counselled them on the virtues of competition and market forces. While this experience may have helped put neoliberal ideas in front of them, their decision to adopt this framework as a basis for critiquing the established political economy cannot be understood without appreciating how it fit into their political calculus. Both hoped to use it to appeal to urban salaried workers, the New Middle Mass.[32]

By the time Sakigake, the Japan New Party, and later the Democrats set out to locate their own challenge to the LDP, therefore, the terrain had already been mapped and slogans tried out. With the LDP having resisted Nakasone's and Ozawa's attempts to shift the party's base, the party was more dependent than ever on its core constituencies – the farmers, the construction industry, and small businesses. Their example suggested that political opportunity lay in appealing to urban salaried votes with promises to cut pork barrel spending, clean up government finances, and make the economy

more efficient. Even the original core of the Democrats, the moderate socialists and Sakigake citizens' activists, were drawn into challenging the LDP
with a promise to shift power from the central government to localities, citizens' groups, and the market. Once they did so, they attracted a host of eager
young politicians who believed in this rhetoric and sought to make the party
platform much more specific (see Figure 2 below).

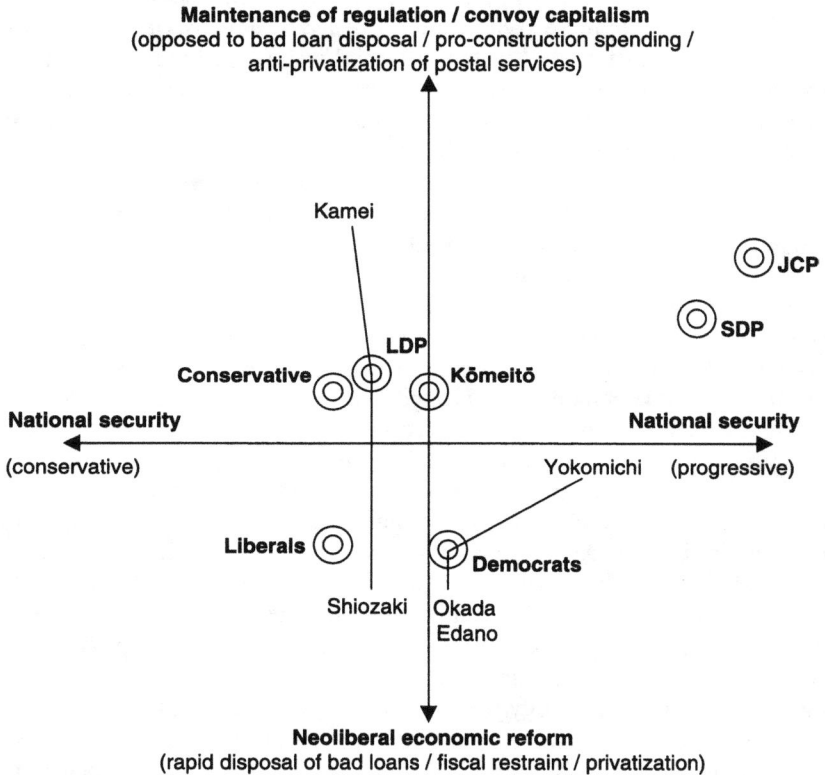

Method: Security policy positions are based on chart in Ikuo Kabashima, 'An Ideological
Survey of Japan's National Legislators', *Japan Echo*, August 1999, p. 14. Positions on
neoliberal reform for parties based on surveys of Diet members reported in Ikuo
Kabashima Zemi (ed.) *Gendai nihon no seijika zo, Vol 1*, Tokyo: Bokutakusha, 2000; and
Junko Kato and Michael Laver, 'Research Note: Party Policy and Cabinet Portfolios in
Japan, 1996', *Party Politics*, 4:2, 1998, 253-260, along with recent policy positions taken by
parties and individual politicians, some of them discussed in this paper.

Figure 2 Two-dimensional positioning of parties and key politicians (2003).

The figure above shows how the LDP and DPJ have yet to develop unified
positions on economic issues. The core of each party, however, has aligned on
opposite sides of the 'economic reform' dimension, with the LDP (despite

Koizumi) continuing to delay banking reform, fiscal reconstruction, and privatization of the postal finance system. Meanwhile, the DPJ has settled (despite Yokomichi) on the neoliberal side of this divide. While the party system continues to evolve and may see more splits and mergers before this paper comes out in print, the processes set in motion by the decision of the DPJ to locate on the neoliberal side of the LDP is now self-reinforcing, virtually guaranteeing that the main party competing with the LDP for the foreseeable future will be attacking it from its right on economic issues.

The self-reinforcing process can be seen at work, first, in the DPJ's response to Koizumi's attempt to steal much of the DPJ's economic reform platform. When Koizumi upset the political world by openly campaigning against his own party in 2001, adopting many of the DPJ's reform proposals, the DPJ moved *further* in the neoliberal direction rather than attempting to stake out a new (social democratic?) position from which to challenge Koizumi. It went from calling for a 20 per cent reduction in public works to calling for a 30 per cent reduction. It attempted to put forward a tax reform plan that was more pro-business than Koizumi's. As Koizumi has compromised on many of his reform promises, the DPJ has called him on it, ridiculing him for his abandonment of his promise to limit deficit spending and criticizing his banking policies for being too lenient on banks and debtors. Once a new party stakes out a direction from which to challenge the established dominant party, it cannot easily change strategies.

Second, the self-reinforcing process can be seen in the way the DPJ has grown since it was founded. Having staked out a position as the neoliberal party relative to the LDP, it began attracting neoliberal candidates to run for open seats. This process began in 1996 when the original DPJ recruited a large class of new young Diet members to run for open seats and continued when the 'new' DPJ recruited another large class to run in the 2000 election. By 2001, there were a total of 66 DPJ Diet members in the Lower House (out of a total of 125) who had not run under any of the four parties that made up the original party union. This large contingent of newcomers, with few attachments to the founding parties, dwarfed all of these groups. By 2001, there were just 20 DPJ members of the Lower House who had originally been members of the Socialist Party, and just 14 who had run under the Sakigake banner. (See Table 1 for a complete list of members and groups.) When the DPJ held its leadership contest in 2002, the leader of the ex-Socialists, Yokomichi, came in fourth on the first ballot and was outpolled by Yoshihiko Noda, who came in third after stepping forward to represent the large bloc of newcomers.[33]

What is interesting about the new faces recruited by the DPJ is how different they are from the types of individuals recruited by the Old Left parties. Six of them were former bureaucrats of the elite ministries, with two each from Finance, Foreign Affairs, and Trade and Industry. Three were bankers with the most elite Tokyo financial firms (see Table 2). Because of their elite backgrounds and rich experience, these new members were given policy influence way beyond their level of seniority. These were the men the party turned to in

134   *Leonard J. Schoppa*

Table 1 Democratic Party of Japan membership in the Lower House (total of 126 as of November 2001)

Former Social Democrats
(20 members)
Kanju Satō (10 temrs)
Ichirō Hino (8)
Takahiro Yokomichi (7)
Chūji Itō (5)
Hidenori Sasaki (4)
Yoshino Hachiro (4)
Akihiro Ōhata (4)
Ritsuo Hosokawa (4)
Taneaki Tanami (4)
Hirotaka Akamatsu (4)
Ryū Matsumoto (4)
Kenji Nakazawa (4)
Mamoru Kobayashi (4)
Tsutomu Yamamoto (4)
Masanori Gotō (4)
Motohisa Ikeda (3)
Yoshito Sengoku (3)
Miyoko Hida (UH-1, LH-2)
Nobutaka Tsutsui (2)
Yutaka Kuwabara (2)

Former Minseitō
(20 members)
Kōzō Watanabe (11 terms)*
Tsutomu Hata (11)
Hajime Ishii (10)
Michihiro Kano (9)
Hiroshi Kumagai (6)
Takao Satō (5)
Katsuya Okada (4)
Ikuo Horigome (4)
Issei Koga (4)
Kiyoshi Ueda (3)
Shigefumi Matsuzawa (3)
Kōichi Yoshida (3)
Osamu Fujimura (3)
Shinji Tarutoko (3)
Eiji Nagai (3)
Masaru Nakagawa (2)
Kimiaki Matsuzaki (2)
Tetsundo Iwakuni (2)
Kazuhiro Haraguchi (2)
Ban Kugimiya (UH-1, LH-1)

Former Sakigake
(14 members)
Naoto Kan (7 terms)
Yukio Hatoyama (5)
Tadamasa Kodaira (4)
Kenichirō Satō (4)
Kōichirō Genba (3)
Yukio Edano (3)
Kō Tanaka (3)
Sakihito Ozawa (3)
Kōki Ishii (3)
Seiji Maehara (3)
Sei'ichi Kaneta (3)
Satoshi Arai (2)
Fumihiko Igarashi (2)
Hiroshi Kawauchi (2)

Former Shintō Yūai
(10 members)
Kansei Nakano (9)
Kazuya Tamaki (7)
Eisei Itō (6)
Tatsuo Kawabata (5)
Keishū Tanaka (4)
Yoshiaki Takaki (4)
Yasusuke Konta (2)
Masamitsu Jōjima (2)
Satoshi Shima (2)
Setsuya Kagita (2)

Other (62 members)
Masamitsu Ōishi (5)
Ryūichi Doi (4)
Kenji Kitabashi (4)
Banri Kaieda (3)
Takashi Kawamura (3)
Yoshihiko Noda (2)
Yukio Ubukata (2)
Hiroyuki Nagahama (2)
Yoshikatsu Nakayama (2)
Yoshinori Suematsu (2)

Akira Nagatsuma (1)
Kōichi Katō (1)
Ikuo Yamahana (1)
Yukihiko Akutsu (1)
Shigeyuki Gotō (1)
Gōshi Hosono (1)
Yasutomo Suzuki (1)
Yoshio Maki (1)
Yūkichi Maeda (1)
Kenji Kobayashi (1)

Shū Watanabe (2)
Motohisa Furukawa (2)
Shōichi Kondō (2)
Hirofumi Hirano (2)
Jun Hayama (2)
Muneaki Samejima (2)
Eiko Ishige (2)
Ken Okuda (2)
Seishū Makino (2)
Satoru Ienishi (2)
Azuma Konno (1)
Sayuki Kamata (1)
Hiroko Mizushima (1)
Kōichi Takemasa (1)
Atsushi Ōshima (1)
Atsushi Kinoshita (1)
Hisayasu Nagata (1)
Hisako Ōishi (1)
Yōichirō Esaki (1)
Jin Matsubara (1)
Yoshio Tezuka (1)

Hisako Ōtani (1)
Takeaki Matsumoto (1)
Hideo Hiraoka (1)
Yorihisa Matsuno (1)
Kakio Mitsui (1)
Zenjirō Kaneko (1)
Toshiaki Koizumi (1)
Hitoshi Gotō (1)
Akira Ōide (1)
Nobuhiko Sutō (1)
Kazuo Inoue (1)
Hirosato Nakatsugawa (1)
Eriko Yamatani (1)
Yutaka Banno (1)
Takeshi Yamamura (1)
Shōgo Tsugawa (1)
Kazunori Yamanoi (1)
Tetsuji Nakamura (1)
Osamu Yamauchi (1)
Toshimasa Yamada (1)
Kinya Narasaki (1)

---

* Watanabe Kōzō was nominally independent because he resigned from the party to serve in the Diet leadership
Source: Compiled by author based on data in Kokusei Jōhō Sentaa, *Shitte okitai kokkai giin no ugoki*, 2001. Thanks also for assistance from Diet Librarian Tarō Kawashima.

1998 when it needed to draft its own legislation to deal with the banking crisis, a team that included first-term member Furukawa, fresh from the Ministry of Finance. They were the ones who staffed the committees that drew up the party's new 'Final Plan' for the banking system, its Economic Revitalization Plan, and its New Strategy for Industrial Revitalization. Katsuya Okada, a former Trade and Industry official with just four terms in office, took over as Secretary General of the party in 2002 and was selected party leader in 2004.

Table 2 Recently elected DPJ members coming from financial sector and elite ministries

	Background
Motohisa Furukawa (2)	Ministry of Finance
Tetsundo Iwakuni (3)	Merrill Lynch (VP)
Takeaki Matsumoto (1)	Industrial Bank of Japan
Hisayasu Nagata (1)	Ministry of Finance
Akira Nagatsuma (1)	Nikkei Business
Katsuya Okada (4)	Ministry of International Trade and Industry
Sakihito Ozawa (3)	Bank of Tokyo
Yoshinori Suematsu (2)	Ministry of Foreign Affairs
Toshimasa Yamada (1)	Ministry of International Trade and Industry
Tsuyoshi Yamaguchi (1)	Ministry of Foreign Affairs

Source: Compiled by author using *japanesepoliticians.com* database (accessed 14 May 2003).

Iwakuni, a former Vice-President of Merrill Lynch, was made party vice-president after just two terms in office. Sakihito Ozawa, a three-term Diet member who was once with the Bank of Tokyo, was made shadow minister for Trade and Industry in 2002.

Another large contingent of newcomers came to the DPJ from the Matsushita Seikei Juku, a school for young people aspiring to enter politics that indoctrinates its graduates with views quite different from those of politicians who were attracted to the parties of the Old Left. The school was established by Kōnosuke Matsushita, the founder of Matsushita Electric, who is reported to have set up this operation in hopes of training a new generation of politicians who would bring business values and management training to government. *Asahi Shimbun* reporter Shinichi Yamada describes Matsushita graduates as advocates of smaller government, deregulation, and competition in an open market. They are committed to bolstering the power of politicians over the bureaucrats who have traditionally dominated the policymaking process in Japan.[34] As Table 3 shows, there were 11 Matsushita graduates among the DPJ's Lower House membership by 2003. Their similar age and common experience in the training school made them another coherent bloc reinforcing the DPJ's neoliberal orientation. These members have also been able to move quickly into leadership positions, with Noda challenging party veterans for the leadership of the party in 2002 and Maehara taking over as the shadow cabinet member for defense the same year.

In 2003, shortly before the most recent Lower House election, this process through which the neoliberal orientation of the party has attracted new members who share this perspective received its most recent reinforcement as the DPJ absorbed Ichirō Ozawa's Liberal Party and added 18 new members, many of them veteran Diet members and all of them to the neoliberal right of the LDP on most economic issues. It is difficult to predict how this

Table 3 Young DPJ members who are graduates of Matsushita Seikei Juku

	Age on 14 May 2003
Koichirō Genba (3)	38
Kazuhiro Haraguchi (2)	43
Seiji Maehara (3)	41
Jin Matsubara (1)	46
Shigefumi Matsuzawa (3)	45
Hiroyuki Nagahama (2)	44
Yoshihiko Noda (2)	45
Satoshi Shima (2)	45
Kōichi Takemasa (1)	42
Shinji Tarutoko (3)	43
Kazunori Yamanoi (1)	40

Source: Compiled by author using *japanesepoliticians.com* database (accessed 14 May 2003); and *Christian Science Monitor*, 15 August, 2002, p. 6.

process will play out in the coming years, but whether the DPJ grows slowly by adding new members over a series of elections or absorbs additional groups of Diet members who are cut loose in future rounds of party splits, the pattern we have observed up to this point suggests it will become more neoliberal over time.

Conclusion

Despite the diverse origins of the Democratic Party of Japan's membership and some disagreements over economic policy positions, the party is coalescing around an economic reform agenda that is distinctly neoliberal. In almost any other party system, a party like the DPJ that opposed the use of fiscal policy to fight recession, called for tax increases on moderate-income citizens while urging cuts in capital gains taxes, and pressed for a get-tough policy with banks that threatened to cause widespread corporate bankruptcy and a spike in the unemployment rate, would be regarded as a party of the Right.[35] Yet in Japan it represents the main alternative to the 'conservative' LDP.

The focus of the paper has been on the forces that lay behind the New Left's move to the neoliberal Right. While American trade pressure and lecturing by foreign officials, combined with the examples of Margaret Thatcher and Ronald Reagan, played a role in placing neoliberal ideas in front of party politicians, the structural context in which new parties had to operate also played a critical role. Faced with an '800-pound gorilla' in the form of the LDP defending a system of Japanese-style capitalism that provided a large measure of social protection for weak segments of the economy, the new parties that preceded the DPJ, and later the DPJ itself, all decided that neoliberal reform had the potential of attracting votes from disgruntled urban salaried workers. Once the party launched its challenge from the right of the LDP on economic issues, the trajectory of its rhetoric, its recruitment of new candidates, and its prospects for growth through party mergers all pushed it further toward the neoliberal Right.

The implications of the developments highlighted here for Japanese democracy are stark. Japanese voters face the prospect of having to vote in elections in which both of the largest parties, the only ones that can succeed under an electoral system that awards the bulk of its seats through first-past-the-post rules, are parties of the Right. The LDP may offer a measure of social protection, but the protection this system can provide is steadily eroding under the weight of mounting public debt and a fragile banking system. More and more workers face the prospect of unemployment even if they vote to keep the LDP in power because the system the LDP supports is unsustainable. Meanwhile, the only electorally-viable alternative Japanese voters are presented with on their ballots is a party that promises to *accelerate* the collapse of Japanese-style social protection, with only meagre and vague promises to replace this system with formal welfare programmes. Until Japanese voters are given the option of voting for a liberal social democratic party that has prospects of actually winning some elections, Japanese democracy will be unable to remedy a situation in which 50 per cent of voting-age citizens report that they support *none* of the established political parties.

Notes

1 Leonard J. Schoppa, 'Japanese Trade Policy In Reaction to U.S. Pressure: The Long-Term Effects of Efforts to Deflect Bilateral Demands', unpublished manuscript, 2002.
2 J. A. A. Stockwin, *The Japanese Socialist Party and Neutralism*, London: Cambridge University Press, 1968; Hideo Ōtake, 'Nihon shakaitō higeki no kigen', *Chūō Kōron*, October 1986, pp. 146–161.
3 Gerald L. Curtis, *The Japanese Way of Politics*, New York: Columbia University Press, 1988.
4 Germaine A. Hoston, 'Between Theory and Practice: Marxist Thought and the Politics of the Japanese Socialist Party', *Studies in Comparative Communism*, 20:2, Summer 1987, p. 184.
5 Ronald J. Hrebenar, *Japan's New Party System*, Boulder, Colorado: Westview Press, 2000, p. 157.
6 J. A. A. Stockwin, 'The Social Democratic Party (Formerly Japan Socialist Party): A Turbulent Odyssey', in Ronald Hrebenar (ed.) *Japan's New Party System*, Boulder, Colorado: Westview Press, 2000, p. 230; Gerald L. Curtis, *The Logic of Japanese Politics: Leaders, Institutions, and the Limits of Change*, New York: Columbia University Press, 1999, p. 198.
7 Interview with the author, 12 December 2002.
8 *Yomiuri Shimbun*, 22 December 2000.
9 *Yomiuri Shimbun*, 6 December 2001.
10 Steven K. Vogel, 'Can Japan Disengage? Winners and Losers in Japan's Political Economy, and the Ties that Bind Them', *Social Science Japan Journal* 2:1, April 1999, p. 12.
11 Gerald L. Curtis, *The Logic of Japanese Politics: Leaders, Institutions, and the Limits of Change*, New York: Columbia University Press, 1999, p. 194.
12 Democratic Party of Japan, 'Policies for the 19th House of Councillors Elections: A Fair Deal for All: Seven Reforms / 21 Key Policies, 17 April 2001', online at <http://www.dpj.or.jp/english/policy/19hc-elec.html>, accessed 10 October 2001.
13 *JEI Report* 3B (21 January 2000), p. 1.
14 DPJ, 'Policies for the 19th House of Councillors Elections'.
15 Ibid.
16 Interview with Nagatsuma, 16 December 2002.
17 *Nihon Keizai Shimbun*, 5 June 2000.
18 DPJ, 'Democratic Party of Japan Economic Revitalization Plan (Key Points), 11 Feburary 2002', online at <http://www.dpj.or.jp/english/news/021115/04.html>, accessed 22 November 2002.
19 Tetsundo Iwakuni, *Minshutō daihyō Hatoyama Yukio sama: keiki taisaku tenkan wo motomeru mōshiireshō*, unpublished memo, 2002.
20 Motohisa Furukawa, 'The Finance Diet of 1998', in Gerald L. Curtis (ed.) *Policymaking in Japan: Defining the Role of Politicians*, Tokyo: Japan Center for International Exchange, 2002, pp. 45–46; Jennifer Amyx, *Japan's Financial Crisis: Institutional Rigidity and Reluctant Change*, Princeton: Princeton University Press, 2004.
21 *JEI Report* 38B, 9 October 1998; see also Furukawa, 'The Finance Diet of 1998', pp. 46–47.

22 *JEI Report* 37B, 2 October 1998, p. 2.
23 Furukawa, op. cit., p. 51.
24 Democratic Party of Japan, 'Final Financial Reconstruction Plan, 24 January 2002', online at <http://www.dpj.or.jp/english/policy/plan.html>, accessed 19 May 2003.
25 Ibid.
26 Iwakuni, op. cit.
27 Amyx, op. cit.
28 Quotations from DPJ, 'New Strategy for Industrial Revitalization, August 8, 2002', On the web at http://www.dpj.or.jp/english/policy/strategy.html, accessed 22 November 2002.
29 Iichirō Asano, Kōhei Ōtsuka, Tetsurō Fukuyama, Kōji Matsui, and Takeaki Matsumoto, 'Sayōnara Koizumi-ryū kaikaku: keizai saisei no kōsō wa ware ni ari'. *Ronza* (May 2002), p. 100 (translated by the author).
30 Interview with Nagatsuma, 16 December 2002.
31 This phrase was used by a wide range of individuals I spoke with during a visit to Tokyo in December 2002, including DPJ politicians, journalists, bureaucrats, and even LDP politicians.
32 Hideo Ōtake, 'Political Realignment and Policy Conflict', in Hideo Ōtake (ed.) *Power Shuffles and Policy Processes*, Tokyo: JCIE, 2000.
33 *Yomiuri Shimbun*, 24 September 2002.
34 *Christian Science Monitor*, 15 August 2002, p. 6.
35 The DPJ's positions supporting environmental regulation, fighting for freedom of information, defending human rights, and calling for an increase in spending on unemployment insurance are more consistent with positions taken by parties of the Left in other systems. I focus on its positions on fiscal policy, tax policy, public corporations, and banking because these are the issues at the top of the economic policy agenda in contemporary Japan. On all of them, the party comes down on the neoliberal Right of the LDP.

8   After Abu Ghraib

American empire, the left-wing intellectual and Japan Studies

David Williams

Americans like to say that the world changed as a result of the September 11, 2001, terrorist attacks on the World Trade Center and the Pentagon. It would be more accurate to say that the attacks produced a dangerous change in the thinking of some of our leaders, who began to see our republic as a genuine empire, a new Rome, the greatest colossus in history, no longer bound by international law, the concerns of allies, or any constraints on its use of military force.

Chalmers Johnson[1]

By the waters of Babylon we sat down and wept

The infamous image of a hooded Iraqi prisoner, arms outstretched, electrodes attached to limbs and genitals by the torturer, should give pause to all students of Japan who have served as intellectual spear bearers for the American imperium. That broken image conjures up the pathetic fate of the raped and butchered Lavinia in *Titus Andronicus*, Shakespeare's most brutal and unforgiving play. At the apogee of American empire, Shakespeare's unsparing critique of Rome and its imperial pretensions, has never been more relevant because the proponents of the war on terrorism may yet plunge the entire planet into the heart of a new imperial darkness.

Violent imperial deeds overtook the initial plan for this essay which was conceived as a conventional 'Old Left' analysis of the three crises that decisively shaped the trajectory of the Japanese Left since the ending of the Pacific War: the 1960 eruption over the Japan–US Security Pact; the student uprising over the renewal of the treaty in 1970, a struggle intensified by demands for the reversion of Okinawa to Japanese control and protests against the Vietnam War; and, finally, the political crisis provoked among pacifists by the Japanese public's reluctant and belated endorsement of Gulf War I (1990–91).

The attack of 11 September 2001, the war on terrorism, the American invasions of Afghanistan and Iraq, and most notoriously of all, the revelations of gross violations of the Geneva Convention by American forces at Abu Ghraib prison and elsewhere call into question many of the fundamental assumptions of the Old Left approach. How the scholar understands the world may never be the same. To recast Thomas Jefferson's epigram on France, every area specialist now has two regions of supreme intellectual concern: his own and the United States of America.

Japan studies must make an imperial turn or *Kehre* because American Empire is the central question in all branches of area studies. Working on the assumption that the implications for Japanese democracy could hardly be greater, this essay is an attempt to push the critique of US base imperialism to new limits.

An empire of bases

> Who hath brought the fatal engine in
> That gives our Troy, our Rome, the civil wound.
> *Titus Andronicus*, Act 5, Scene 3

The terrorist attack on the World Trade Centre opened a new chapter in the world's understanding of itself. The war on terrorism and the invasions of Afghanistan and Iraq have revolutionised perceptions of American power, and encouraged a new scepticism, even hostility, towards our increasingly un-pacific *Pax Americana*. This revolution in perception may prove to be historically more significant than the physical devastation of Lower Manhattan or the two vicious wars against Asia provoked by Islamic resistance to US interference in Middle Eastern affairs. It is clear to all that almost the entire world is trapped, one way or another, under the eagle's wing.

If we are all subjects of America's empire of bases, the lives and destinies of the globe's billions are, in the military and economic sphere, vulnerable to any clique of politicians, however fanatical or self-serving, which may seize the levels of power in Washington. US laws and electoral plebiscites that involve less than one percent of the world's population restrain such cabals only fitfully.

Yet the profounder truth is that neo-conservative juntas may come and go in Washington, but if the American establishment, Republican or Democratic alike, has its way, the whole world shall remain subject to American power for the indefinite future. Without a diplomatic concert to curb US power, the world's only effective ally at the moment in this unequal struggle is America's fiscal weakness, mounting trade deficits and its poor savings habits. In the global context, Iraqi resistance is a pinprick. It may wound US pride and make Washington temporarily more cautious, but it does not alter the imbalance of military and cultural power between America and the rest of the world.

The story of the consolidation of America's global military hegemony is the most important obscured truth of postwar diplomacy. This story challenges the orthodox view that international relations since 1945 have been a struggle between the forces of light (America) and darkness (Communism and Islamic fundamentalism). Ronald Reagan's famous quip about 'the evil empire' has proven to be only half right: the Soviet Union *was* evil but America *is* the empire.

An exercise in 'deep revisionism' (Ernst Nolte) is therefore proposed, one that seeks to bring a series of neglected truths to light. If the United States helped to crush the Axis, Germany and Japan also stood in the way of America's nascent global hegemony. If World War II delivered deathblows to the Asian empires of Japan and Europe, the United States also assumed the imperial prerogatives of both in the wake of decolonization. If the United States contained Soviet subversion, Moscow shielded the world from unipolar American domination until the fall of the Berlin Wall. If American imperialism rarely depends on colonies, it has turned base imperialism into an art form.

NATO's war against Serbia brought down a cruel and aggressive regime in Belgrade, but it has also resulted in the Balkans passing firmly into America's sphere of military domination. Gulf War II overthrew Saddam Hussein, but it has also given the United States an excuse to strengthen its grip on the Gulf and introduce base imperialism into Iraq itself, both to secure its oil and to threaten the only remaining focus of resistance to American hegemony in the Middle East: Iran. Any defender of America's postwar world who insists that virtue is the only factor in this story is wrong. There are two stories, two narratives of power, that shape the *Pax Americana*.

In principle, there are no reasons why two grand narratives *à la Lyotard* – the United States as our protector and America as our *dominatrix* – should not inform how the world understands itself but, in fact, the orthodox view cannot withstand the subversive pressures of the new discourse of anti-hegemonic criticism. The point is easy to illustrate. George Bush *fils* boldly declared in August 2002 that 'Our nation is the greatest force for good in history'; but try rereading the sentence without the phrase 'for good'. The statement is still true; perhaps even more so. But the first loses all conviction in the shadow of the second.

Bush's 'greatest force' remark echoes an ageing orthodoxy, one that has prevailed so long because the alternative view has been, consciously or otherwise, suppressed or ignored. The subversive powers of this new discourse will be demonstrated by re-examining one of the key chapters in the consolidation of American power, the relationship of Japan and the United States since Pearl Harbour and, more specifically, the role of the Japanese Left in this poorly understood chapter in world history.

Republic or empire?

Before examining the Japanese case in detail, we must be clear about three key issues. First, what is the nature and scale of American base imperialism? Second, what is the impact of American empire on the national sovereignty of states such as Japan that have played host to American bases? Finally, there is the question of interpretative rubrics: one must decide whether this new empire is better understood as a threat to American democracy (thereby requiring an American solution) or subversive to the security and freedom of the whole world (thus necessitating an international remedy).

The global reach of American military power can be factually demonstrated. Ten years *after* the Cold War ended, the US officially maintained 725 overseas military bases, with many more disguised as host facilities but in fact manned and operated entirely by Americans. In Britain, Chicksands Priory is an excellent example of such exclusive deployments. The number of US facilities in the United Kingdom has never been officially disclosed and apparently the British Parliament has never voted to authorise their presence. One 'well-informed' source claimed that there were 104 US bases in the United Kingdom at the end of the Cold War.[2] As the defence budget remained at near Cold War levels under the Clinton administration and overseas military expenditure has soared under the presidency of Bush *fils*, there may be even more US facilities in Britain. But either way, the question needs to be posed: Just whom is Britain being defended from?

Turning to the issue of sovereignty, it is obvious that the American electorate and policymaking establishment are in denial about their global imperium.

As distinct from other peoples on this earth, most Americans do not recognise – or do not want to recognise – that the United States dominates the world through its military power. Due to government secrecy, they are often ignorant of the fact that their government garrisons the globe. They do not recognise that a vast network of American military bases on every continent except Antarctica actually constitutes a new form of empire.[3]

In short the issue of whether America has colonies or not is a red herring. Washington rules via bases. The number of US bases maintained, officially and secretly, in this country or that provides an index of whether the host government possesses anything but the outward trappings of national sovereignty. China (no US bases) is a sovereign power; Japan with 75 is not.[4] As France plays host to almost no US military facilities, it has more sovereign powers than Britain which has so many. With 37 'military communities', 10 air bases and 213 other American installations on its soil, Germany barely knows what the idea of sovereignty means. But the larger truth, to repeat, is that America maintains an empire of bases; not colonies.

One of the most telling examples of base imperialism is found in Japan, and Okinawa in particular. The anti-hegemonic critic of American empire does not fault the old Japanese Left's attacks on the US military presence in Japan. The cataloguing of the dangers posed to Japan's security and the travails the US military has inflicted on Japanese communities living near American bases has been exhaustive and telling. But the old Left critique has proven less acute about the motivations behind the American drive for global hegemony. More damning, the old Left critique has refused to consider the scale of resistance that may be necessary to redress the intolerable power imbalance between the United States and the rest of the world, including Japan.

This brings us to our third issue: the nature of the threat itself. To revise our understanding of postwar Japanese politics in the light of the anti-hegemonic critique of American power requires that we choose between two contrasting interpretations. One is the American isolationist case as updated by Chalmers Johnson in *The Sorrows of Empire*, where he concludes his case thus:

> There is one development that could conceivably stop this process of [imperial] overreaching: the people could retake control of Congress, reform it along with the corrupted election laws that have made it into a forum for special interests, turn it into a genuine assembly of democratic representatives, and cut off the supply to the Pentagon and the secret intelligence agencies. We have a strong civil society that could, in theory, overcome the entrenched interests of the armed forces and the military-industrial complex. At this late date, however, it is difficult to imagine how Congress, much like the Roman senate in the last days of the republic, could be brought back to life and cleansed of its endemic corruption. Failing such a reform, Nemesis, the goddess of retribution and vengeance, the punisher of pride and hubris, waits impatiently for her meeting with us.[5]

In a brilliant polemic, Johnson is renewing the century-old American domestic debate over the choice between republic and empire that began with the Spanish-American War (1898). Although he is acutely aware of the perilous impact of US imperialism on the rest of the world, his primary concern is the corrosive effects of militarism on his country's republican virtues and democratic institutions. His model is ancient Rome and the classic argument over how the transition from Republic to Empire undermined the powers of the Rome Senate, thus leading to imperial tyranny.

In *Defending Japan's Pacific War*, I propose an alternative remedy for American imperialism; one grounded in respect for the classical doctrine of the balance of power in world affairs and that does not assume that the world is helpless unless Americans rebel against their military-industrial-media complex.[6]

> For Americans, therefore, the question is whether democracy within can be squared with imperialism without. For the rest of the world, the problem is different. American hegemony violates the central doctrine of modern diplomacy: the balance of power. A hegemonic power that towers above all its potential military opponents poses a threat to the liberty of the rest of the world. *The imbalance is of itself unacceptable.*[7]

This means that reversion to the more benign approach of the Clinton presidency, however welcome, would fail to address the fundamental problem, which is the excess of American power. The liberal imperialist argument that American empire is desirable (an argument made by such non-Americans as Ignatieff and Niall Ferguson) because this colossus will always act benignly, is not true in fact nor acceptable in principle.[8]

> The collapse of the Soviet Union and the surge in U.S. expenditure on defence since the fall of the Berlin Wall means that the balance of power between America and the rest of the world has decisively altered in a way that no thinking person, American or otherwise, should accept. . . . Furthermore, if the US will not unilaterally disarm to restore the relative balance between itself and the rest of the planet. . . . One day soon Western Europe, Russia, Japan, China and the rest of the globe may have to consider how they might be able to contain the American juggernaut.[9]

Pace Ignatieff, we do not live in an age of terror. However irrational and murderous al-Qaeda, Bush is the greater, not the lesser, evil. American empire is the power that matters. How can this giant be tamed?

> The hitherto unthinkable may have to be thought. An audit of non-American military and economic assets may have to be undertaken. This will require casting a hard eye over the state of Europe's conventional military forces, Russia's nuclear arsenal, Japan's financial leverage over the U.S. Treasury, and the capabilities of China's ground and air forces. America's dependence on Middle Eastern oil will be a factor in this sober calculation to determine how the rest of the world might be able to compel America, peacefully, to ease the fetters of its global domination.
>
> The implied alliance of Europeans, Russians, Japanese, Chinese and the rest would be as unholy as it is necessary. But the hope must be that the shock of such a diplomatic initiative might encourage the United States to slash its nuclear arsenal and substantially reduce its military spending. Failing this, the fundamental global imbalance of power may have to be addressed in still other ways.[10]

In contrast to the neo-isolationist critique of American empire, I argue that it is the world outside America that is the main victim of US base imperialism. In *Defending Japan's Pacific War*, I develop the case for global resistance against the excesses of American power in the short and middle term but suggest that the ultimate cure for America's global domination will be found only when the non-West acquires the values and means to govern the globe successfully without relying on White or Western authority or leadership. In the end, the only permanent cure for American hegemony is 'post-White power'.

If Japan offers one of the most telling examples of base imperialism, it also provides fundamental instruction in the challenges and perils nurturing post-White power. This essay proposes a new interpretation of postwar Japan, and the Left's role in its relationship with the United States, one that reflects the power and aggressive character of the American empire.

American empire and moral disarray on the Left

> What's the news from Rome?
> *Titus Andronicus*, Act 5, Scene 1

In the wake of the American crusade in the Middle East, the neo-conservative ideologue is not the only intellectual under pressure. The liberal imperialist – the New Labour advocate of global intervention, the Israeli Labour Party supporter who wants to expel the Palestinians from Jerusalem or the American Democrat who lusts to confront the 'Axis of evil' – has testing questions to answer as well.

This liberal crisis has a British dimension. In the wake of the revelations about Abu Ghraib Prison in Baghdad in the spring of 2004, Mary Dejevsky, commenting in the *Independent* (London), asked 'How was the intelligentsia fooled so easily?'.[11] She took to task some of the most prominent names in the British media – 'the historian, Andrew Roberts, the academic, Michael Ignatieff, the writers, William Shawcross and John Lloyd, and a whole clutch of columnists, including the editor and MP Boris Johnson'.[12] She concludes that these writers 'are contorting themselves, Houdini like, to extricate themselves from the jungle.'[13]

No convincing definition of liberalism can be squared with Ignatieff's slippery justification of torture.[14] Two hundred years after Voltaire and Cesare Beccaria demolished the moral defence of torture, Ignatieff toys with the idea that the brutalising and murder of prisoners may be justified in ways that betray one of the supreme moral legacies of the European Enlightenment. His casuistic attempt to deny national self-determination to the Palestinian and Iraqi peoples while arguing the ethical 'pros' and 'cons' for the horrors being perpetrated in American and Israeli military prisons suggests that this liberal has lost his moral compass. Behold the new treason of the intellectual.

Granted: the road *to* Abu Ghraib Prison was paved by the malevolent intentions of neo-conservative ideologues who captured the ear of George W. Bush. But the road *from* Abu Ghraib may come to torment the liberal intellectuals who have supported the expansion of the American Empire since 1945. The interventionist heirs of John F. Kennedy and ideological mainstays of Bill Clinton stand exposed. Like the IMF consensus that they have supported in the economic sphere, the liberal ideology of America's global hegemony is proving increasingly threadbare.

History is the key. Influential figures in the British media were easily fooled for more than transient reasons. The rhetoric of 'empire lite' (cf. 'torture lite'), naïve trust in the intentions of the Bush and Blair administrations, blind loyalty to Zionism, revulsion against Islamic terrorism and unthinking solidarity with the United States after the events of 9.11 all made it easier for the proponents of American empire to justify aggression against Iraq. But viewed from the perspective of the *longue durée*, the British intelligentsia was misled by a false, because incomplete, understanding of the history of the world beginning with the causes and significance of World War II.

The principal academic task generated by the war on terror and America's high-risk strategy in the Middle East is the writing and dissemination of what I call 'the new history' of the globe since 1939. The academic Left, by virtue of its values and its dominant place in the British university, is well placed to advance this revisionary enterprise. In America, Japan studies has already begun the attack. In *Blowback* and *The Sorrows of Empire*, Chalmers Johnson has opened a breach in the imperialist barricades.[15] It is time for the political historians on the radical Left to pour through this breach.

Johnson has shattered many of the assumptions that have blinded world public opinion, to cite a key example, to the intolerable burdens being inflicted on the Okinawan people in the name of American empire. But, the scales having dropped from our eyes, the great task before us is not journalistic critique but revolutionary scholarship. Our goal is the systematic demolition of the ideology of American imperialism.

With the demise of Soviet communism, imperial America represents the greatest threat to world peace, global development and ecological sanity. But the 'New Left' or post Abu Ghraib scholar – someone who keeps a portrait of Max Weber on his wall, a copy of *Science as a Vocation* on his book shelf, and has the Weberian warning about politicised scholarship engraved on his heart – brings strict discipline to his labours.[16] Because of the cultivated weakness among traditional left-wing academics for criticism over research, political advocacy over objectivity, the responsible 'New Left' intellectual who is a serious scholar commits himself to empirical exactitude and ideological debunking in equal measure. One must be on constant guard against the paranoid style; the beguiling tendentiousness of the academic Left's past has no place in our future. But one thing is certain. If Hegel described the newspaper as the morning prayer of modern man, each day the Japan specialist will henceforth need to begin the day with the question: 'What is the news from Rome?'

The Middle East crisis as a crisis in Japan Studies

> Why, foolish Lucius, dost thou not perceive
> That Rome is but a wilderness of tigers?
> *Titus Andronicus*, Act 3, Scene 1

To study Japan is to criticize America. The assault of the administration of George W. Bush on the Middle East has given fresh life to this neglected left-wing mantra. Not since the Vietnam War have the faults of US society – its militarism, imperialism and aggressive self-righteousness – been so exposed to almost universal ire. This sudden reversal of critical perspective suggests that the neo-conservative revolution in American foreign policy may have paradigmatic implications for the left-wing student of Japanese politics. Today we need to ask 'what went wrong?' not with pre-war Japan but with postwar America.[17]

To dwell on the failings of the United States is to break with the traditional Orientalist assumption that Japan is a morally inferior society, an assertion at work in the widely held belief, certainly in Japan studies in Britain, that, in the political sphere, Westerners have nothing to learn from Japan. Recent events in the Middle East suggest that the proposition should now be reversed: the world will not learn by averting its eyes from the dark side of American politics. This new proposition has the potential to recast our fundamental approach towards Japan and its place in modern history. Here is to be found yet another unintended intellectual consequence of the reckless neo-conservative hour in American life.

For the area or regional specialist, the fact of American power is *the* political fact of our time. In all the regions of the earth, from Western and Eastern Europe to Africa and the Middle East, from Central and South America to the Indian subcontinent and East Asia, the United States is now the pre-eminent power and dominant force. Whatever else World War II and the Cold War were, they were also stages in the growth and consolidation of American empire. 'Good War' nostalgia must not obscure this truth.

American hegemony has reduced every region of the globe to an actual or potential province of imperial rule or manipulation. From the vantage of the American homeland, foreign continents are best understood as a series of bicycle spokes all linked to a single *hyper puissance*. The truth of the clichéd observation that Latin American relations with the rest of the world consist of 'the United States and nothing else' now reaches beyond the New World. Thus, China, the Koreas, Russia and Southeast Asia may all figure in Japanese assessments of its national security, but none of these powers matters as much as the United States.

America's nuclear superiority over the rest of the world means that neither Japanese rearmament nor Japanese nationalism poses any danger of major consequence to the world community. Old Left carping about prime ministerial visits to the Yasukuni Shrine or the conservative criticism of Article 9 or revisionary textbooks have served only to deflect attention from the fact that the most dangerous beasts live in Washington.

It is time therefore for the scholar to concentrate on the singular character of American power in order to recast our understanding of the role of the Left in the making of modern Japanese history. In the light of developments in Iraq and elsewhere, the radical scholar has begun to see old faults as virtues, not only because the pernicious influence of American empire occludes the flaws of Japanese politics and society, but also because certain aspects of Japanese government and thought previously regarded as negative, even fascist, take on an entirely different character when assessed in the light of the unipolar dominance that has emerged since the collapse of the Soviet Union.

The grim revelations from US military prisons in Iraq, Afghanistan and Guantanamo Bay have exploded the conventional pro-American and anti-Japanese assumptions that have governed Japanology since Pearl Harbor. It should be obvious to all that whatever else the United States may be, this new Rome is also a wilderness of tigers. The hoary irrelevancies of *Japanokritik* must be set aside in favour of the urgent necessities of *Americanokritik*.

Shifting attitudes towards a string of conflicts – the Pacific War, the Cold War, the Vietnam debacle, the unbroken history of US interference in Latin America, the Bosnia–Kosovo civil wars, the US invasion of Afghanistan, the War on Terrorism and Gulf War II – provide the decisive bellwethers. There is a world of difference between the moral and imperial complacencies of the various assessments of US-Asian relations produced by the Council of Foreign Relations in the 1960s and a recent study such as *America's Asian Alliances*, in which Robert D. Blackwill and Paul Dibb deconstruct a web of self-serving historical myths about US involvement in the Western Pacific from the wartime decisions of Franklin D. Roosevelt down to the end of the 1990s.[18]

The rise of American empire has exposed harsh moral truths, thus unsettling the hierarchy of facts – the hierarchy that distinguishes between facts that count and facts that do not – that organise our interpretation of the world. This essay is an attempt to reassess which facts should count as decisive facts or (true) phenomena and which should be judged to be merely marginal facts or epiphenomena in our understanding of Japan as an American protectorate.

An example. In *Okinawa: Cold War Island* Johnson, writing in 1999, offers this summary of American military policy towards Okinawa:

> Fifty years ago, without any Okinawan being asked or even being part of either the Japanese or American political systems, the American military seized Okinawan property for its numerous military bases, espionage centers, and housing estates for American families. It is important to understand that the Americans did not requisition or pay for this land; they simply seized it at bayonet point and then bulldozed the houses on it. Any Okinawan who protested this American seizure of land was charged with being a communist, and some 'troublemakers' were shipped off to Bolivia and dumped in a jungle area near the headwaters of the Amazon.[19]

Hitherto the liberal imperialist has either dismissed such claims as anti-American propaganda or insisted that such episodes are mere exceptions to the normally benign actions of a great democracy acting with the needs and interests of the world at heart. After the torture stories from Iraq and elsewhere, this Okinawan story seems as fresh as today's revelations from Afghanistan or the West Bank. Stripped of his liberal blinkers, the suspicious sceptic becomes keener to ask whether there were similar incidents in the past or where equally repellent episodes are taking place at this very moment. Such probing is loosening the previously confident grip of the liberal imperialists not only on the moral high ground but also on factual reality itself. Where once one hoped and believed that the maintenance of the *Pax Americana* did not require illegal or barbaric measures, now one wonders what malicious deed or uncivilised act has not been committed in its defence.

In the wake of the Iraq war, liberal *mea culpae* are in order, including my own. During the first Gulf War, I was an editorial writer for *The Japan Times* in Tokyo. I vigorously supported the Allied effort to expel Iraq from Kuwait before, during and after the conflict when a majority of the Japanese electorate still refused to endorse the war. I was naïve. Gulf War I was more than a struggle to liberate Kuwait or a battle to control the world's supply of oil. It was also a war to strengthen US hegemony over the Middle East. Litres of ink were used by the mass media to debate the defence of Kuwait and the nasty side of oil politics, but the threat of American base imperialism was almost wholly ignored. Such neglect was a major lapse.

Wishful thinking about American empire has influenced my criticism of other writers on Japan. Before my own ideological conversion or *tenkō* from Right to Left in the late 1990s, I regularly took 'radical' writers to task for their loose reasoning and poor evidence when assessing Japan. In *Japan and the Enemies of Open Political Science*, influential examples of Left-wing criticism of one aspect or another of Japanese life are sceptically examined.[20] In many cases, Western critics of Japan resort to specious reasoning and thin evidence. But this critical spirit can find its feet by challenging the complacencies of the America's global hegemony while examining how Japanese on both the Left and Right have sought to resist Washington's excesses.

Whatever the divisions between the pro-American modernization school led by Marius Jansen and Edwin O. Reischauer and their anti-Japanese Left-wing critics, both sides have been suffered from what I have called 'The Allied Gaze'.[21] This gaze (the notion derives from Foucault) embodies the naïve notion that sixty years after the ending of the Pacific War, it is still possible to discuss this conflict solely in terms of our high ideals and low Japanese conduct. The New Left historian of wartime Japan insists that the low Allied conduct and the high ideals of Imperial Japan also figure in our understanding the Pacific War.

Johnson's break with the Cold War stands as the outstanding example of an American 'Right to Left' conversion or '*tenkō*' but he continues to endorse the Allied Pacific War orthodoxy. Here I argue that deep revisionism requires that the radical doubts that Johnson has brought to bear on the Cold War and the war on terrorism should be applied to the Pacific War as well. All of America's wars since Pearl Harbor have also been efforts to expand and consolidate a global imperium. The Pacific War is no exception.

Japanese resistance to American empire: the Pacific War

Hail Rome, victorious in thy mourning weeds!
Titus Andronicus, Act 1, Scene 1

The disciplined and precise understanding of postwar Japan's place within the American imperium defines our task. This is a canonic exercise of the first order. Its main branches include the philosophy of subjectivity after Hegel, Max Weber's argument on the sources of the West's supremacy over the rest of the planet, Tocqueville's reading of the early history of the United States from its violent colonial beginnings, the story of Asian resistance to Western expansion and the dismal history of its failure to achieve self-mastery, the moral history of Europe's evolution from martial imperialism to mature restraint, and, finally, the demographic challenge of post-Whiteness.

In my own work on the wartime Kyoto School, the struggle to overturn the foundations of the American ideology (cf. Marx's and Engels' *The German Ideology* and Jun Tosaka's *Japanese Ideology*) has led irresistibly to the deconstruction of Pacific War orthodoxy.[22] In *Defending Japan's Pacific War: The Kyoto School Philosophers and Post-White Power*, my work as a historian has focused on the errors of neo-Marxist historiography, the faulty interpretations and translations of Kyoto School texts, and the failures of religious scholars to deal credibly with political ideas of the Kyoto School. On all these fronts, the principal obstacle has been the Allied Gaze.

Here, by contrast, the history of the postwar Japanese Left will be reassessed as a case study in the new revisionist history of the rise and consolidation of American empire since the Japanese attack on Pearl Harbour. The radical historian of Asia should seek to dislodge his liberal imperialist colleague from his hitherto dominant place in the discipline. It is time for the Old Left, the worthy keepers of the critical flame during the past half-century, to be applauded into early retirement and to take their utopian notions that could never be realised with them. The world must be addressed in an enlightened but realist fashion. In our intellectual labours, we place race above class, subjectivity over pacifism, and power over dreams.

Transwar history offers the key rubric. The Japanese Left, both as a parliamentary and intellectual force, grew lasting roots during the prewar period, but it was the Pacific War (1941–45), or if you will, the Great East Asian War (1931–45), that decisively shaped its ideological and political outlook. The critic of American hegemony is the natural ally of the Pacific War revisionist because he judges the Pacific War to be simultaneously a struggle to establish American ascendancy over East Asia as well as a war to defeat Japanese expansionism. The Pacific War was crucial to the transformation of the world's greatest ocean into an American lake that began with the Spanish-American War (1898). In the eyes of the critic of American hegemony, President Franklin Roosevelt was the father of his country's 'total empire' (Louise Young) in the Pacific.[23]

The Pacific War revisionist is also an uncompromising foe of Japanese reactionary revisionism because the radical revisionist is a proponent of Asian subjectivity (*shutaisei*), that is demonstrated self-mastery. Like the wartime Kyoto School philosophers, the Pacific War revisionist and the advocate of 'post-White power' insist that there is no point in resisting American hegemony if a viable post-White order cannot be constructed in its place. The pragmatic realism of this argument marks another significant break with the utopianism of the Old Left.

Just as Kyoto School thinkers such as Hajime Tanabe and Iwao Kōyama insisted that the ideals behind a Greater East Asian Co-Prosperity Sphere would never be realised unless the interests of non-Japanese East Asians were comprehensively addressed and Imperial Japan exercised proper moral leadership over the region, so the proponent of 'post-White power' rejects irrationalist Japanese chauvinism as the enemy of an effective and humane form of regional autonomy for East Asians.[24]

The revisionist stresses the weakness of Imperial Japan. In 1941, Franklin D. Roosevelt held almost all the cards; Tōjō almost none.[25] Washington's conditions for ending the fatal embargo of oil and steel to Japan contained in the Hull Note of late 1941 effectively required that Japan fight or concede that the United States would henceforth act as hegemon in the Western Pacific. Roosevelt knew that Japan would either be brought to its knees with economic sanctions or provoked into fighting a war it could not win. For Tōjō, Pearl Harbor was a desperate gamble. He took his stand against American imperialism and lost. Imperial Japan thus joined the long and still growing list of nations that tried to resist US expansion.

Nevertheless, it is also true that the programme of Japanese national expansion between 1937 and 1942, as conceived by the Tōjō clique and implemented by the Imperial Army, was a disaster for East Asia and Japan. Aside from ousting Western power from the region, the Imperial Japanese Army offered even less to East Asians than Hitler's legions delivered by their brutal unification of continental Europe. Such facts do not relieve the burden on the Left to weigh the historical evidence carefully and realistically. The critic of Japanese history textbooks will never succeed unless he learns to respect the need for Japanese *amour propre*, but this need must not be confused with the justification or denial of what was brutal Japanese aggression, particularly against China. Only a notion of Japan's role as regional hegemon grounded in geo-political realism and a measure of political respect offered a programme of regional unity that had any chance of success. This the Kyoto School argued forcefully and correctly.

But if there is no love lost between the liberal revisionist and the Japanese reactionary, the critic of American hegemony needs to exploit the revisionist's gifts for thinking beyond the conventional limits of Allied World War II orthodoxy. It is the revisionist who has demonstrated that the Pacific War helped accelerate trends in American society, for example, that may sweep away the demographic pillars of the White Republic over the course of the present century.[26] The Pacific War saw the first mass migration of Mexicans to work the fields of wartime America. The struggle against Japan made it impossible for the US authorities, and more particularly state governments, to ban immigrants from China. Finally, the very language of the Atlantic Charter, the 'Four Freedoms' for example, helped erode the will of American society to discriminate against its Black minority or continue to preserve middle class professions, let alone the commanding heights of government, the bureaucracy and the economy, for Whites alone. In this sense, the Pacific War inaugurated the self-deconstruction of the White Republic.

At the same time, it is the revisionist who challenges one of the fundamental tenets of neo-isolationism: the self-serving assumption that the conquest of North America and the subjugation of the native peoples of the continent was not an act of imperialism, and that therefore the 'Republic' of the contiguous 48 states is an unstained achievement that bears no comparison with the sins of oceanic imperialism abroad. Rare among neo-isolationists, Johnson reluctantly concedes the implicit hypocrisy of the 'republic or empire' debate among so-called liberal imperialist circles.[27]

The critic of American empire also has a quarrel with the old Japanese Left. The most influential ideas of the postwar Left – neutralism and pacifism, negative liberty *à la* Isaiah Berlin and the evasion of sovereignty – have stoked Japanese criticism of American hegemony, but at a price. At work in the ideal of pacifism is the implicit denial that Japan should ever exercise subjective power over itself or East Asia. The role of regional hegemon is thus conceded, in principle, to the United States forever. This was one of the more unacceptable consequences of Japan's embrace of defeat after 1945.

If the American empire poses the greatest challenge to the balance of power since the Soviet Union, the radical revisionist needs to revitalise his support for national self determination and non-White subjectivity because a new post-White world order cannot be constructed unless regional blocs and powers learn to manage their affairs, domestic and external alike, in a manner akin to the European Union. Nothing strengthens the position of the United States in Northeast Asia more than the Japanese fear of North Korea and China. Unless Sino-Japanese relations can be placed on a footing closer to the kind of ties that now bind Germany and France, an unhealthy Japanese dependence on the United States will continue. Only such bilateral *Asian* reconciliations hold out the prospect of easing the burdens of the US military presence on Okinawa. Similar arguments apply to Taiwan and the Philippines.

The radical revisionist proposes a parallel thesis regarding 'American empire as the lesser of two evils' argument. In Japan studies, for example, there has been relentless criticism of Japan's wartime conduct and the potential threat Japanese armament poses for the peace and stability of the Western Pacific. The revisionist does not support the notion that it would have been better if Tōjō's Japan had won the Pacific War. Indeed, the revisionist has no time for historical hypotheticals because they depart from the facts of history. But endless carping about the failures of Imperial Japan deflects attention from the dangers of American power today. Contemporary Japan poses no threat to the world order because no other country can act without regard for America's nuclear superiority. To dwell on the most important military consequence of the Pacific War – the creation of America's atomic arsenal – is to return the argument to the events of August 1945 and beyond.

Japanese resistance to American empire: the postwar struggle

> Let Rome herself be bane unto herself,
> And she whom mighty kingdoms curtsy to,
> Like a forlorn and desperate castaway,
> Do shameful execution on herself
> *Titus Andronicus*, Act 5, Scene 3

On 3 September 1945, nearly a month after the first atomic bomb was dropped on a large civilian population, a British journalist revealed to the world in a celebrated telegram that there was 'No more Hiroshima'. The phrase became an anti-war, anti-militarist and, eventually, anti-American slogan in Japan. During the occupation, the full horrors of the final phase of the Pacific War gradually became apparent to the Japanese people despite the efforts of the Allied censors. The firebombing of Tokyo in March killed some 80,000 people while injuring, displacing or otherwise directly affecting another ten million.[28] Nearly 100,000 civilians, a quarter of the population, perished during the battle for Okinawa. The atomic destruction of Hiroshima and Nagasaki claimed another quarter of a million lives. As the full scale of civilian suffering became clear and the number of radiation victims steadily climbed, the imperative to reject war and all its horrors seared itself in the Japanese consciousness, particularly on the Left.

Allied orthodoxy holds that the first atomic destruction of a city saved the lives of thousands of American soldiers as well as the lives of still more Japanese who might have perished in the battle for the mainland. The left-wing pacifist viewed it as compelling demonstration of the horrors of war. The New Left revisionist sees Hiroshima together with the bombing of Nagasaki as the final drama in the Japanese Holocaust. The purpose of these atomic bombings was to demonstrate American hegemony over the region, warn off Stalinist Russia and break the Japanese will to resist.

These three interpretations, or schools of history – Allied, Pacifist and Revisionist – define the debate over the significance of the Pacific War and the character of postwar Japanese foreign policy and domestic politics. A fourth school – the Japanese nationalist school of revisionist history – is treated less seriously here because of its often-unscholarly character. If the Allied view holds that defeating Japanese expansion was the *essence* of the Pacific War, the pacifist sees the war as *essentially* evil, and therefore never to be repeated for however worthy ends. The New Left revisionist places supreme emphasis on the threat to global liberty posed by the American empire, and therefore takes resistance to US hegemony as its defining concern, an approach that at once complements and challenges the other two schools.

Take, for example, the revisionist understanding of the cult of Article 9 that dominated left-wing thinking after 1945. From a revisionist point of view, Article 9 represents more than an intolerable dilution of Japanese national sovereignty; it concedes military hegemony of the Western Pacific to the United States. Should it become necessary for the world to confront the American empire militarily, such pacifist doctrines would have to be abandoned. But, short of a military clash, Article 9 has provided successive Japanese governments with a tool for resisting Washington's more extreme demands for a deeper Japanese involvement in the American policing of the rest of Asia.

The Left's broad if somewhat uneasy acceptance of the judgements handed down by the Tokyo War Crimes Tribunal (25 so-called 'A Class' war criminals, including Hideki Tōjō, were sentenced in November 1948) highlights another contrast with the revisionist approach. The Pacific War was more than the last gasp of Japanese imperialism; it was a struggle to resist American power. The Tokyo trials were 'victors' justice'; no liberal can defend this judicial travesty and remain a liberal.

Tōjō was an early, if very flawed, proponent of post-White power. This war criminal was also a kind of hero. Both interpretations of the man and his conduct are historically credible. To describe him as a hero is not to ignore his failings. Tanabe and the leading lights of the second generation of Kyoto School philosophers, particularly Kōyama, Keiji Nishitani, Shigetaka Suzuki and Masa'aki Kōsaka, were right to conspire with the Yonai faction of the Imperial Navy to bring Tōjō down as prime minister because of his erratic judgment and brutal policies. But his wartime role and postwar execution make him a pivotal figure for the revisionist historian because he links the two eras of Japanese resistance to America's Pacific hegemony. Tōjō also invites warts and all comparisons with other nationalist leaders across the colonised and Third World. The Japanese leader's strengths and weaknesses need to be weighed against those of Indonesia's Achmad Sukarno, Pakistan's Mohammed Ali Jinnah, Egypt's Gamal Abdel Nasser, Argentina's Juan Peron, Vietnam's Ho Chi Min, Palestine's Yasir Arafat and Iraq's Saddam Hussein. Like Indonesia's General Radin Suharto, Zaire's Colonel Joseph-Désiré Mubuto and Pakistan's General Pervez Musharraf, the Japanese leader was, to borrow S. E. Finer's famous phrase, another 'man on horseback'.[29] The force of nature that was Tōjō cannot be responsibly confined to the self-serving Allied category of 'fascist warlord', and the student of comparative politics can tell us why.

Even this does not exhaust the possibilities for still other arresting studies in compare and contrast. When one recalls V. S. Naipaul's damning assessment of the *naïveté* and unworldliness of Mohandâs Gandhi, and the damage his ideas inflicted on the political culture of post-colonial India, fresh methods to probe Tōjō's mindset suggest themselves.[30] The Japanese pacifist shuns such comparisons because national pride will not tolerate placing Japan on the same level as a 'developing country'. Allied orthodoxy evades such analysis because it invites unsettling questions about the nature of the Pacific War while exposing the under-theorised nature of the term 'Axis'.

The revisionist is willing to think boldly about the historical record in ways that neither the pacifist nor the Allied historian is prepared to do. But, at the same time, the revisionist does not reject Allied and pacifist analysis but rather he insists that both are radically incomplete without a parallel critique of American empire. Take the benefits that the American Occupation conferred on the Japanese Left: classroom democracy, genuine parliamentary power and influence (Japan's first socialist prime minister, Tetsu Katayama, took office in June 1947), permission for labour union activity on a nation-shaping scale, land reform and political equality for women created a programme of reform and constituencies to support it. The revisionist does not deny the genuineness of such progressive gains but he is ever mindful that 'soft power' gains conspired to make the Left less aggressive, and therefore, less effective opponents of American hegemony. Thus, when SCAP turned reactionary in the late 1940s, the Japanese Left proved too divided and too feeble to sustain a general strike to resist the impact of MacArthur's reverse course. The broad perception that the Supreme Allied Commander in the Pacific was abandoning his campaign to compel Japan to break with its feudal and conservative past deepened doubts about America's intentions in the Pacific. For the Left, SCAP's decision to ban the general strike planned for 2 February 1947 was a psychological blow. But, instead of weeping radio broadcasts, the unions should have faced down SCAP with spontaneous strike actions across the country.

This diagnosis can be applied less easily to the Japanese Left's response to the crises in East–West relations during the early 1950s, but the revisionist can sustain a telling critique of the thinking pacifist. The international background to SCAP's 'reverse course' decisions are well known and widely accepted by most historians. The deepening of tensions over Central Europe, particularly the divided city of Berlin, between the Soviet Union and its former Western allies in Europe was very influential. In East Asia, the triumph of Mao's forces in Mainland China in 1949 was a major reverse for America in its new imperial role as Japan's successor as regional hegemon. Then in June 1950, North Korean forces invaded South Korea.

When the Cold War had turned hot in Asia, many of the idealistic expectations raised among leftist politicians and voters, intellectuals and their readers, in the four years of the Occupation collided with their fears for the future. These anxieties inspired the publication of 'A declaration by the peace study group on the problems of the peace treaty' on 15 January 1950 in the influential monthly *Sekai* (World). The authors, Yoshishige Abe, Hyōe Ōuchi and Shigeru Nambara, called for a total peace settlement (one that included the Soviet Union and Communist China), as well as a neutral and unarmed Japan. This declaration affirmed the Left's commitment, and not just among intellectuals and students, that Article 9 was not a temporary reaction to defeat.

Japan's commitment to pacifism was becoming, in Glenn Hook's phrase, an 'embedded norm' of Japanese political life.[31] Launched in February 1950, the activities of the *Heiwa o Mamoru Kai* (Peace Defence Council) led to a massive campaign to gather millions of signatures calling for the banning of nuclear weapons, a movement linked to the Stockholm Appeal launched in May the same year. The fears that fuelled these various and often-disputatious peace groups were proven justified by a set of tumultuous developments over the next two years. A border clash between the armed forces of North and South Korea along the 38th parallel was followed by a declaration of war by Pyongyang in June 1950. The subsequent invasion of South Korea plunged the world into the largest international conflict since the end of World War II. The involvement of US forces in the defence of South Korea inevitably transformed Japan into an advanced staging area and supply depot for the United Nations. Within three weeks of the outbreak of hostilities on the Korean peninsula, General MacArthur wrote to Prime Minister Shigeru Yoshida calling for the creation of a 75,000-man preparatory police force (*keisatsu yobitai*). Amidst great controversy, the Japanese authorities put the plan into effect early in August. The force was oversubscribed with volunteers and became the core body of the Japanese Self Defence Force in 1954.

The revisionist focus on the imperative of resisting US military domination of the globe inevitably encourages a different interpretation of the troubled birth of the Japanese Self-Defence Force. The strong recruiting response affirmed Japanese military potential. At the same time, the restrictions imposed on this nascent Japanese army served to limit its usefulness to the military planners in Washington. Viewed from the standpoint of the critic of American empire, strengthening Japan's capacity for independent military action is essential if US power is to be curbed.

The revisionist historian also takes an unconventional view of another key event of the summer of 1950: SCAP's Red Purge targeting members of the Japan Communist Party and its closest allies. Whatever the Stalinist tendencies of the JCP, the party's links (however tentative) with the Eastern bloc may be judged, from a post-Cold War perspective, as part and parcel of the balance of power function of the old Soviet Union. A similar analysis might be applied to Castro's Cuba: repressive and stagnating within but still a thorn in Washington's side. With the military imbalance between the United States and the rest of the world so lopsided, every thorn counts.

Reflecting on the significance of this Red Purge for domestic Japanese politics, the revisionist concludes that the failure of the country's labour movement to resist this attack on the Left marked a further demoralization of 'progressive' political forces in the country just as the Cold War had turned hot. There appears to be a shortage of effective leadership, commitment, courage and sheer 'bolshieness' on the part of the left-wing forces that allowed them to be co-opted at this critical juncture in the occupation.

Revisionism: beyond Left or Right in Japanese politics

> A speedier course than ling'ring languishment
> Must we pursue, and I have found the path.
> My lords a solemn hunting is at hand
> *Titus Andronicus*, Act 2, Scene 1

Given the schema of interpretations developed to rethink some of the most important events during the American occupation of Japan after World War II, we are in position to discuss the importance and meaning of one of the most serious crises to engulf the Japanese Left after the return of sovereignty to Japan: the 1960 struggle against the conclusion of the Japan–US Security Treaty. Events that year took a dramatic turn once the ruling Liberal Democratic Party (LDP) announced its intention to push ratification of the new treaty through the lower house of the Diet despite the intense opposition of minority parties, most notably the Japan Socialist Party and Japan Communist Party. This provoked scuffles between Left and Right politicians in the Diet. Later even some members of the ruling party boycotted the final vote. In preparation for a state visit of President Dwight Eisenhower to Japan on the occasion, his press secretary flew into Tokyo's Haneda Airport only to be greeted by some 20,000 protesters. His official car was rocked and damaged by the demonstrators, and Eisenhower's advance representative had to be rescued by a US Marine helicopter team. The state visit was subsequently cancelled.

Emotions reached a peak on 16 June when, during one of the most spectacular days of protest in modern Japanese history, 111 separate student and labour groups mobilised an estimated 5.8 million demonstrators across Japan to protest against final passage of the bill. Amidst threats of intervention by violent right-wing extremists, the police sought to contain the protest through the night and into the next morning. Eventually 4,000 demonstrators managed to break into the Diet itself. In the ensuing struggle, 589 people were injured, 43 of them severely, and one student was killed. Although some 330,000 demonstrators surrounded the Diet to protest on 18 June, the day before the treaty automatically completed the legislative process, the crisis demoralised the Left. Nevertheless, Prime Minister Nobusuke Kishi eventually had to resign and Japan's parliamentary Right never again acted so aggressively to exploit its Diet majority over so divisive an issue.

Many of the classic strategies of the American empire of bases contributed to this crisis. As elsewhere, Washington used conservative political forces, sometimes reactionary but almost always corrupt, to support policies that provoked widespread public resistance. Later, when the treaty had to be renewed in 1970, the country's universities erupted and violent student protesters repeatedly took to the streets and rail links of the capital. Public antipathy towards the Japanese government and America was inflamed by the refusal of the US authorities to relinquish administrative control over Okinawa and by the use of US bases, particularly on Okinawa, to bomb North Vietnam.

In 1960, Washington displayed prudent flexibility, and quietly endured the humiliation of the president. In 1970, the Nixon administration gave way and agreed to return Okinawa to nominal Japanese control. In 1960, the US negotiators had effectively exploited Cold War fears, both at home and in Japan, to secure its military hold over an old Pacific rival in what was in effect a major victory for base imperialism over democratic idealism and national sovereignty. In 1970, an economically more vulnerable America, a nation bitterly divided over its war in Vietnam, outwardly pursued a less aggressive form of diplomacy. Washington had learned through the warm stages of the Cold War that base imperialism did not require colonies or the direct administrative responsibility for regions but merely effective 'status of forces agreements' that secured immunity from prosecution by the local legal authorities for offences against the local population and freedom of movement of American military personnel, their weapons and supplies. The complex process by which the Japanese political establishment and the general public embraced and learned to live with the consequences of defeat worked in uneasy tandem with the pressures of the Cold War on the United States. But analysed retrospectively, the student of American empire sees both incidents as victories for base imperialism. Japanese resistance did curb some US demands, but by and large, Washington got what it wanted. The privileges America won in 1960 and 1970 remain largely undiluted to this day. In some cases, they have even been enhanced. Militarists worship a jealous god.

What is to be done?

As we have seen, in *The Sorrows of Empire*, Johnson asks whether America's republican institutions can be revitalised in ways that might curb the militarism, imperialism and secrecy of the defence-security establishment. In Japan, the problem is partly ideological and partly historical. American empire gives the Right security in place of subjectivity, and the Left has bought a partial realization of its pacifist dream by diluting national sovereignty. In their different ways, Right and Left have offended each other's deepest aspirations. But resisting American empire requires the end of these Right-vs-Left divides in Japanese political life. Sovereignty and subjectivity must be reclaimed and revitalised, and not only in Japan but almost everywhere that finds itself trapped under the eagle's wing. If the liberty of the world is to be restored and the forces of our new Rome vanquished once more, a solemn hunting is at hand. In the sphere of the intellect, this is the supreme political calling and duty of the revisionist.

Notes

1 Chalmers Johnson, *The Sorrows of Empire: Militarism, Secrecy, and the End of the Republic*, London and New York, Verso, 2004, p. 3.
2 Ibid., p. 164.
3 Ibid., p. 1.
4 Ibid., p. 202. Johnson cites the claim of anti-base Japanese activists that the true total may be 91.
5 Ibid., p. 312.
6 David Williams, *Defending Japan's Pacific War: The Kyoto School Philosophers and Post-White Power*, London and New York: RoutledgeCurzon, 2004.
7 Ibid., p. 8.
8 See Michael Ignatieff, *The Lesser Evil: Political Ethics in an Age of Terror*, Princeton, New Jersey: Princeton University Press, 1994; and Niall Ferguson, *Colossus: The Rise and Fall of the American Empire*, Harmondsworth, Middlesex: Penguin Allen Lane, 2004.
9 Williams, op. cit., p. 8.
10 Ibid.
11 Mary Dejevsky, 'How was the Intelligentsia Fooled', *The Independent*, 18 May 2004, p. 31.
12 Ibid.
13 Ibid.
14 Michael Ignatieff, 'Evil under Interrogation', *FT Magazine, The Financial Times*, 15 May 2004, p. 25.
15 Chalmers Johnson, *Blowback: The Costs and Consequences of American Empire*, New York: Metropolitan Books Henry Holt and Company, 2000, and *The Sorrows of Empire*, op. cit.
16 Weber, Max, '*Wissenschaft als Beruf*', *Gesammelte Aufsaetze zur Wissenschftslehre*, Tübingen, 1922, (a translation may be found in H. H. Gerth and C. Wright Mills (eds), *From Max Weber: Essays in Sociology*, New York: Oxford University Press, 1946).
17 The question was made famous by Edwin O. Reischauer in his essay 'What Went Wrong? in James W. Morley (ed.), *Dilemmas of Growth in Prewar Japan*, Princeton, New Jersey: Princeton University Press, 1971, pp. 489–510, but the question itself was posed by Ron Dore in his contribution (co-authored with Tsutomu Ōuchi) in the Morley volume, titled 'Rural Origins of Japanese Fascism'. On reflection, it is clear now that one of the consequences of imprecise left-wing talk of Japanese 'fascism' was doubly wrong: a misconceived obsession with the Japanese past that has encouraged the field to turn a blind eye towards the contemporary realities of US imperialism.
18 Robert D. Blackwill and Paul Dibb (eds), *America's Asian Alliances*, Cambridge, Massachusetts and London: MIT Press, 2000.
19 Chalmers Johnson, 'Foreword', in Chalmers Johnson (ed.), *Okinawa: Cold War Island*, Cardiff, CA: Japan Policy Research Institute, 1999, p. 5.
20 See the chapter titled 'Criticism' in David Williams, *Japan and the Enemies of Open Political Science*, London and New York: Routledge, 1994, pp. 172–197.
21 See 'Chapter 11, Nazism is No Excuse: After Farías – The Allied Gaze and the Second Crisis', in David Williams, *Defending Japan's Pacific War: The Kyoto School Philosophers and Post-White Power*, London and New York: RoutledgeCurzon, 2004, pp. 151–165.
22 Karl Marx and Frederick Engels, *Die deutsche Ideologie*, Berlin: Dietz Verlag, 1959, Vols 3 and 4, translated into English as *The German Ideology*, Moscow: Progress Publishers, 1968. Jun Tōsaka, *Nippon Ideorogii-ron* (The Japanese Ideology), Tokyo: Iwanami Shoten, 1977 (originally published in 1935).

23 Louise Young, *Japan's Total Empire: Manchuria and the Culture of Wartime Imperialism*, Berkeley, Los Angeles and London: University of California Press, 1998. The term 'total' as in the expressions 'total war' or 'total empire' apparently derive from the usage of Carl Schmitt. In a way that Old Left historiography never imagined but the war on terrorism has made obvious, there is hardly a chapter title or theme from Young's book that could not be applied to contemporary America.

24 See Williams, *Defending Japan's Pacific War*, op. cit., for a detailed discussion of this issue (Chapter 5) and a translation of Tanabe's secret wartime lecture on the ideals at work in the notion of a genuine Greater East Asian Co-Prosperity Sphere. See also the invaluable documents and analysis presented in Ryōsuke Ōshima, *Kyōtō Gakuha to Nippon Kaigun: Shin Shiryō 'Ōshima Memos' o Megutte* (The Kyoto School and the Japanese Navy on the New Historical Documents, *The Oshima Memos.*), Tokyo: PHP, 2001.

25 Among his few cards, Tōjō had one potential trump; the possibility that Japanese defeat would draw America so deeply into Asia that Washington would eventually suffer a fatal form of 'imperial over-stretch, while at the same time, the multi-cultural-multi-ethnic nature of empire would cause a demographic revolution at home, thus undermining the racial pillars of Roosevelt's White Republic.

26 For a summary presentation of the evidence and argument for this interpretation, see Williams, *Defending Japan's Pacific War*, op. cit., especially chapters 1 and 2.

27 Johnson, *Sorrows*, op. cit., p. 191.

28 The historical information discussed in this section is drawn from Shunichi Uno (ed.) *Nihon Zenshi (Japan Chronik)*, Tokyo: Kōdansha, 1991.

29 S. E. Finer, *Man on Horseback: The Role of the Military in Politics*, New York: Transactions Publishers, 2002.

30 Criticism of Gandhi, as an inverted version of the third world 'mimic man', is the *Leitmotif* of Naipaul's writings, the novels, the essays as well as the travel writings. See particularly the *vignettes* of Gandhi in 'Indian Autobiographies' and 'A Second Visit' in *The Overcrowded Barracoon and Other Articles*, Harmondsworth, Middlesex: Penguin Books, 1976.

31 Glenn Hook, Julie Gilson, Christopher W. Hughes and Hugo Dobson, *Japan's International Relations: Politics, Economics and Security*, London and New York: Routledge, 2001, pp. 65–68.

9 The Left in the shaping of Japanese democracy

Historical review

Junji Banno

Introduction

The results of the general elections for the House of Representatives held in November 2003 show that the collapse of the Left may substantially alter the character of Japan's postwar democracy, which has now lasted for 59 years. The Social Democratic Party (SDP) and Japan Communist Party (JCP) together won a mere 15 seats out of a total of 480. This was less than the proportion held by the social democratic forces in 1937, just before the outbreak of the Sino-Japanese War. At the general elections held in February 1936, the social democratic parties won 22 seats and in the general elections of April 1937 they received 37 seats. Moreover, this was out of a total of 466 seats, less than the present total. The number of seats held by socialist parties in parliament at the beginning of the twenty-first century was less than half that of prewar Japan, over which the Peace Preservation Law held sway.

The Japan Socialist Party (JSP, predecessor of the SDP), and the JCP (which has consistently held on to its 'Communist' label) were one crucial wing of the 59-year-old 'post-war democracy'. The combined total of seats won by these two parties has now fallen to 15 out of 480 (3.1 per cent). Thus the Japanese Left seems to be gradually turning into an object of study for historians.

This sense of loss is premised on the 59 years since the war in which the Left did rather well. From an analysis of the JSP and JCP at the height of their powers in the period of postwar democracy, it seems difficult to draw lessons useful to those two parties in their current state. Even so, the prewar Japanese Left had an even harder time of it. We have shown that the prewar Left had more seats than the Left had in the general elections of 2003, and in the general elections of 2005 the two parties failed to make significant progress, winning between them 16 seats.

The problem is that the Left in prewar Japan (just a handful of people) constantly insisted on the purity of their vision, and continued to attack even those reformers who might be considered close to their own position. As a result, the prewar Left tended to drive itself into a corner within the progressive camp, and, at the height of its isolation, it would be subjected to

repression by the government. It is generally agreed that those who perpetrated this repression were worse than those on whom it was perpetrated.
In the twenty-first century, unlike the situation under the prewar Imperial
Constitution, however much the Left might be isolated, it was not going to
suffer from repression. But since the prewar Left chose the road of isolation,
in general the development of democracy was retarded and weakened. This
could happen again at the beginning of the twenty-first century.

The prewar Left suffered serious repression at the time of the Great Treason
Trial in 1910, at the 15 March Incident in 1928 and in the Popular Front
Affair of 1937. In the Great Treason Affair, anarchists in Nagano Prefecture
were arrested in 1910 on suspicion of preparing bombs with which to assassinate the Emperor. Shūsui Kōtoku and others were arrested for having
allegedly made an unsuccessful attempt to kill the Meiji Emperor, and the
following year (1911) Kōtoku and 12 others were executed. As a result of the
15 March Incident, when in March 1928 the *Seiyūkai* Cabinet of Giichi
Tanaka arrested 1,600 associates of the JCP under the Peace Preservation
Law, the JCP was no longer able to engage in overt activities. In the Popular
Front Incident, just after the outbreak of war between Japan and China
in 1937, a little under 500 socialists (linked with what became the left wing
of the JSP after the war) were arrested under the Peace Preservation Law
on the ground that they were promoting a united front. This chapter will not
seek to analyse these cases as such, but will investigate the role of the 'Left' in
democratic and social democratic movements around the time of those
events.

The general elections of November 2003 show that the oft-repeated mantra
about the 'end of post-war democracy' had finally come to pass. The election
was a major step towards a party system based on two major parties. It
resulted in the dramatic collapse of the Left in the elections, while overseas
despatch of the Self Defence Forces was no longer regarded as a major issue
in the voting behaviour of the electorate. We may thus analyse not only the
'postwar democratic system' – now approaching its end – but also 'prewar
democracy' – which failed and came to an end – and in particular the role
within it of the Left, and this exercise may afford us unexpected insights.

The Left and the end of Meiji

Nobody would disagree that the Left in the Meiji period means the Shūsui
Kōtoku group. Even though Kōtoku rejected Marxism and espoused anar-
cho-syndicalism, he was the representative figure of the Left in the Meiji
period. The execution of Kōtoku and his supporters in the Great Treason
Affair resulted from a frame-up by the second Katsura Cabinet. There was in
fact no concrete plan to assassinate the Emperor.

On the other hand, the Kōtoku group, in the socialist movement that
preceded the Great Treason Affair, attacked the parliamentary faction of
Tetsuji Tazoe (1875–1908), Mitsujirō Nishikawa (1876–1940) and others.

This internal strife weakened the power of both sides, and in the end they were buried by the regime.

Two years after the Great Treason Affair, a popular democratic movement arose, calling itself 'The First Constitutional Defence Movement'. If the parliamentary socialism of Tazoe and others had lasted up to the time of the popular movement, demands for universal suffrage and social improvement might have been added to it, as it was only calling for party cabinets. But because of the executions resulting from the Great Treason Affair, not only the Direct Action Faction, but also the Parliamentary Faction – indeed, virtually all social democrats – were forced into silence. Hitoshi Yamakawa, one of the very few survivors from the Direct Action Faction (he had been spared association because, at the time of the Great Treason Incident, he was in prison in connection with a different affair), from 1916, resumed activism in favour of freedom of speech.

Those interested in the modern history of Japan will all be familiar with the First Constitutional Defence Movement of 1912–13. Its principal leaders were Yukio Ozaki and Tsuyoshi Inukai. They were praised even then as the 'gods of constitutional government', and today Ozaki's bronze statue surveys the Parliament building from the Constitution Memorial Hall. In terms, however, of what was meant by democracy, the demands made by this, the greatest popular movement of the time, were extremely weak. Their slogans 'Down with the aristocratic clique' and 'Support constitutional government' had not progressed beyond the *Proposal to Establish a Popular Assembly* of 1874: 'When we, the loyal citizens of the Emperor, humbly consider to whom power belongs today, we have to realise that it does not belong to the Emperor himself, nor does it belong to the common people, rather it belongs to the government officials.'

Democratization movements gradually developed in the Meiji period by way of the *Proposal* of 1874, the Popular Rights Movement of the early 1880s, the activities of the popular parties (Liberal Party and Progressive Party) in parliament in the early 1890s, and the first party cabinet launched in 1898 (the first Shigenobu Ōkuma Cabinet). By comparison, the aims of the movement that was active in 1912–13 ('Down with the aristocratic clique', 'Support constitutional government') represent, rather, a retreat from democracy.

Sakuzō Yoshino, the Tokyo University professor, pointed this out in an outspoken fashion, soon after his return from a study tour of Europe and America. He made the following criticisms of the First Constitutional Defence Movement:

> First of all, only when a movement of the masses is spontaneous and positive, is it likely to be taken seriously at a political level. . . . An approach lacking specific demands, and confined to destructive violence, is extremely deplorable. . . . There have been many instances overseas of mass demonstration movements. But in foreign countries

these movements for the most part have positive ideologies and demands. For instance, the mass movements in Austria before 1907, and the mass movements in Belgium which broke out explosively in April of last year (and are still taking place to some extent) aim to expand the suffrage and amend the election law. . . . French workers sometimes mount demonstrations, but they put forward anti-war arguments and oppose expansion of armaments, or take issue with three years of military service. They do not merely make a big noise in vague opposition to the Government. Given that in Japan we only have negative demonstrations, whose methods are always both negative and revolutionary, demonstrators just end up setting fire to things and clashing with the police. This hardly differs from the rabbles rioting at the time of the French Revolution.[1]

Just to read this extract makes us acutely aware of the superior insight of this Tokyo University political scientist who, stayed in Europe between 1910 and 1913 and witnessed social movements there with his own eyes. He urged Japan's popular movements not to shout 'Down with the aristocracy', but to promote universal suffrage.

If, however, parliamentary socialists together with 'direct action' socialists had not been forced into silence as a result of the Great Treason Affair of 1910, what would have been the outcome? There were Meiji period parliamentary socialists, who had not spent three years overseas at public expense, but knew from documents the Western European situations that Yoshino had seen for himself, and tried to turn these into objectives for the Japanese socialist movement to pursue. One of these was Mitsujirō Nishikawa, who wrote as follows in *Shakai Shimbun* of September 1907:

People say that socialists only dream of fundamental reform, and oppose small reforms. Even some socialists advocate this position. Our view differs, however. The way we see it, if our ideal is radical reform, minor reforms should not be inconsistent with this basic aim. . . . We used to say that, without universal suffrage, socialism was like a ship beached on a sandbank. . . . Among European nations, socialist parties in states that have already achieved universal suffrage operate with that as a base, but in states where it has yet to be achieved (like Sweden and Norway), socialist parties fight hard to bring it about. In Austria, universal suffrage was introduced last year after 40 years of struggle by the Socialist Party. The German Socialist Party opposed a general strike. But last year, when the Kaiser hatched a plan to eradicate universal suffrage, the party held a congress at Jena and issued a declaration that: 'Should the Kaiser lay a finger on universal suffrage, we shall organise a general strike'. This shows just how vital European socialist parties regard universal suffrage. Thus, both in logic and in fact, since universal suffrage is crucial for socialist parties, socialism in Japan also must act to bring it about.[2]

What is advocated here implies an affirmation of social reformism, and is basically similar to Yoshino's observations cited above and also to his *min-ponshugi* (politics having the people as its base), first put forward in 1916, and which we shall refer to in the next section. Indeed, it may be regarded as its precursor.

The left-wing socialists not only opposed parliamentarism and advocated direct action, but also, by their imprudent actions, invited the frame-up perpetrated by the second Katsura Cabinet in the Great Treason Affair. Kōtoku and his friends did not make concrete plans to assassinate the Meiji Emperor but it is undeniable that they acted in such a way as to make it possible for the government to reach its distorted interpretation.[3] As a result, they not merely invited the repression of their own faction, but also took away the freedom of action from the parliamentary socialists who should have been those responsible for Taishō democracy.

Taishō 'Democracy' and the Left

It was at the beginning of 1916 that Hitoshi Yamakawa, the survivor of the Direct Action Faction from the end of the Meiji period, was able to resume his activities. Of the central figures in the Parliamentary Faction, Tetsuji Tazoe died of illness in 1908, before the great Treason Affair, Mitsu-jirō Nishikawa changed his views through 'conversion' (*tenkō*), and Sen Katayama in 1914 went to the United States where he had previously spent years as an impoverished student. Thus, the socialists in the Taishō period (1912–26) were composed principally of members of the Direct Action group. This was most unfortunate for the universal suffrage movement around 1920. The 'Taishō socialists', led by Yamakawa, persistently and maliciously criticised the *minponshugi* of Yoshino and others, and persistently rejected political democratization through universal suffrage.

Hitoshi Yamakawa was suddenly made famous by an article he published in the April 1918 issue of the journal *Shin Nippon* (New Japan), entitled 'Criticism of the Democracy of Dr [Sakuzō] Yoshino and Professor [Reikichi] Kita'. In the article, Yamakawa, in an ironic fashion, portrayed Yoshino as a scholar serving the government and rejecting popular sovereignty:

> Democracy (according to Dr Yoshino) has become two separate doctrines, that of democracy concerning the location of sovereignty and democracy concerning the exercise of sovereignty. According to Dr Yoshino, however, since the Japanese Constitution says clearly that sovereignty lies with the Emperor, there is no room to allow democracy. Political science, which is the objective study of the state, explains that the state is as it is today, and the scientific study of politics says that because something is as it is, so it must be as a matter of duty. The scientific study of politics does not require the highest level of truth concerning the political life of human beings, but takes as its universal

starting point the present constitution of the country where his university is. According to him, the constitution is not just a historical phenomenon in political life, but is an accomplished fact for all time. . . . Political science does not embrace great hopes, such as seeking to direct the Constitution through searching for the truth, but determines what is truth and what is not as a reflection of the present Constitution. . . . According to Yoshino, Japan's present Constitution plainly does not permit democracy. Therefore scientific political analysts have no responsibility to advocate democracy. Happily, Dr Yoshino has been a scientific political analyst![4]

In this long-winded text, the point of Yamakawa's criticism is simply that the Meiji Constitution and people's sovereignty were incompatible. The assessment by the editor, Katsuyuki Tanaka, that 'I was really excited to read Yamakawa's sharp, clear-cut criticism of Yoshino' is wide of the mark.[5]

Given that among postwar historians the Emperor System was seen as the root of all evil, Yoshino's *minponshugi*, which accepted the Emperor System, had a poor reputation, and Yamakawa's criticism of it was extremely well regarded. But in applauding Yamakawa, they failed to probe deeply, first, how he planned to create popular sovereignty in Japan in practice, and, secondly, whether what is called Yoshino's acceptance of imperial sovereignty was really what Yamakawa was criticising.

Concerning the first point, Yamakawa and his fans forget that, in the prewar Constitution, parliament did not possess the right to propose constitutional amendments. According to Article 73, the power to revise the Constitution rested entirely with the Emperor. If constitutional revision through parliament was impossible, the only way of changing imperial sovereignty into popular sovereignty was either by revolution or by the self-destruction of the emperor system. In practice, in 1945, through the defeat and allied occupation, imperial sovereignty was indeed transformed into popular sovereignty, but that was not a path advocated by Yamakawa. Thus, Yamakawa was merely making the criticism that Yoshino was not supporting revolution.

So far as the second point is concerned, it may be resolved by reading an article, long like its title, published in *Chūō Kōron* in January 1916.[6] In this article Yoshino defines democracy in the famous words of Abraham Lincoln: 'Government of the people, by the people and for the people', and argues that, except in a republic, democracy in the sense of 'government of the people' cannot be achieved. But in the belief that even in a country with monarchical sovereignty, it was possible to create 'government by the people' through universal suffrage and party cabinets, Yoshino gave this the name *minponshugi*. From this perspective, Yoshino, while occupying his position at Tokyo University, worked hard appealing to the people with his advocacy of universal suffrage in speeches given all over the country and to all sorts of groups. According to the chronology in *Yoshino Sakuzō Chosakushū* (his collected works), in 1918 he made 60 speeches in Tokyo, Osaka, Kyoto and eight other prefectures on 49 separate occasions, and in 1919 he gave 89 speeches in Tokyo, Osaka, Kyoto and 14 other prefectures on 81 occasions. Most of these related to *minponshugi* and universal suffrage.

While Yoshino, subjected to criticism by Hitoshi Yamakawa, was working actively for universal suffrage, what were the attitudes of Yamakawa towards universal suffrage? By comparison with the many articles attacking the *minponshugi* arguments of Sakuzō Yoshino and Ikuo Oyama, there are not so many articles by Yamakawa directly criticising universal suffrage as such. But Yamakawa's attitudes, as shown in his small numbers of articles about universal suffrage, are extremely clear. In an article published in the journal *Zenei* for March 1922, entitled 'Universal Suffrage and the Tactics of the Proletarian Class', Yamakawa wrote as follows:

> Universal suffrage may be brought about in the near future. This will probably happen. But today, even if the door were opened, that would not be enough to lure the main stream of the working class movement into parliament. By contrast, if universal suffrage had been realised several years earlier, the order of battle of the workers' movement would have been greatly disrupted, and it would have taken at least ten years to set it back on the right path.[7]

The conclusion of the socialist, Yamakawa, who thought that universal suffrage would 'emasculate' the working class movement, was that there should be a 'clear and conscious abstention from voting'. He continues:

> Nevertheless, if the tactic of the proletarian class not to use parliament as an arena for struggle resulted from a lack of interest in politics on the part of the working class, this would have no value from the point of view of class struggle. If we decide not to use the vote that is given to us, this must be a clear and positive decision to abstain. If we abstain from voting, then at least, rather than placing our vote in the ballot box, we must abstain in a more effective way. In other words, if abstention itself is not a positive, conscious mass movement, it has no value as class struggle.[8]

It was in 1920 that demands for universal male suffrage in Japan became insistent, and this movement was given a big boost by Yoshino's promotion of *minponshugi*. Reacting to this, Prime Minister Kei Hara, known as 'the commoners' premier', dissolved parliament and appealed to the electorate on the ground that to introduce universal suffrage would be premature. The result was that Hara won handsomely. With universal male suffrage the electorate would increase to 12 million, whereas at the time the electorate totalled 3 million. By appealing to this privileged electorate of three million with the argument that it was too early to introduce universal suffrage, the

Seiyūkai party, which he headed, won 281 out of 464 seats. This was 60 per cent of the total, as against 45 per cent at dissolution.

But Sakuzō Yoshino, the person who most hated the party-first-ism and government suprematism of Kei Hara, the Seiyūkai President, was the proponent of *minponshugi*. In an article he wrote in *Chūō Kōron* for April 1920 (publication date, 20 March), he literally reviled Hara:

> The justifications given by the Hara government for dissolving parliament have been strange from the start. . . . They are almost impossible to understand and lack any kind of logic. . . . Perhaps it is pointless to address oneself to this, the world's most malformed politician, who cuts politics off from philosophy or science, and operates in a completely haphazard fashion. There seems no point in discussing whether his arguments are logical or illogical.[9]

Among the arguments for dissolution of parliament that Yoshino could not understand was Hara's statement that universal suffrage would spell the end of the class system. It is worth noting that Yoshino was not arguing that political participation through universal suffrage would contribute to the diminution of class struggle. On the contrary, he maintained that it was correct to argue for the abolition of the class system, and that universal suffrage was political reform for that purpose. There are many people who read criticism by a socialist such as Hitoshi Yamakawa, and believe that Yoshino's *minponshugi* was a doctrine of compromise and accommodation with the regime. Let us then allow Yoshino to speak in his own words:

> There is a minority of people who hate like poison the idea that the class system should be abolished, but most people firmly believe that the class system ought to go. The argument of Prime Minister Hara that because it will result in the end of the class system it is no good converting to universal suffrage becomes the argument of the majority of the people that universal suffrage ought to be introduced quickly. Without investigating in depth whether ending the class system would be a good thing or a bad thing, he (the Prime Minister) seems to have listened to government officials and others to the effect that it would be a bad thing, and thus he puts this argument straight into the public arena. It is like a country person wearing an old-fashioned kimono and thinking he is smart.[10]

Of course Yoshino was not arguing for an end of the class system through revolution. The central proposition of his *minponshugi* was that political equality should be established through universal suffrage, and thus social and economic inequalities should be corrected. As a socialist, Yamakawa not only did not give support to Yoshino's *minponshugi*, but he attacked what he saw as Yoshino's lack of an argument for popular sovereignty. He argued that, with the introduction of universal suffrage, Japanese socialism would be 'emasculated', so the working class should engage in 'positive abstention'.

Just as Yamakawa criticised Yoshino, and Yoshino criticised Hara, the Seiyūkai during the Hara period criticised the so-called Yamagata bureaucrats, namely the Army, the Privy Council and the House of Peers, which constituted the extreme conservative wing of Japanese politics. The difference between the Yamagata bureaucrats and Hara's Seiyūkai concerned the interpretation of the 'right of command' (*tōsuiken*), in other words, the Emperor's right to command the armed forces directly, overriding cabinet. Kei Hara, as prime minister in a party cabinet, held a position close to the 'organ theory of the Emperor' proposed by Dr Minobe Tatsukichi. On this point, Hara wrote in his diary at the beginning of September 1920:

> Anyway, the fact that the Military General Staff Headquarters is receiving support from (Aritomo) Yamagata, the *genrō*, does not fit the spirit of the times. The present era is quite different from that of the previous Emperor (Meiji), and it is dangerous to exercise the right of command, etc., for future prospects. The government, in order not to have a bad influence on the Imperial House, should take full responsibility. In other words, in the essence of constitutional government, it is for the sake of the Imperial Household. The Imperial Household has no direct connection with politics, but rather is the branch of government concerned with charity, honours, etc. This is my view and it is the policy we adopt. But the military men around the Military Staff Headquarters do not understand this, and are inclined to place burdens on the Imperial Household in their political activities. This is extraordinarily mistaken.[11]

On the other hand, Yamagata, the grand old man of the conservative faction, and Hara, the Seiyūkai President, were of the same mind concerning the question of universal suffrage. In October 1920, on the day when he had a meeting with Yamagata, Hara wrote the following in his diary:

> Yamagata as usual said that universal suffrage would destroy the country, while my view is that it would destroy the country if the timing of it is not right. The danger in hastening the introduction of universal suffrage lies not in the rural areas but in the cities. From ancient times, revolution has originated in the cities, and if we introduce universal suffrage too quickly, Tokyo will become a scene of disorder. I said this was greatly to be feared, and Yamagata agreed with me.[12]

We have broadened the argument to include relations between Kei Hara and Yamagata Aritomo, neither of whom had a direct relationship with the role of the Left. This is in order to establish the position of the Left in the

Taishō period in the context of relations between the Left, the centre Left, the centre Right and the conservatives, around the end of the First World War. If we sum up their mutual relations on the basis of what we have described above, Yamakawa (Left) criticised Yoshino (centre Left) with malice, Yoshino (centre Left) maliciously criticised Hara (centre Right), while Hara (centre Right) in part agreed with and in part criticised Yamagata (conservative). After Hara's death, the Seiyūkai invited General Giichi Tanaka, the former Army Minister, to be its President (1925), and the differences between the centre Right and the conservative faction became narrower. At the same time, the Seiyūkai cabinet now became more conservative, moved to suppress the Japan Communist Party (in effect founded in December 1926), which had just expelled Hitoshi Yamakawa and moved to the far left. The 15 March Incident (1928) was the realization of this policy of repression, and it took place during the period of the Tanaka Giichi Cabinet. So the attacks by the Left on the centre faction, attacks by the centre Left on the centre Right, and by the centre Right on the Right, extended in a direct line from Left to Right. And with the Right also attacking the Left, what was a straight line was extended into a circle. Moreover, just as at the time of the Great Treason Affair of 1910, now a 'winter season' began for the Left. The two-party period that went from the Tanaka Seiyūkai Cabinet, through the Minseitō Cabinets of Osachi Hamaguchi and Reijirō Wakatsuki, then to the Seiyūkai Cabinet of Tsuyoshi Inukai began with repression of the JCP on the left. As has become clear from the above analysis, 'Taishō Socialism', led by Yamakawa, was not responsible for its repression under the Peace Preservation Law, but it bore some responsibility for the Left becoming isolated, which was one reason for its being subjected to repression. If Yamakawa had not devoted himself to attacks on the *minponshugi* of Yoshino, who appears to have been closest to his position, but rather they had worked together to bring about universal suffrage, and if as a result they had won a certain number of seats in the first general elections held under universal male suffrage (on 20 February 1928), even the Tanaka cabinet might have found it difficult to carry out the mass arrests of Communists on 15 May of the same year.

What had happened once happened a second time, and what happened twice happened a third time. In the general elections held on 30 April 1937, a mere two months before the outbreak of the Sino-Japanese War on 7 July, the Social Masses Party (SMP) increased its total of seats to 36 (initially 37 seats, but one member dropped out). But we shall now investigate the related Popular Front Faction, which only elected one of its candidates, Kanju Katō, in the same elections. The principal reason for the large-scale arrests of Popular Front Faction members between December 1937 and January 1938 (much resembling the arrests on 15 March 1928) lay in the outbreak of the war with China in July. But if the Popular Front Faction had done well in the elections of 30 April in conjunction with the SMP, any suppression of the Popular Front Faction in December would certainly have assumed a different form. On this occasion also, the repression took place at a time when the Left had become isolated.

'Shōwa Democracy' and the Left

Even though the term 'Taishō Democracy'[13] exists, there is no such expression as 'Shōwa Democracy'.[14] Where such a term is used, it has the sense of 'postwar democracy'. Concerning 'prewar Shōwa', the terms normally used are 'ultra-nationalism', or 'Emperor-system fascism' – in other words, concepts having the very reverse meaning from democracy. An article, however, was published in the September 1937 issue of the journal *Kaizō* by the Marxist philosopher, Jun Tosaka (1900–45), which showed that it was possible to use the term 'Shōwa Democracy' even in relation to the prewar period. Incidentally, Tosaka, along with Yoshitarō Ōmori and Itsurō Sakisaka, was an advocate of the Popular Front, and was not a turncoat (*tenkōsha*):

> It was the Social Masses Party that pointed out the contradiction between a huge military budget and a budget that makes the people's standard of living secure. . . . Those who, somewhat instinctively, pursued these relationships were the established parties and the so-called 'liberals'. In Japan, however, 'liberalism' is in practice the normal outlook of the masses. In other words, attention to these contradictions was prevalent among the people at this time. . . . It is impossible to obscure the fact that liberalism and democracy are the common view of the people. If we look at the content of electoral speeches, this is demonstrated without ambiguity.[15]

Since monthly journals were actually published about ten days before the official publication date, Tosaka's article would have been published about 20 August. If we add to the calculation the time taken for printing, it must have been written in the first half of August, or about a month after the Marco Polo Bridge Incident. The 'content of electoral speeches' mentioned in the article would have referred to the 20th general election that took placed about three months previously, as well as the big city assembly elections of June. Incidentally, in a round table discussion that took place on 8 May for the June issue of the journal *Chūō Kōron* (just after the elections of 30 April) the SMP parliamentarian, Miwa Jusō (1894–1956), wrote: 'Bringing the discussion back to the elections, what really resonate with the common people are statements of opposition to fascism. . . . Opposition to fascism pervades the masses.'[16] This may be regarded as background to Tosaka's arguments.

It is well known that, in the last general elections before the war (30 April 1937), the SMP had increased its representation from 18 to 36. And it had already been pointed out that the expectations of the electors voting for that party were anti-fascist. This was seen in the context, however, that the SMP betrayed the expectations of the masses, as shown by its linking up with the

Army and its use of the slogan 'broad national defence'. The most recent *Dictionary of Japanese History* writes as follows about the SMP:

> Proletarian party formed in July 1932 from a merger of the National Labour-Farmer Masses Party (NLFP) and the Social Masses[17] Party (SMP). Chairman: Isoo Abe; Secretary-General: Hisashi Asō. The leadership group, consisting of Asō and Teruaki Tadokoro of the former NLFP and Kanichirō Kamei of the former SMP, developed a change in policy by establishing links with part of the Army and with the progressive bureaucrats. The party made good electoral progress in the general elections of 1936 and 1937, when it won its best total of 37 [previously given as 36, as one member dropped out soon after the election] seats. When war with China broke out it co-operated with the war. During the cabinet of Fumimaro Konoe, it behaved as a pro-government party, and supported the National Mobilization Law.[18]

The SMP is here being described as a thoroughly fascist party. This description is diametrically opposed to that of Jun Tosaka, who, at the time, gave it the image of a social democratic party, opposed to the military and defending the living standards of the people and democracy.

While the views of a contemporary writer and those of post-war historians differ so radically, we should perhaps be somewhat cautious in making Tosaka a representative example of the former. But as a writer who, in the same period as Tosaka, gave an almost identical evaluation of the electoral success of the SMP in the 1937 elections, let us quote Eijirō Kawai, the liberal Socialist and Tokyo University economics professor. Just after the elections he wrote the following in an article published in *Chūō Kōron*:

> An unpredictable aspect of the electoral results was whether the SMP would make a substantial advance. But in the elections, the party gained 930,930 votes[19] and returned 36 MPs. This result was not entirely unexpected. But the fact that these hopes and expectations were realised and that the party leapt ahead was a major event in Japanese political history, and deserves to be given wide publicity. It resembles the success of the British Labour Party in 1906, when it won 43 seats a mere six years after its foundation in 1900, and thus attracted attention from the political world.[20]

The evaluations made by Jun Tosaka and Eijirō Kawai were practically the same. On the other hand, at that time there were those who stubbornly attacked the 'fascist' character of the SMP. These included Mosaburō Suzuki and others of the Japan Proletarian Party (JPP), arrested in December 1937 in the Popular Front Affair.

This group, which continued on into the left wing of the postwar JSP, split from the SMP in May 1936, and formed the JPP in March 1937. From the time of the preceding Labour-Farmer Proletarian Conference, it advocated a popular front, and persistently criticised the SMP, which refused to join such a front. In its 'Struggle Policy for the 70th Session of Parliament' (January 1937), the JPP criticised the SMP in the following words:

> The fact that the fascists have built a nest within one part of the SMP is widely known. Our party, whatever the SMP may do, will have nothing to do with fascist ideology. . . . The SMP, in its self-opinionated fashion, deliberately denounces a popular front and has obstructed alliance with the liberal elements in the bourgeois parties.[21]

In 1935 the Comintern (the international communist organization) mandated all communist parties to pursue a united front. This was in order to foster anti-fascist united fronts and stop attacks by communist parties on social democratic parties. In Japan, however, instead of the banned Communist Party, the JPP and the Marxist intellectuals known as the Labour-Farmer Faction (*Rōnō ha*) attacked the SMP and backed bourgeois parties. Before the general elections of 30 April 1937 the Labour-Farmer Faction intellectual, Yoshitarō Ōmori, in an article published in *Kaizō* of 20 April, made this position perfectly clear:

> Preferably return candidates of the JPP to parliament! If there are some JPP candidates available, choose those who are most clearly anti-fascist. Then vote for the small anti-fascist elements in the established parties. . . . But what should you do if such candidates are not available? Go ahead and vote for members of the usual established parties.[22]

What he meant by 'established parties' was the Seiyūkai and the Minseitō – the two major parties. These two parties, since the young officers' uprising in February 1936, were openly criticising the military. But, at the same time, both parties were persistently opposing social legislation, including a labour union bill, an unemployment insurance bill, and a retirement reserve fund bill. Even though they were anti-war and anti-fascist, they were parties conspicuously dependent on capitalists. Even if workers and small farmers were told to vote for those two parties for the sake of anti-fascism, they would find this advice hard to accept.

On this point the message of the SMP was unambiguous. The party's electoral slogans were as follows:

- First, effect domestic reform!
- Stabilise the people's standard of living!
- Broad defence or narrow defence?
- *Seiyūkai/Minseitō* alliance, or SMP?
- A vote for parliamentary renovation should be a vote for the SMP!
- Absolutely oppose tax increases!

- Establish worker parliamentary politics!
- Establish popular diplomacy![23]

To oppose war and fascism, the JPP advocated support for capitalists and bourgeois parties, while the SMP placed 'war' and 'fascism' in brackets. For workers and small farmers, the choice was clear. The JPP returned only one MP (Kanju Katō), whereas the SMP had 36 of its candidates elected. The difference in popularity of the two parties is shown most clearly by comparing the votes for Bunji Suzuki (SMP) and Mosaburō Suzuki (JPP) in the 6th district of Tokyo. Bunji Suzuki obtained 392,000 votes and came top of the poll, whereas Mosaburō Suzuki (JPP) won 20,000 votes and failed to be elected. Should we conclude from this that the SMP and Bunji Suzuki, because they were co-operating with 'war' and 'fascism' had won popularity among the people, while the JPP and Mosaburō Suzuki, opposing fascism, experienced honourable defeat? Analysis by the contemporary intellectuals, Jun Tosaka and Eijirō Kawai, cited above, shows quite the opposite. There is a high probability that workers and small farmers saw 'war' and 'capital' as linked together, and voted for the SMP, soundly defeating candidates of the JPP.

In postwar democracy, which from the start was presented as 'peace and democracy', the evaluation was turned on its head. The JPP, which had won just a single seat, and Mosaburō Suzuki, who had obtained a mere 20,000 votes, became the 'heroes who had opposed war and fascism'.

If we assume the premise of parliamentary democracy, however correct a candidate may appear to be at first glance, if that candidate is unable to persuade the electors, he is in some sense wrong. On the other hand, however dangerous a party may seem, electors may vote for it wagering on the possibility of reform. The image of Mosaburō Suzuki and the JPP in April 1937 overlaps with the image of the SDP under Takako Doi in November 2003, when her party, proclaiming only 'Defence of the Constitution', won a mere six out of 480 seats. On the other hand, the image of the SMP, which won 36 seats even though it was known to be close to the fascists, somewhat resembles that of the Democratic Party in 2003, which won 177 seats even though it was known to be dangerous on matters of security. The Japanese Left, both before and after the war, intoxicated with correct doctrine but ignoring the feelings of the electorate both in historical and contemporary politics, surely requires reassessment.

Notes

1 Sakuzō Yoshino, *Gendai no seiji* (Modern Politics), Tokyo: Jitsugyō no Nihon sha, 1915, pp. 28–30 (originally published in *Chūō Kōron*, April 1914).
2 Shiryō Nihon shakai undō shisō shi hensan iinkai (ed.), *Shiryō Nihon shakai undō shisō shi* (Materials on the History of the Thought of the Japanese Social Movement), Aoki Shoten, 1971, vol. 6, pp. 58–9.
3 F. G. Notehelfer, *Kōtoku Shūsui*, Cambridge: Cambridge University Press, 1971, p. 171.

4 Katsuyuki Tanaka and others (eds), *Yamakawa Hitoshi Zenshū* (Collected Works of Yamakawa Hitoshi), Keisō Shobō, 2003, vol. 1, p. 453.
5 Ibid., p. 581.
6 Sakuzō Yoshino, *Kensei no hongi o toite sono yūshū no bi o nasu no michi o ronzu* (Explaining the Real Meaning of Constitutional Politics and Arguing How to Bring It to Perfection), *Chūō Kōron*, January 1916.
7 Kikue Yamakawa and Shinsaku Yamakawa (eds), *Yamakawa Hitoshi Zenshū* (Collected Works of Yamakawa Hitoshi), Keisō Shobō, 1967, vol. 4, p. 213.
8 Ibid., p. 218.
9 Yoshitake Oka, *Yoshino Sakuzō hyōron shū* (Collection of the Criticism Written by Yoshino Sakuzō), Iwanami Shoten, 1975, p. 152.
10 Ibid., p. 157.
11 Keiichirō Hara (ed.), *Hara Kei nikki* (Diary of Hara Kei), Fukumura Shuppan, 1965, vol. 5, p. 276.
12 Ibid., p. 302.
13 Translator's note: The Taishō period lasted from 1912 to 1926.
14 Translator's note: The Shōwa period lasted from 1926 to 1989.
15 *Kaizō*, September 1937, pp. 30–2.
16 *Chūō Kōron*, June 1937, p. 106.
17 Translator's note: 'Masses' in the earlier party was *minshū*, in the merged party *taishū*. It is difficult to make the distinction in English.
18 Nihon shi kō jiten henshū iinkai, *Nihon shi kō jiten* (Comprehensive Dictionary of Japanese History), Yamakawa Shuppan sha, 1993, p. 1033.
19 The correct figure was 928,934.
20 Shakai Shisō kenkyūkai (ed.), *Kawai Eijirō zenshū* (Collected Works of Kawai Eijirō), Shakai Shisō Sha, 1969, vol. 19, pp. 201–2.
21 Naimushō Keihōkyoku Hoan Ka, *Tokkō gaiji geppō* (External Affairs Monthly of the Special Police), February 1937, pp. 100–1.
22 *Kaizō*, May 1937, pp. 75–6.
23 Naimushō Keihō Kyoku (ed.), *Shakai undō no jōkyō* (The Circumstances of Social Movements), 9, 1937, pp. 583–4.

Index

For Product Safety Concerns and Information please contact our EU
representative GPSR@taylorandfrancis.com
Taylor & Francis Verlag GmbH, Kaufingerstraße 24, 80331 München, Germany